Authority and History

Also available from Bloomsbury

Anachronism and Antiquity, edited by Tim Rood, Carol Atack and Tom Phillips
Antiquity and the Meanings of Time, Duncan F. Kennedy
After the Crisis: Remembrance, Re-anchoring and Recovery in Ancient Greece and Rome, edited by Jacqueline Klooster and Inger N. I. Kuin

Authority and History

Ancient Models, Modern Questions

Edited by Juliana Bastos Marques
and Federico Santangelo

BLOOMSBURY ACADEMIC
LONDON • NEW YORK • OXFORD • NEW DELHI • SYDNEY

BLOOMSBURY ACADEMIC
Bloomsbury Publishing Plc
50 Bedford Square, London, WC1B 3DP, UK
1385 Broadway, New York, NY 10018, USA
29 Earlsfort Terrace, Dublin 2, Ireland

BLOOMSBURY, BLOOMSBURY ACADEMIC and the Diana logo are trademarks of
Bloomsbury Publishing Plc

First published in Great Britain 2023
Paperback edition published 2024

Copyright © Juliana Bastos Marques, Federico Santangelo & Contributors, 2023

Juliana Bastos Marques and Federico Santangelo have asserted their right under the
Copyright, Designs and Patents Act, 1988, to be identified as Editors of this work.

For legal purposes the Acknowledgements on p. viii constitute an extension
of this copyright page.

Cover design: Terry Woodley
Cover image © Paul Cézanne, *Portrait of Gustave Geffroy* (detail), 1895–96.
Wikimedia Commons

All rights reserved. No part of this publication may be reproduced or transmitted
in any form or by any means, electronic or mechanical, including photocopying,
recording, or any information storage or retrieval system, without prior
permission in writing from the publishers.

Bloomsbury Publishing Plc does not have any control over, or responsibility for, any
third-party websites referred to or in this book. All internet addresses given
in this book were correct at the time of going to press. The author and publisher
regret any inconvenience caused if addresses have changed or sites have
ceased to exist, but can accept no responsibility for any such changes.

A catalogue record for this book is available from the British Library.

Library of Congress Cataloging-in-Publication Data
Names: Marques, Juliana Bastos, editor. | Santangelo, Federico, editor.
Title: Authority and history : ancient models, modern questions /
edited by Juliana Bastos Marques and Federico Santangelo.
Description: London : Bloomsbury Academic, 2023. | Papers from two conferences, one
held at Newcastle, England, in February 2019 and the other, at São Paolo, Brazil, in July
2019. | Includes bibliographical references.
Identifiers: LCCN 2022030727 | ISBN 9781350269446 (hardback) |
ISBN 9781350269484 (paperback) | ISBN 9781350269453 (ebook) |
ISBN 9781350269460 (epub) | ISBN 9781350269477
Subjects: LCSH: Classical literature–History and criticism–Congresses. |
Authority–Congresses. | Historiography–Congresses. | Historiography–History–To 1500–
Congresses. | Civilization, Modern–21st century–Classical influences–Congresses.
Classification: LCC PA3009 .A98 2023 | DDC 880.09—dc23/eng/20220920
LC record available at https://lccn.loc.gov/2022030727

ISBN:	HB:	978-1-3502-6944-6
	PB:	978-1-3502-6948-4
	ePDF:	978-1-3502-6945-3
	eBook:	978-1-3502-6946-0

Typeset by RefineCatch Ltd, Bungay, Suffolk

To find out more about our authors and books, visit www.bloomsbury.com
and sign up for our newsletters.

Contents

List of Contributors	vi
Acknowledgments	viii
Introduction *Juliana Bastos Marques*	1

Part One Ancient Models

1	Authority and Authenticity *John Marincola*	9
2	Poetry as History: The Authority of Lucan as a Historian *Leni Ribeiro Leite*	29
3	Truth and Authority *Roger Chartier*	43
4	The Time of Restitution of All Things: Past as Future in Michael Servetus *Elaine C. Sartorelli*	69

Part Two Modern Questions

5	Classics and Western Civilization: The Troubling History of an Authoritative Narrative *Rebecca Futo Kennedy*	87
6	"The Society That Separates Its Scholars from Its Keyboard Warriors…": Tracking Thucydides on Twitter *Neville Morley*	109
7	Is Livy a Good Wikipedian? Authority and Audience in Ancient Historiography and Contemporary Anonymous Writing *Juliana Bastos Marques*	127
8	The New *Agora*? Online Communities and a New Rhetoric *Catalina Popescu*	143
9	Classical Literature and Contemporary Classics *Ayelet Haimson Lushkov*	159

Bibliography	171
Index	191

Contributors

Roger Chartier is Emeritus Professor at the Collège de France and Annenberg Visiting Professor in History at the University of Pennsylvania. His current research interests focus on the mobility and materiality of texts in early modern Europe. His most recent publications are *Editer et Traduire* (2021) and *Won in Translation* (2022).

Rebecca Futo Kennedy is professor at Denison University, Ohio, in the Department of Classical Studies. Her research interests focus on the social, political, economic, and cultural history of ancient Athens, on race and ethnicity in antiquity and its modern legacy, and on women and gender. She has published widely on Athenian tragedy, immigration and women, race, ethnicity and environment, and modern receptions of ancient ideas and texts. Her most recent monograph is *Immigrant Women in Athens* (2014).

Leni Ribeiro Leite is Associate Professor of Classics at the University of Kentucky. Her research interests focus on the Flavian period, classical receptions, and Latin in the Latin American colonies. She has published numerous articles and book chapters in Brazil and abroad, including a recent contribution to *The Routledge Handbook of Literary Translingualism* (2022).

Ayelet Haimson Lushkov is Associate Professor of Classics at the University of Texas at Austin. Her research interests focus on Latin historiography, reception studies, and political narratives in the Roman republic and early empire. She has published on various aspects of Latin literature, including on Ennius, Cicero, and Vergil, as well as Livy; and on modern receptions of the classics, including in *Game of Thrones*. Her monographs include *Magistracy and the Historiography of the Roman Republic: Politics in Prose* (2015) and *You Win or You Die: The Ancient World of Game of Thrones* (2017).

John Marincola is Leon Golden Professor of Classics, Emeritus, at Florida State University. He has interests in Greek and Roman historiography, rhetoric, and literary criticism. His publications include *Authority and Tradition in Ancient Historiography* (1997), *Greek Historians* (2001), and (with M. A. Flower) *Herodotus: Histories Book IX* (2002). He has edited *On Writing History from*

Herodotus to Herodian (2017). He is Managing Editor of *Histos: The On-Line Journal of Ancient Historiography.*

Juliana Bastos Marques is Associate Professor of Ancient History at Universidade Federal do Estado do Rio de Janeiro. She published her first monograph in Portuguese in 2012, *Tradição e renovações da identidade romana em Tito Lívio e Tácito*, and has been working in the fields of Roman historiography, theory of history, reception of Classics, and digital public history.

Neville Morley is Professor of Classics and Ancient History at the University of Exeter. His research interests include ancient economic and social history, historiography, and the reception of antiquity, especially the influence of Thucydides in modern historical and political thought. His most recent books are *Thucydides and the Idea of History* (2014) and *Classics: Why It Matters* (2018).

Catalina Popescu is Lecturer-Collaborator at the University of Bucharest's Department of Classics, where she teaches an undergraduate workshop on Apuleius. Her current research interests focus on Ovid's poetry and the function of memory in literary expression. She has published on Greek plays, heroic memory, and metamorphosis, as well as gender and fantasy. Her most recent published articles include "Overflowing Bodies and a Pandora of Ivory: The Pure Humors of an Erotic Surrogate" (2021) and "*Ta Klea Andron*, (Dis)Embodiment and Heroic Peregrinations in Ovid" (2021).

Federico Santangelo is Professor of Ancient History at Newcastle University. He works mainly on the political and intellectual history of the Roman Republic, the civic and municipal life of the Roman world, Roman religion, and the history of classical scholarship. His most recent book is *La religione dei Romani* (2022). He is editor of *History of Classical Scholarship.*

Elaine C. Sartorelli, former president of the Brazilian Society of Rhetoric (2013–14), is a professor in the Department of Classics at Universidade de São Paulo. Her research interests focus on classical reception by Christian authors, the rhetoric of the Christian plain style, and the sixteenth-century polemics, both literary and religious. She has translated from Latin into Portuguese works by Erasmus of Rotterdam, Pico della Mirandola, Michael Servetus, Giordano Bruno, and John Calvin. Her postdoctoral project at the Université Bordeaux-Montaigne studied the role of Erasmus in Montaigne's *Essais.*

Acknowledgments

This volume stems from two conferences that took place at Newcastle in February 2019 and at São Paulo in July 2019, under the framework of a Newton Advanced Fellowship granted by the British Academy. We are very grateful to the Academy for supporting this project and enabling several visits of Juliana Bastos Marques to Newcastle in the academic year 2018/2019. We should like to thank the colleagues at our institutions—UNIRIO, Universidade de São Paulo, and Newcastle University—for the invaluable administrative and logistical support they have offered in the run-up to both events: at São Paulo, Norberto Luiz Guarinello, Sarah Fernandes Lino de Azevedo, and the student members of the Laboratório de Estudos sobre o Império Romano e Mediterrâneo Antigo (LEIR-MA/USP); at Newcastle, Elizabeth Bell, Vic Christie, and Claire Holden. Juliana Bastos Marques would also like to thank the Fulbright Commission and Florida State University for enabling and hosting a research stay during which some of the ideas behind this volume were initially scoped.

Alice Wright, Georgina Leighton, and Lily Mac Mahon at Bloomsbury have offered us valuable guidance and support throughout. We have benefited greatly from the comments of two referees. We have a special debt of gratitude to John Marincola, who has generously offered his advice on the framing and development of this project at several crucial junctions.

Juliana Bastos Marques
Federico Santangelo
Rio de Janeiro and Newcastle, March 2022

Introduction

Juliana Bastos Marques

The early twenty-first century has been a time of bitter, polarized disputes, and few disciplines have witnessed this as acutely as Classical Studies. Fierce defenses of the timeless classical canon and its mastery through extensive knowledge of Greek and Latin seems to be competing with a pressing challenge to the centrality of Classics to a world history that has ties with decolonial and intersectional theory. As difficult and divisive as the debate has been, it is also a sign of the vigorous relevance that the classical tradition continues to have in shaping contemporary times, for better or for worse.

Given the many potential perspectives that can be brought to bear on this debate, any answer stems ultimately from an issue of authority, either within academic circles or from outside. Who gets to establish what Classical Studies are? How should they be approached? What is their relation to whatever is "non-Classical" in the ancient world or to other traditions that get in conflict with them?

Therefore, the broader questions of who is (or should be) an authority, to whom, and how they impose their authority successfully need to be urgently examined. After all, this is the age of fake news—not just any local or innocent gossip, but a discourse that can be actively created and used to ostracize or acclaim any person, and, most dangerously, to shape national and international policies, or global health. In the intellectual realm, established mechanisms of imposing authority, through recognition of one's place and prestige among peers, have changed in ways that could not have been predicted decades ago. A curious little tale will suffice as an example of this trend.

In 2012, the American novelist Philip Roth published an open letter in the *New Yorker* complaining about the Wikipedia article on his 2000 novel, *The Human Stain*.[1] At that time, the article mentioned several literary critics who had published reviews and articles crediting Roth's inspiration for the main character to the *New York Times*' literary editor, Anatole Broyard. Having read the article, Roth demanded this information to be removed from the page, claiming it was incorrect; the removal was denied, however, because the attribution had been referenced via a verifiable authorial third party. Outraged to be told that his own word was not accepted as the true source of the reference for the character he himself wrote, Roth presented his arguments in the *New Yorker* letter, claiming that not only did Anatole Broyard have no connection to the character, but that it was actually based on another person, his friend Melvin Tumin. The Wikipedia editors did add this information following the letter's publication, but did not remove the (by then disproven) claim that Broyard was the inspiration for the character.

Roth had not realized a fundamental rule of the "encyclopedia that anyone can edit": the authority of any information written by anonymous editors can be accepted *only if it is already published by a third party*: hence the need for referencing every piece of information in the entry. The literary critics who had pointed to Broyard as the inspiration for the character were still mentioned in the article, because their reading was backed by an acknowledged newspaper that had published them. Roth's first correction, which came from private correspondence, would not be approved until it was published and, thus, openly verifiable.

This strange story of an author whose word was not trusted as the interpretation of his own text exemplifies important aspects of the problem of authority today. Roth was not aware of the rules in that medium which dictated the validity of the text about Broyard; they were not established by a group whose codes he knew and associated himself to, but by another, almost random group, which is not necessarily associated with literary academia. Different discourse settings presuppose different languages and audiences, but what if these end up blending? What is clear about this story, as with many others, is that the author is not in total control of authority about his speech—it is granted by the receiver, the audience. This is not a new conclusion, but we should now also ask: who is this audience? Do they belong to the same group (however that is defined) as the author, or do they hold different assumptions, goals, and values? What happens if they do, and how does the author negotiate their authority with different kinds of groups?

The key terms "authority" and "authorship" are etymologically related. *Auctoritas* in a broader sense denotes an attribute of the *auctor*, which in many instances means 'initiator', 'inventor', somebody who begins or declares something—the word shares the same etymology as key religious terms such as *augur* and *augustus*.² Although the word was used in Plautus, Cicero, and Vergil, the role and meaning of the author as initiator—as a producer of new material and new ideas versus a translator or a mere collector of previous sources and citations—became a major topic in the medieval period,³ and also led to the birth of copyright in early modern times.⁴ The association of authorship and textuality then becomes indistinctly linked in modern romanticism to the triumph of the individual, breaking with the anonymous position of the author in the Middle Ages.⁵ The medieval audience, however, granted authority to the text by transcending the importance of the (anonymous) author, in favor of the message of the text itself. In that sense, modern romanticism can be viewed as an interlude of triumph of the author as an individual, one with complete power and control of the weight of their words over their audience(s).

However, in 1968, in the pulsating middle of the postmodern rupture, Roland Barthes suggested another point in this history of authorship and authority, declaring the "death" of the romanticist author.⁶ Although his manifesto mostly deals with this theme, and its reception was widely focused on what happens with the deceased, he suggests at the very end what we have already hinted: "*la naissance du lecteur* [our emphasis] doit se payer de la mort de l'auteur." At the same time, reader-response theories provided several sets of interpretations, from individualist to uniformist approaches, which led to the same interpretation of the agency of the audience in determining the authority of a text.⁷ Although feminist, queer, Black, and decolonial studies present several critiques of the reader-response approaches, they all have in common the breach proclaimed by Barthes. What sets them apart can be summed up in terms of authority, in the sense that these new and different audiences may confirm (or rather not confirm) the intentions of the author in getting themselves and their discourse recognized.

Contemporary rhetoric has also contributed to this centrality of the audience, as in Kenneth Burke's concept of *identification*, or *consubstantiality*.⁸ For Burke, the whole effectiveness of the speech lies not with the speaker's *pathos*, or the intrinsic merits of the *logos*, but with the identification of the audience with the speaker's *ethos*, even prior to the contact with the text. This identification, from the point of view of the successful speaker, comes from belonging to and/or accepting the same premises of the group from which they take their model of authority, or, as Burke puts it, mastering a common *substance* of ideas, values, interests and concepts between author and audience.⁹

Burke still centers his view on the centrality of the speaker/author, and the way in which they grasp the methodological strategies required to fit in with the audience's expectations. A change in the set of values from a determined audience would thus have to be correctly perceived by the author in order to adapt their discourse successfully. However, Burke's linguistic theory is not focused on the mechanisms by which the audience changes, looking rather as if it was some sort of spontaneous movement, nor does it consider the social and cultural forces in conflict between different audiences. This problem was raised by sociology, one example being Pierre Bourdieu's criticism of the previous limitations of linguistics as not being able to recognize the role of structures in communication beyond speech itself. Thus, according to Bourdieu,

> The whole truth of the communicative relation is never fully present in the discourse, nor even in the communicative relation itself; a genuine science of discourse must seek that truth within discourse but also outside it, in the social conditions of the production and reproduction of the producers and receivers and of their relationship.[10]

In sum, in the words of philosopher Linda Alcoff, "who is speaking to whom turns out to be as important for meaning and truth as what is said; in fact, what is said turns out to change according to who is speaking and who is listening."[11]

With this background in mind, this volume will proceed to examine ways in which the ancient author is in control of their authority over the discourse they produce, after negotiating with a certain level of expectations from their intended audience, and ways in which this control is accepted or challenged through modern times. This collection of essays results from two conferences held in 2019, in Newcastle and São Paulo, and aims to put forward a collective reflection on how we may understand the effectiveness and authority of discourse strategies built in classical times to the present day. The scope of the essays is diverse and encompasses specific topics, but they should be understood as parts of a shared underlying examination of the strategies for historical discourses built by the ancients, which have been accepted by audiences to varying degrees through the ages. Notably, we should like to examine how contemporary times have offered unprecedented challenges to this authority, through the widening of audiences and their expectations.

Notes

1   Roth (2012).
2   Nettleship (1889: 360–5); Ernout-Meillet (1951: 56–8).

3 A standard reference is St. Bonaventure's discussion of the four categories of writers: scribe, compiler, commentator, and author, as cited in Minnis (2012: 94–103).
4 See Chartier (1994, 2014); Lowenstein (2002); Rose (1993). On a discussion about "ancient copyright," see Selle (2008).
5 An introductory analysis of the issue can be found in the third chapter of Scanlon (1994).
6 Barthes (1977); see also Foucault (1977).
7 Some of the foundational texts are Jauss (1982), Iser (1978), and Fish (1980).
8 Burke (1969).
9 Burke (1973).
10 Bourdieu (1977).
11 Alcoff (1991).

Part One

Ancient Models

1

Authority and Authenticity[1]

John Marincola

There can be little doubt that ours is an age in which authority is in crisis. The mass "democratization" brought about by the internet has resulted not only in radically new ways of packaging and conveying information, but also in contesting and competing sources of authority. A repudiation of traditional elites in the political sphere has been matched by an increasing suspicion of "expert" knowledge and those sources (including institutions of higher learning) from which they have traditionally sprung. It has got to the point, of course, where people consider themselves entitled to their own understanding of the external world and claim without irony to have "alternative facts."[2]

It is all too easy to bewail this state of affairs and to warn of the long-term consequences of the breakdown of scientific consensus. To be sure, these are serious matters. Yet without in any way minimizing these, one could point out that in the ancient world, with its reliance on rhetoric and persuasion, contestation was a ubiquitous phenomenon. For the essence of a rhetorical society is that everything in it is subject to examination from various sides, and from various perspectives. What is "true" is not very different from what you can get your audience to believe—or at least that is the way it is often portrayed. Plato, of course, was troubled by this, but it is not clear that others were. Indeed, aspects of performance so dominate the ancient world that we can hardly be sure in many cases where performance ends and reality begins.[3]

The authority of the ancient historian, at least as I have argued,[4] is one constructed by such rhetorical means: it is an authority that emerges from the text and from the ways in which people construct the "person" whom they imagine to be behind the text. Very few people in antiquity ever met Thucydides and so had a chance to assess his temperament and personality. But the vast majority of his readers had a very particular view of his reliability, his impartiality, and his devotion to the truth. Such a picture of Thucydides, in the absence of any concrete biographical detail or personal acquaintance, can have come only from the picture that was formed in people's minds as they read his work.[5] It is, of course, what we continue to do today. Yet for modern readers there may well be, as there may not have been for the ancients, a questioning of the extent to which the character we construct from the work can be said to be "authentic," and modern literary criticism distinguishes between the implied and actual author.[6]

Now just as authority is under contestation in these times, so is the notion of "authenticity." While the internet and modern social media have had some effect here, concerns about the notion of authenticity arose even before the electronic revolution, though the internet has increased interest in the concept and brought to light new issues.[7] It is generally agreed that the notion of authenticity is a modern one. In his classic book published some fifty years ago, Lionel Trilling traced the ways in which individuals came to be seen not as placeholders in a system of social relations but rather as individuals responsible to themselves and deriving their individual autonomy from a unique inner self. Sincerity and authenticity came to be understood as a congruity between one's inner and outer self, the way one felt inside and the way one came across in the public sphere. Not coincidentally, of course, this concept arose in conjunction with the development of the notion of the modern self. In the pre-modern world, by contrast, there was a notion of authenticity but this was not about the individual self but rather about the ways in which one fitted oneself to the larger purposes of the world, and how one defined oneself within the existing social, religious, and political structures.[8]

The question of authenticity is not without interest when thinking about ancient historiography. The issue has long been recognized, even if not in such terms. We may well ask ourselves to what extent the narrators of historiographical works are "authentic" and whether that matters at all in the construction of their authority. Scholars have long been aware that there is sometimes a significant dichotomy between what historians profess and what they actually do. It has been noted that historians, on the one hand, in their prefaces and in methodological remarks throughout the work, profess a fidelity to truth, which they claim to honor highly by making it the aim of their work. When they come to write their histories, on the other hand, such professions seem to count for little, and they write in seeming ignorance or even defiance of the principles they so eloquently espouse elsewhere in their work. And the problem may be said to affect all historians to some degree, not only those less highly regarded such as Dionysius or Livy, but even those who are more highly esteemed such as Polybius or Tacitus. When Frank Goodyear, for example, remarks:

One can hardly doubt that there is some conflict between Tacitus' judgement of these writers [sc. his predecessors] and his use of them, and also between the rigorous standards he implies in his prooemia and those he in fact attains[9]

would it be appropriate to speak of Tacitus' "insincerity" or "hypocrisy" here? Or consider the way in which Sallust depicted how he came to write history:

> As a young man, I at the beginning, like very many, was carried by eagerness towards public affairs, but many things were opposed to me there. For in place of modesty, in place of restraint, in place of virtue, there flourished recklessness, bribery, greed. And although my spirit, unfamiliar with evil practices, spurned such things, nonetheless among such vices my frail youth was led astray and held by ambition. And although I dissented from the evil behaviour of the others, still the desire for distinction troubled me with the same reputation and jealousy as the rest. And so when my spirit had settled down after many afflictions and dangers, and I had decided that I would live the rest of my life far from the public sphere, … I would return to that undertaking and pursuit from which evil ambition had kept me back, and I decided to compose a detailed account of the deeds of the Roman people, etc.[10]

As is well known, Sallust did not leave public life "voluntarily," nor was he quite as averse to the evils around him as he suggests: after his provincial governorship in Africa, he barely escaped conviction for extortion, and that thanks only to Caesar's intervention.[11] Surely this has the whiff of hypocrisy, if not outright falsehood, and perhaps some sense of this is hinted at in Macrobius' *Saturnalia*, when Sallust is characterized as a "very stern scold and censor of other men's luxury."[12] But this line of thought is not very pronounced in the ancient judgments on Sallust, and he is again and again lauded as a learned, reliable, and honest writer.[13] This might suggest that the ancients cared somewhat, but not very greatly, about whether Sallust's work was congruent with his actual life.

Nor might this seem surprising, given that a fundamental characteristic of classical historiography was its rhetorical nature and underpinnings. For history followed the rules of rhetoric in the way that it conceived of, structured, and actually composed its material.[14] This meant that for the "speaker," whether an actual speaker or one composing a written work, it was necessary in some sense to take on a "role." He needed to speak and behave in a way that the situation demanded, and thus took less thought for what he "really" believed and much more on how he could effectively accomplish the task that he was set or set himself.

A good example of how such thinking might reveal itself can be seen in Dionysius of Halicarnassus' evaluation of Pericles' last speech in Thucydides' history. Here Pericles addresses an angry populace suffering from war and the plague, and defends himself against their anger and dissatisfaction with the war's course and with himself (2.60–64). He asserts the consistency of his policy—he makes a point of saying that he remains the same as ever—and chides the people for their inconsistency: they behaved and thought one way before the war actually started, but have changed both their thought and their behavior now that they are actually experiencing the hardships and losses that war brings. Pericles thus concludes that the people have no right to be angry with him.

Many modern scholars would agree that this is one of the most powerful speeches in Thucydides, rivaling even the Funeral Oration. For Dionysius, however, the speech is not to be admired: it is poorly crafted and is not "true" because this is not the kind of speech that someone in that situation would have given. He believes that much of what Thucydides puts in Pericles' mouth was Thucydides' own opinion and he ought to have stated it as such (Thuc. 45.6):

> But just as I said at the beginning, the historian displays his own opinion about Pericles' virtue and seems to have said it in the wrong place. What he should have done was say what he wished about the man but give to one who was in a dangerous situation words that were humble and sought to avoid the people's anger: for this was appropriate for the historian who wished to imitate real life (τῷ μιμεῖσθαι βουλομένῳ συγγραφεῖ τὴν ἀλήθειαν).

For Dionysius, then, it seems that the speech lacked authenticity because it did not conform to what the tenets of rhetoric had told him people in that situation would or should say. We could rephrase this by saying that for Dionysius what was "authentic" was dependent on the social and literary contexts and the agreed-upon conventions.

We may then genuinely wonder to what extent the audience of a work of history was looking for an "authentic" individual voice. One way to approach this is to look at the kinds of attacks that writers actually level against historians. Polemic, a characteristic feature of classical historiography, begins with Hecataeus' opening manifesto against Greek accounts which he finds 'many and ridiculous' (*FGrHist* 1 F 1a) and continues through to the end of antiquity.[15] Historiographical criticism embraced virtually all aspects of the writing of history, both specific and general. The style of historians was criticized, as we can see already from the enigmatic remarks of Duris of Samos against Ephorus and Theopompus (*FGrHist* 76 F 1), as was they way in which they arranged their material and organized the various elements of his history. Far and away the most common polemic, however, revolved around questions of bias and impartiality, framed consistently in terms of fear or favoritism: the historians were charged with an improper motive in writing, either the desire to flatter and glorify the subject or subjects of history (who might still be alive when the history was being written) or the opposite wish to vilify a figure (one who was often dead) and his actions.[16] Favoritism would be adopted so that a historian might reap some reward, especially if he were writing about a living king or despot who could benefit him. Vilification, on the other hand, could be used to settle scores against a political enemy, especially if he were dead and unable to take action against the writer.

The criticisms made by some historians seem to have veered often towards the personal, attacking writers for their habits (including sexual ones) or challenging their social status. Timaeus of Tauromenium seems to have polemicized vigorously in his history, not only against political figures but even against previous writers, and he in turn was criticized by Polybius, who devoted his entire Book 12 to elucidating Timaeus' faults and shortcomings. Polybius criticized not only the contents of the work but also the author's disposition, his attitude towards his subject matter and, more generally, towards history itself. Timaeus is faulted for failing to engage in the travels and inquiries necessary for writing history; he is ignorant of topography; his narratives of battles are ludicrous, and he is no better in his accounts of the foundations of colonies. He attributes improbable and puerile speeches to his characters, uncritically includes mythological material, and towards men in power he is alternately fawning and scathing. He is everywhere blinded by his "bitterness" such that he cannot speak fairly or measuredly about historical figures.[17]

Polybius' criticisms of Timaeus proceed on the assumption that Timaeus' work is a good, indeed unproblematic, reflection of his character, and that his character can be inferred from what he writes about and how he writes about it. Timaeus had himself done no less, though sometimes with ludicrous conclusions: he argued that the many descriptions of feasting in the *Iliad* and *Odyssey* show that Homer was clearly a glutton; and that Aristotle was obviously a gourmand, since he has numerous descriptions of rich food in his writings.[18] Now while Timaeus may have taken this to comical lengths, he was not doing anything qualitatively different from other critics, namely reading an author's character from his work. For Polybius at any rate, Timaeus' work revealed his "authentic" self, and his work was congruent with his character. No one claims that Timaeus is inauthentic; indeed, it is not common at all in antiquity to suggest that an author is inauthentic, that is, that he is other than what he claims to be. The man's true nature is revealed in the work. The sole exception, I would suggest, is the essay that has come down to us ascribed to Plutarch and bearing the title *On the Malice of Herodotus*.

The structure of the work is straightforward: a general statement asserting Herodotus' malice; "tokens and signs" by which one can determine whether a historian is malicious;[19] discussion of individual passages in Herodotus pointing out their malice; and a conclusion that reaffirms the remarks of the preface. Plutarch sets himself a double task in this essay. He must not only "correct" the record of Greek action in the Persian Wars, offering a "better" account than did Herodotus; he must also show that Herodotus *deliberately* told a false story, that the historian knew that his account was wrong even as he was offering it. For only if he can show Herodotus to be a deliberate liar can he then demonstrate that the historian did indeed possess a malicious character.[20]

The essay has had a nearly unanimously negative reception in earlier and even more recent scholarship.[21] With very few exceptions, scholars have dismissed it and believed that it has little to teach us about the writing of history in the ancient world; or if it teaches us anything, it is perhaps that serious, independent, reliable history in antiquity was always precarious and consistently under threat from the type of romantic, hagiographic approach exemplified by Plutarch's "rewriting" of Herodotus' history. Plutarch's portrait of the Persian Wars is as romantically unrealistic as he claims that Herodotus' account is. Plutarch's criticisms are those of an out-of-touch bystander looking back at events of half a millennium earlier that he could not possibly understand. For reasons that I cannot get into here, I think this is a misapprehension both of the essay itself and of Plutarch's intentions.[22] Instead, I want to focus on how Plutarch's criticisms differ from previous attacks on Herodotus, and how that might relate to the question of authority and authenticity.

Now it is, of course, the case that a work purporting to criticize Herodotus would hardly have raised an eyebrow in antiquity. The first historian was an enduring object of attack, and Josephus exaggerates only slightly when he says that "everybody corrects Herodotus."[23] Criticisms of him, while not uniform, generally fell into two categories. The first was the correction of factual errors by later writers who felt they had more accurate information. These attacks were generally defined closely, and limited to this or that detail; this is not surprising, given that the enormous range of Herodotus' inquiries in space and time would have provided many opportunities for correction. Even in the first generation after Herodotus' work appeared, Thucydides seems to single him out (though not by name) when he "corrects" two errors of his and uses these as emblematic of the failure of people to pursue accurate inquiry (Thuc. 1.20.3). Thucydides' focus, however, was the Peloponnesian War, and he did not directly contest Herodotus' account of the Persian Wars. Ctesias of Cnidus, on the other hand, *did* treat the Persian Wars though from the Persian perspective, and he offered a very different account of those wars: Photius says that he differed with Herodotus on practically everything, and going so far as to call Herodotus "a liar in many things."[24] This would indicate that just one generation on, Herodotus was the historian to be reckoned with in matters dealing with Persia. In the third century, Manetho claimed to offer a history of Egypt based on native sources and superior to that of Herodotus, faulting the earlier historian for his "ignorance."[25] Indeed, an important locus for the correction of Herodotus was his account of Egypt and the Nile. This drew forth many of the criticisms directed against him, as can be seen in Diodorus who in the first century claimed that he could improve Herodotus' account of Egypt thanks to his own inquiry of the priests and their records.[26]

Such criticisms, however, were only one strand of the attack on Herodotus. He was also faulted regularly for being a purveyor of fantastic or tall tales. This is first explicitly attested in the fourth century, where the same Ctesias mentioned above called him a *logopoios*, while Aristotle referred to him as a *muthologos*.[27] Both terms were clearly derogatory and meant to suggest a predilection for *muthoi* which were—to use the categorization later developed in ancient literary criticism—neither true nor like the truth, and were characterized especially by supernatural events or physical transformations.[28] This second strand was perhaps the more prominent one in Herodotean criticism, even though it is clear that such attacks on this front did not affect his reputation as a historian, as we can see from Cicero's famous remark that "even in Herodotus, the father of history, there are innumerable tall tales (*fabulae, Leg.* 1.5)"—*fabulae* in this case being the appropriate Latin term corresponding to *muthoi*. Yet as has often been pointed out, Herodotus—for all the criticisms directed towards him, whether of factual detail, tall tales, or his general approach—continued to be read. He was never dislodged from his place as the "father of history," and his account of the Persian Wars remained the canonical one.

The fact, then, that Plutarch criticizes Herodotus was neither surprising nor new, at least when viewed in *general* terms. Yet it is essential to recognize the important ways in which Plutarch in this essay is doing something new and distinctive. To take only the most obvious example: the criticism of *muthoi*, so prominent in critics before Plutarch, plays no role whatsoever in Plutarch's essay. The word itself appears only once, at the very end, not in the narrator's own voice but in a quotation from Homer's *Odyssey* (874B). Thus, what was for many before Plutarch a fundamental characteristic of Herodotus' history has no interest for him. What he cares about are Herodotus' "falsehoods and fictions" (ψεύσματα and πλάσματα, 854F). He believes that Herodotus invented things wholesale, and not just in matters concerning the ends of the earth (where exaggeration and invention were prevalent and recognized, even if not always approved)[29] but rather at the heart of his work, in the account of the battles of the Persian Wars—the very narrative on which Herodotus' fame rested. The aim of Plutarch's work is not primarily a matter of incidental correction to what is otherwise an overall reliable account. Rather, the purpose is to show that Herodotus' account is consistently and persistently unreliable, no matter where one looks or what kind of material Herodotus treats. And Plutarch concludes that to explain this pervasive unreliability, one cannot assume innocent error; on the contrary, such pervasive mendacity can only be the result of the historian's intentions and disposition.[30] The essay is, therefore, in many ways a "psychological" study, an attempt to probe Herodotus' personality so as to come to a more accurate view of the man and his work.

It begins with a condemnation of Herodotus' character, saying that he has deceived many by his fine style and that his work conceals the true nature of his character, namely that he is κακοήθης, a term that means "malevolent" or "malicious" or perhaps more accurately "mean-spirited,"[31] a fact that has escaped the majority of his readers (854E–855A):

> The style of Herodotus <of Halicarnassus>, my dear Alexander, because it is simple and lacking in effort and easily runs over events, has thoroughly deceived many people. And more people have experienced this with regard to his character. For not only is it, as Plato says, the greatest injustice to appear to be just when one is not, it is also an act of the greatest malice to mimic a good nature and simplicity in a way that is hard to detect. <...> he has especially employed <his malice?> against the Boeotians and the Corinthians, nor has he refrained from any of the others, I think it is appropriate for us to come to the defence both of our ancestors and of the truth in this very part of his work – since those who wished to go through in detail all the rest of his falsehoods and fictions would require many volumes. But as Sophocles says, 'the face of Persuasion is fearsome', especially when, in a narrative that has such great charm and power, it is able to cover up all the other absurdities as well as the character of the historian. Philip used to say to those Greeks who were breaking their alliance with him and going over to Titus that they were putting on a collar that was smoother but would last longer. The malice of Herodotus is smoother, to be sure, and softer than that of Theopompus but it fastens onto its object and causes

pain more, like winds that blow in secret through a narrow opening compared with those that are dispersed in the open.

Plutarch here makes three initial points: first, many readers have been thoroughly deceived by Herodotus' style; second (and following from the first), Herodotus' character has been misapprehended by readers; and third, contrary to the usual evaluation of Herodotus, he is not fair-minded but malicious, and, moreover, his malice is all the more effective because of its covert nature. The three points are emphasized by a series of dichotomies: between Herodotus' reputation and the reality of his account; between the 'many' who have been deceived and the knowledgeable speaker who will now, by contrast, evaluate things as they really are (and so establish the truth of the matter); and between the more overt type of malice which is easily apprehended, and the subtle form practiced by Herodotus.

In this opening paragraph, Plutarch draws on two long-standing beliefs in ancient literary criticism: first, that any writer, including a historian, reveals something of his personal character in his style, a "simple" style being the mark of a straightforward character, one which is reliable and lacking artifice; second, a writer reveals his character also by his choice of subject matter, his own interests being reflected in what he chooses to write about.

In the matter of style, it was a truism of ancient literary criticism that the style was the man himself: words were the image of the soul, summed up in Seneca's epigrammatic "as is a man's speech so is his life."[32] To be sure, there were occasionally counter-claims: poets who composed iambic or comic attacks sought to make clear that their verses should be kept separate from their own personal character, but they did this precisely because they knew that their audience would be judging them in this way.[33]

But words could also be deceptive. They could be considered magical and charming, and yet could also (and often did) deceive those listening.[34] As early as the *Iliad*, Achilles chides the man "who hides one thing in the depths of his heart and speaks forth another," while the *Odyssey* presents a figure skilled at composing false speeches that sound like the truth.[35] The sophistic revolution brought forward men who could "make the weaker argument the stronger," and in such a context, where "fancy" words could be equated with deception, simplicity, by contrast, could serve as an indication of straightforwardness and a guarantor of truth.

Using this as a guide, Herodotus' "simple" style ought to be a guarantor of truth.[36] Plutarch concedes this aspect of Herodotus' style: it is "simple and unlaboured and easily runs over events" (ἀφελὴς καὶ δίχα πόνου καὶ ῥαδίως ἐπιτρέχουσα τοῖς πράγμασιν, 854E); it has persuasiveness, charm and power (χάριν ... καὶ δύναμιν, 855A). But whereas earlier critics had made a direct connection between Herodotus' style and his character—which was likewise thought to be "simple" and "sweet"—Plutarch breaks this long-held tenet of literary criticism. In this case the style does *not* indicate the man; on the contrary, the man has adopted a style best designed to *conceal* his actual character.

The second belief—that subject matter also indicated the historian's character— is perhaps most clearly seen in Dionysius of Halicarnassus' preface of his *Roman Antiquities* (A.R. 1.1.2–3):

> I am convinced that those who choose to leave behind to future generations monuments of their intellect which will not perish together with their bodies, and especially those who write histories—works which we all consider to be the very seat of truth, which is the beginning of reason and wisdom—should first choose topics that are noble and grand, and that will bring much benefit to their readers; and that they should then procure for themselves with great care and effort the sources which are appropriate for the composition of their topic. Those who compose treatises containing matters that are inglorious, wicked, or not worthy of our attention, whether they do so because they desire notoriety or to win some sort of name for themselves, or because they want to display the power of their eloquence, are neither admired by posterity for their notoriety nor praised for their talent; instead, they leave behind for those who take up their histories the belief that they approved of the sorts of lives which they treated in their works: for everyone rightly thinks that words are the image of each person's mind.

The choice of a "noble" subject therefore indicates a "noble" disposition. Here again Herodotus would be evaluated very positively, since he chose a topic—the united Greek defeat of Persia—that was clearly noble and grand, as indeed Dionysius states elsewhere.[37] Refuting Herodotus on this score, then, will take more effort, for Plutarch will have to show that far from treating the events of the Persian War in an ennobling manner, Herodotus did everything he could to impugn the motives and actions of the Greeks of that time.

He sets the stage for this immediately at the outset by quoting, within the first few lines, Plato's remark that it is the height of injustice to appear to be just while not actually being so. In using this remark of Plato's, Plutarch can place front and center the dichotomy between seeming and being, between appearance and reality. And indeed a look at the particular passage of Plato which Plutarch here cites shed additional light on the issue. For in that passage from *Republic* 2

Glaucon proposes to Socrates two different kinds of character, one wholly just, the other wholly unjust. Now in characterizing the just man, Glaucon says that he is "simple and noble," and in Aeschylus' words, "he doesn't want to seem best but to actually be so." These lines of Aeschylus, from the *Seven Against Thebes*, are a favourite of Plutarch's, and he uses them in particular when talking of Aristides the Just, though he there changes the wording from "best" (*ariston*) to "just" (*dikaion*), and this brings it more into line with what he is suggesting about Herodotus here: unlike the truly just man, Herodotus simply wishes to give the appearance of justice.[38]

After the opening paragraph, Plutarch offers a series of "tokens and signs" by which one can distinguish a malevolent historian. He gives eight of these, and they cover a variety of approaches.[39] For example, even the choice of words, the use of "harsher" instead of "milder" terms, can indicate a bad character. More substantially, the introduction of discreditable but irrelevant material or the omission of noble and relevant matter are also signs of a malicious historian. If a historian always assumes the worse motive by a character, or always chooses the less creditable version of an event, these too can indicate one who is always looking to find fault and criticize.

Having begun with these "tokens and signs," Plutarch then immediately goes through individual events narrated by Herodotus in roughly the order of Herodotus' own work, and discussing incidents from each of the nine Books but one. The treatment of Books is not equal, and the space allotted to individual incidents grows as Plutarch progresses through the *Histories*: only slightly more than a quarter of the essay deals with the earliest Books, and Plutarch arrives at Book 5 of Herodotus (more or less the second half) with still more than two-thirds of the essay to go. This is not surprising, of course, since the more historical Persian War material would have been of greater interest both to Plutarch and his audience, and he had said at the outset that he was especially keen to engage Herodotus in the latter's treatment of the Persian Wars.

A few examples can show how Plutarch goes about demonstrating that Herodotus is not only wrong but deliberately and maliciously wrong. A simple and straightforward example is Herodotus' treatment of Pactyes, who was entrusted by Cyrus with the task of conveying the Lydian booty to the Persian court after Cyrus had defeated the Lydians. But Pactyes induced the Lydians to revolt and then fled to Cyme. When the latter demanded him from the Cymaeans, they sent him to Mytilene. The Mytileneans in turn were intending to hand him over to Cyrus, but then the Cymaeans took him from there and brought him to Chios. At Chios he fled to the temple of Athena in supplication, but the Chians dragged him from the temple and handed him over to the Persians (Hdt. 1.154–60). It is this "sacrilege" with which Plutarch is here concerned (859A–B):

> He [Herodotus] says that when Pactyes revolted from Cyrus, the Cymaeans <…> and the Mytileneans were preparing to hand the man over "for a certain price, though I cannot say exactly how much": well done this, to claim ignorance of what the amount was and yet to cast such a reproach against a Greek city, as if he knew clearly. He then says that the Chians, when Pactyes was brought to them, removed him from the temple of Athena the City-Guardian and handed him over, and when they had done this they received Atarneus as their reward. Yet Charon of Lampsacus, an older writer, when he comes to treat Pactyes, has attributed no such pollution to the Mytileneans or the Chians. Here are his actual words: "When Pactyes realized that a Persian army was marching against him, he took flight and went first to Mytilene and then Chios. And Cyrus got hold of him."

Plutarch here uses the "older" writer, Charon, to refute Herodotus, suggesting that the story before Herodotus was a simple one (or at least there were no details about the actual surrender of Pactyes), but that Herodotus added particular slanders to the story, first that the Mytileneans were going to hand him over to the Persians for a reward, and second (and more seriously) that the Chians committed a sacrilege by forcibly removing him from the temple.

In this first example, Herodotus is accused of inventing false material to the detriment of particular characters. In the second example, Herodotus is faulted for omitting things that he "must have" known. This concerns the account of the Greek attack on Sardis in Book 5 (97–102), at the beginning of the Ionian Revolt. Plutarch writes (861A–D):

> In the account of Sardis that follows, he did everything he could to do away with and despoil the deed. He dares to call the ships which the Athenians sent to the Ionians to assist them in their revolt from the king "the beginning of evils" because they tried to free so many and such great cities from the king. And remembering the Eretrians only in an aside, he is completely silent about their great and renowned success. For when there was confusion around Ionia and a royal force was sailing against them, the Eretrians went to meet the Cypriots outside, in the Pamphylian sea, and fought a naval battle against them. Then turning back and leaving their ships at Ephesus, they attacked Sardis and besieged Artaphernes who had taken refuge in the citadel, trying thereby to raise the siege of Miletus. They accomplished this and they caused the enemy to withdraw in astonished fear. And when they were then attacked by a great force, they retreated. Others have spoken of this, especially Lysanias of Mallus in his

On Eretria. And it would have been a fine thing to have noted this brave deed and display of prowess if for no other reason, then at least to mark the capture and destruction of the city. But he says that they were in fact defeated by the barbarians and driven back to their ships, although Charon of Lampsacus records no such thing, but writes exactly as follows: "The Athenians sailed with twenty triremes intending to bring help to the Ionians, and they marched against Sardis and captured everything except the royal wall. And having accomplished these things, they withdrew to Miletus."

So here once again other authors are used as a way of showing that Herodotus must have known something but deliberately wrote something different. Here Plutarch uses a local historian in addition to Charon, and the double citation is meant to suggest even more so than in the first example that Herodotus is striking out on his own, contradicting what had been in the tradition before him.

The third example is somewhat more complicated, in that Plutarch here uses a variety of sources to refute Herodotus' account. This concerns Herodotus' account of the battle of Salamis, and in particular the treatment of the Corinthians in the battle. Before the battle of Salamis, Herodotus lists the Greek contingents who took part in the battle, but in the actual narrative, Herodotus focuses on just two Greek states, Athens and Aegina. Only when he has completed his narrative of the battle does Herodotus add a story about the Corinthians (8.94):

> The Athenians say that right at the beginning of the action the Corinthian commander Adeimantus got sail on his ship and fled in panic. Seeing the commander making off, the rest of the squadron followed; but when they were off that part of the coast of Salamis where the temple of Athene Sciras stands, they were met by a strange boat. It was all very mysterious, because nobody, apparently, had sent it, and the Corinthians, when it met them, knew nothing of how things were going with the rest of the fleet. From what happened next they were forced to conclude that the hand of God was in the matter; for when the boat was close to them, the people on board called out, "Adeimantus, while you are playing the traitor by running away with your squadron, the prayers of Greece are being answered, and she is victorious over her enemies." Adeimantus would not believe what they said, so they told him he might take them as hostages, and kill them if the Greeks were not found to have won the battle. On this, he and the rest of the squadron put about, and rejoined the fleet after the action was over. This, as I said, is the Athenian story, and the Corinthians do not admit the truth of it; on the contrary, they believe that their ships played a most distinguished part in the battle—and the rest of Greece gives evidence in their favour.

It is this account that Plutarch must refute (870B–D):

> Well, let us take no account of his lies in general but examine instead those lies which are told to someone's detriment. He says that the Athenians claim that Adeimantus, the Corinthian general, when the enemy were at hand, was overwhelmed with terror and fled, not by backing water or quietly slipping through the enemy ships but raising sail openly and turning all his ships around; but then a boat speeding along met up with him as he approached the end of Salamis and from the boat a voice spoke, "Adeimantus, in your flight you are betraying the Greeks. But they in fact are winning and they have mastered the enemy just as they desired." This boat, it seems, fell down from heaven: and indeed why should he have spared the tragic crane when everywhere else in his history he surpasses the tragic poets in imposture? And Adeimantus, trusting the voice, returned to camp when it was all over. This is the Athenians' story but "the Corinthians do not agree but consider themselves to have played a most distinguished part in the sea battle; and the rest of Greece bears witness to them". The man is like this in many places: he offers different slanders and accusations against different people, with the result that he cannot fail to make someone, at any rate, seem wicked. Just as here the net result for him is that the Corinthians are disgraced if the slander is believed, and the Athenians if it is disbelieved. But I don't think the Athenians ever made this charge against the Corinthians; I think Herodotus made these false allegations about both at the same time. Thucydides, at least, where he has an Athenian speaking in opposition to the Corinthians in Lacedaemon, and the Athenian is taking great pride in Athens' deeds in the Persian Wars and in the battle of Salamis, has levelled no charge of treason or desertion against the Corinthians.

The first point that Plutarch wishes to make is that this kind of 'slander' must redound to one or the other's discredit. But the evidence he brings in is really an argument from silence, namely that Thucydides does not have the Athenians mention Corinthian desertion when they are discussing the Persian Wars. It may not seem a terribly sound argument, but Plutarch does not simply rely on the argument from silence. He also has positive evidence to bring (870D–871A):

> And it's not likely that they would defame the Corinthians in this matter when they could see the name of the Corinthians engraved third, after the Lacedaemonians and themselves, on the dedication of spoils taken from the Persians; and on Salamis itself they gave permission for the men to be buried near the town and to have this elegy inscribed: "Stranger, we once dwelt in the well-watered city of Corinth, / but now Salamis, the isle of Ajax, holds us. / Here, capturing the ships of Phoenicians and Persians / and Medes, we saved sacred

Hellas." And the cenotaph at the Isthmus has this inscription: "When all Hellas was standing upon the razor's edge / we saved her with our lives, and here lie dead." And the following is inscribed on the dedications of Diodorus, a Corinthian commander, in the temple of Leto: "These weapons from the enemy Medes the sailors of Diodorus / dedicated to Leto as memorials of the sea battle." And as for Adeimantus himself, whom Herodotus continually reproaches for "being the only general to resist, saying that he would flee from Artemisium and not remain", look at the renown he held: "This is the grave of that Adeimantus, through whom / all Hellas put on the crown of freedom." Now it was not likely that a coward and a traitor would have received such honours when he died, nor would he have dared to name his daughters Nausinike, Acrothinion and Alixibian and his son Aristeus if he had won no renown or brilliance from those deeds.

And further, the Corinthian women, alone of Greek women, made that beautiful and divine prayer, asking the goddess to implant in their husbands a passionate desire to fight against the Persians. It is not credible that Herodotus was ignorant of this; it must have been known even to the remotest Carian, since the matter was widely publicized and Simonides wrote an epigram when bronze statues of the women were dedicated in the temple of Aphrodite, the temple Medea had built either when she was no longer in love with her husband (as some report) or (as others say) when the goddess ended Jason's love for Thetis. This is the epigram: "Here stand the women who, for the Greeks and their / stalwart fighting citizens, prayed to the divine Cypris: / for shining Aphrodite took care that the citadel of Greece / should not be betrayed to the bow-bearing Medes." It was these things he should have written and remembered . . .

As we saw earlier, Plutarch here uses sources other than Herodotus—in this case, the poetic tradition—to refute the historian. He can thus show that already at the time when Herodotus was writing his work, there was much information that could be gleaned from dedications and dedicatory epigrams. That some of these epigrams can be ascribed to Simonides, a contemporary and well-known witness to the wars, only increases their value. Plutarch is thus able to suggest again not only that Herodotus got it wrong but also that he *deliberately* got it wrong: with so much positive evidence already available to him when he came to write his history, he nonetheless deliberately omitted it so as to write an account of the Wars which denigrated the reputation of its greatest heroes.

This, then, will give some sense of how Plutarch goes about the business of showing not only that Herodotus is wrong but that he is wrong on purpose. I do not wish here to enter the question of the extent to which Plutarch's criticisms in this work are valid or effective; that is another subject.[40] Rather, I wish for now only to say again that Plutarch's refutation must combine both the notion of falsity and the notion of intentionality.

The final paragraph sums up the work, reiterating the influence of Herodotus' fine style on the reader, and warning again that this style is misleading (*Her. Mal.* 43):

> What can we say, then? The man knows how to write, his account is pleasurable and there is charm, force, and grace in his narrative, and he has 'recounted his tale like a poet' not 'knowledgeably' but instead sweetly and with polish. It is no doubt these aspects that beguile and win over everyone; but just as one must watch out for the rose-beetle amongst the roses, so one must be on one's guard against Herodotus' defamation and abuse, which lie beneath a smooth and soft appearance, lest we unwittingly accept absurd and false notions about the best and greatest cities and men of Greece.

Plutarch here returns to the style of Herodotus as the tool of his deception, and here too, as in the opening, Plutarch warns that one would be misled by taking this charm at face value, and one would arrive at a false evaluation of Herodotus' character. He picks up the earlier characterization of Herodotus' style, noting here that Herodotus' account "is pleasurable [ἡδὺς ὁ λόγος], and there is charm, force, and grace [χάρις . . . καὶ δεινότης καὶ ὥρα] in his narrative," and he tells his story "sweetly and with polish" (λιγυρῶς δὲ καὶ γλαφυρῶς), and the whole has "a smooth and soft appearance" (λείοις καὶ ἁπαλοῖς σχήμασιν). As a simile from nature had opened the work, so one from nature closes it. At the end of the essay, Plutarch wants to emphasize what is at stake in all of this: because of Herodotus' reputation and the fact that for most readers he is *the* historian of the Persian Wars, trusting his account will lead one to have the wrong ideas about the best and greatest of cities and men: the glory of the events, the greatness of the men and cities who did those unforgettable deeds, and in short the very meaning of the Persian Wars for the Greeks' sense of themselves is at stake.

Just as it was not by chance that Plutarch in the opening of the work cited a remark by Plato, so too here at the conclusion the adaptation of a Homeric line is also not accidental. The original line is spoken by Alcinous to Odysseus in Phaeacia, and it comes after Odysseus has recounted his wanderings: "you have recounted the tale knowledgeably," says Alcinous, "like a poet" (*Od.* 11.368). In Homer, of course, the comparison to a poet is meant to be seen positively. But Plutarch's citation, or rather manipulation of the line, shows us that it is meant to be read in a very different sense. And if we combine this with the opening reference to Plato, we can see the origin of Plutarch's criticisms of Herodotus.[41]

Pleasure, charm, grace—all of these Herodotus possesses, but he is also false and deceptive. He is, in other words, exactly what Plato thought the poets were. For Plato all poetry is imitation, and an imitation of an imitation, at two removes from the Forms and ultimate reality. Poets compose in ignorance, they represent objects unworthy of imitation, and their employment of emotion corrupts the souls of their audience. And although Plutarch's views on literature are not uniform or simple, it is nevertheless the case that there are many passages in both the *Lives* and *Moralia* that indicate a Platonic approach to literature.[42] His references to tragedy, for example, contain criticism of the genre and its recourse to effects that create absurd situations,[43] as in the criticism above of Herodotus' "little boat" that appears to Adeimantus and the Corinthians, which is immediately compared to the absurd stage effects of tragedy. Like Plato, Plutarch thought that poetry was powerful and for that reason could be dangerous. In a passage from the *Life* of Solon, Plutarch portrays the elder statesman attending a tragic performance by no less than Thespis (*Solon* 29.6–7):

> At this time Thespis was beginning to develop performances of tragedy and the novelty of his enterprise attracted most of the city to watch, although it had not yet been made the object of a regular competition. Solon had always been a good listener and ready to learn something new, and now in his old age had become even fonder of leisure and entertainment, and, by God, of wine and song, too, and so he went to watch Thespis act in his own play, as the ancient poets usually did. After the performance was over, he went up to Thespis and asked him whether he was not ashamed to tell such lies in front of so many people. When Thespis replied that there was no harm in speaking or acting in this way in amusement, Solon struck the ground angrily with his staff and exclaimed, "Yes, but if we allow ourselves to praise and honour this amusement, the next thing will be to find it creeping into our serious business."

In the Herodotus essay, therefore, what we see is a unique approach to the great historian, an attempt to get at him from an angle different from any that had gone before. Plutarch does not wish to improve on this or that fact, nor does he concern himself with the "tall tales" so dear to previous Herodotus critics. He may well have thought that no one believed such tales anyway, and in those cases their obvious appeal to "entertainment" meant that they could easily be dismissed or understood for what they were: in terms of the passage from *Solon*, they would be in Thespis' terms "speaking or acting in amusement." Instead, Plutarch acknowledges Herodotus' "poetic" virtues of charm and grace, which encourage persuasion in the reader. Nor again is it accidental that Plutarch employs this trope: for Herodotus was generally recognized as 'very Homeric'.[44] In other literary critics, this is clearly meant as a compliment, an acknowledgement that Herodotus reached the peak of history as Homer had of poetry. But in the world of Plato and his disciples, Homer is indeed an ambivalent figure: powerful, brilliant, persuasive, but ultimately false and dangerous. So too was Herodotus, at least in Plutarch's eyes.

Historiography, as a rhetorical genre in antiquity, not surprisingly used rhetorical means to establish the authority of the historical narrator. It was a given that people would read a writer's character from his or her words, and would construct an image of the personality of the writer as they read. In many cases, the author's "nature" would emerge in what seemed to be a simple way: the incessant criticisms of Theopompus or the barbed attacks of Timaeus were easily assimilated to an "angry" or even "bitter" character. The writings of a Xenophon, by contrast, showed charm and grace, and a simple and philosophical character. In *On the Malice of Herodotus*, by contrast, Plutarch set himself the task of showing that the character of Herodotus, which appeared on the surface to be genial and generous, was in fact not the writer's actual character, and that only a careful reading and examination of what lay beneath the surface could show the inner—that is, real—nature of the historian. His attack on Herodotus represents an inversion of the defence made by iambic and comic poets: they assert that their verses are bad but they are good, while Plutarch asserts that Herodotus' narrative is (or pretends to be) good but his character is bad. Modern scholars are nearly unanimous in believing that Plutarch makes absolutely no dent in Herodotus' reputation. But even if he doesn't, it would be well for us to recognize precisely what has gone into this essay. Plutarch has built on traditional notions of authority as they developed in classical antiquity, but also introduced heretofore unused notions of authenticity (though that is not, of course, a word he could or would have used), with the result that he produced a piece of historiographical criticism unique in the Greco-Roman tradition.

Notes

1 This chapter is a reworked version of the paper delivered (by Federico Santangelo in my absence) in São Paulo on July 11, 2019. I am very grateful to the editors for the invitation to contribute to the conference and the volume. Translations, unless otherwise noted, are mine (most are from Marincola (2017)).
2 Nichols (2017) is a useful recent overview.
3 See Damon (2009); Marincola (2009: 18–22).

4 Marincola (1997).
5 There was, of course, a biographical tradition about Thucydides eventually, but this comes into being long after his reputation is assured.
6 Booth (1983: 149–65); Bal (2017: 12–22); de Jong (2014: 17–42).
7 See, e.g., Hogan (2010).
8 Trilling (1972); Varga and Guignon (2020) offer an excellent overview and full bibliography on the topic of authenticity.
9 Goodyear (1972) 98.
10 Sall. *Cat.* 3.3–4.2: *sed ego adulescentulus initio, sicuti plerique, studio ad rem publicam latus sum ibique mihi multa aduorsa fuere. nam pro pudore, pro abstinentia, pro uirtute audacia, largitio, auaritia uigebant. quae tametsi animus aspernabatur insolens malarum artium, tamen inter tanta uitia imbecilla aetas ambitione corrupta tenebatur; ac me, cum ab reliquorum malis moribus dissentirem, nihilo minus honoris cupido eadem, qua ceteros, fama atque inuidia uexabat. igitur ubi animus ex multis miseriis atque periculis requieuit et mihi reliquam aetatem a re publica procul habendam decreui ... igitur de Catilinae coniuratione, quam uerissume potero, paucis absoluam ...*
11 Cass. Dio 43.9.2; [Sall.] *Inv. in Sall.* 7.19.
12 Macr. *Sat.* 3.13.9: *Sallustius, grauissimus alienae luxuriae obiurgator et censor* (trans. R. A. Kaster).
13 The testimonia on his reputation are collected in Kurfess (1957: xxvii–xxxi) and Duursma (2019: 204–7).
14 See esp. Wiseman (1979); Woodman (1988).
15 Marincola (1997: 218–36). The historians, of course, had good precedent in the poets themselves, as we can see from the famous opening of Hesiod's *Theogony*, where the Muses already warn that they can say "many false things that resemble true" (1–11).
16 Woodman (1988) *passim*; Luce (1989).
17 The passages are perhaps most easily accessible in Marincola (2017: 77–109).
18 *FGrHist* 566 F 152 (= Pol. 12.24.1–2).
19 On these, see Kirkland (2019: 480–4).
20 Polybius emphasizes that different reactions are necessary for those who make errors inadvertently and those who deliberately lie: the latter 'deserve inexorable prosecution' (Pol. 12.7.6).
21 Bibliography at Marincola (2015) 83 n. 1, to which add Ingenkamp (2016); Marincola (2016); and Kirkland (2019).
22 I hope to provide a full study of this essay in a forthcoming work.
23 Jos. *c. Ap.* 1.16; on the criticism of Herodotus in antiquity see Jacoby (1909: 506–13); Riemann (1967); Priestley (2014).
24 *FGrHist* 688 T 8 = T 8 Lenfant.
25 *FGrHist* 609 T 7a.

26 Diod. 1.37.4; cf. 1.69.7.
27 Ctesias, *FGrHist* 688 T 8 (λογοποιός); Aristot. *Gen. An.* 3.5, 756b (μυθόλογος).
28 See, e.g., [Cic.] *Herenn.* 1.13.
29 On the whole topic, see Romm (1992).
30 See above, n. 18.
31 This last is Ewen Bowie's felicitous translation: Bowie (2016: 71).
32 Sen. *Epist.* 114.1: *talis hominibus oratio, qualis uita*, with Berti (2018) 59–61.
33 See Dickie (1981).
34 See de Romilly (1975).
35 Hom. *Il.* 9.312–13: "For as I detest the doorways of death, I detest that man who / hides one thing in the depths of his heart, and speaks forth another" (trans. Lattimore). On the false speeches of the *Odyssey*, see Grossart (1998).
36 Excellent discussion of the relationship between style and character here in Kirkland (2019: 484–90).
37 Plutarch also believed that it was a noble theme: *Comp. Arist.-Cat. Mai.* 5.1.
38 As it happens, the word δίκαιος has a rather wider connotation in historiographical texts, and is closely connected with impartiality, as can be seen in a passage of Lucian, where he compares the flatterer Ctesias of Cnidus with the "just" (i.e., non-flattering) Xenophon (*hist. conscr.* 39).
39 The complete list: (1) a preference for words too severe; (2) inclusion of discreditable acts irrelevant to the history; (3) the omission of what is good and noble; (4) when accounts differ, a preference for the worse version of some action; (5) a preference for the more discreditable explanation; (6) the assertion that luck, not valor, is responsible for success; (7) indirect attack, e.g. reporting a matter but denying belief in it; (8) use of small praises to make great criticisms believable.
40 Bowen (1992) many of the criticisms of Plutarch and defences of Herodotus often advanced by scholars.
41 See Kirkland (2019: 504–6).
42 See Van der Stockt (1992) on Plutarch's approach to literature; Kirkland (2019: 490–6) on "Platonic presences" in this essay.
43 See de Lacy (1952).
44 [Long.] *Subl.* 13.3, Ὁμηρικώτατος; *SEG* XLVIII.1330 (= *SGO* I, 01/12/02), line 43: Ἡρόδοτον τὸν πεζὸν ἐν ἱστορίαισιν Ὅμηρον.

2

Poetry as History: The Authority of Lucan as a Historian

Leni Ribeiro Leite

The way in which poets determine their own authority is an area that has received scholarly attention for many years.[1] However, as Vieira and others have argued, epic poetry in Rome was, at its inception, an historical genre.[2] A poet writing this kind of poetry would have a double insertion, and therefore a double claim to authority—but how could he affirm it? This chapter looks at Lucan's *Pharsalia* as the earliest example of Roman history in verse to survive to the present day in more than fragmentary form, in order to try and answer this question.

It is always worth remembering that categories such as History or Literature are in themselves historically determined by their discursive fields, so that the same text can variably belong to genres and forms depending on the moment in which it is observed.[3] As Conte affirms, genres are not static forms, but strategies of representation, fluid and mutable[4]—and History is one such genre. In their essay on historiography of India in early modern times, Rao, Shulman, and Subrahmanyam describe how European historians, arriving at the South of India as part of the British invasion, found (to their modern eyes) a region with no conscience or narrative worth the name of History, just a collection of "myths, legends, literature, puranic stories, folklore and phantasmagoria of various types and forms."[5] Therefore, in order to write the history of pre-colonial India, nineteenth-century European historians used what they called empirical data, offered by inscriptions, coins, and other such materials, besides the tales told here and there by European visitors—considered much more trustworthy than the natives. In this way, one could divide the sources between those adequate, "hard" ones, in opposition to the sources from the Indian tradition, which are regarded as "literary" and "recalcitrant." The Indian people were thus denied not only the conscience of their own historicity, but also the existence of a proper textual form through which their historicity was decanted. In the same work,

Rao, Shulman, and Subrahmanyam state their opposition to this portrayal, returning to the category of History a significant quantity of texts produced in the southern part of India which were discarded by nineteenth-century historiography, which considered them too colorful, too rich, and too dramatic to count as History.

Since European historiographic tradition has always seen its own roots as being planted in Greek and Roman soil, drawing a comparison between this situation in India and Roman historiography might at first seem unfair, or at least unfruitful.[6] However, ancient authors have also had their fair share in the very exclusive club of challenged historians. Of course, there were rules and assumptions for the writing of history in the ancient world itself, since claims to authority are frequent in writers such as Sallust, Livy, Cicero, and Caesar, to cite just a few Roman authors.[7] Even then, as Laird[8] points out, Cicero's affirmation in the *De legibus* (1.5) that history is a task for orators has been used by modern scholars to justify not only that history was a branch of rhetoric, but to support a picture of Roman history as not committed to veracity, and therefore outside the realm of history. By equating rhetoric and fiction—as if all discourses were not, by their own discursive nature, fictionalizations[9]—this modern view marking a gap between Roman historiography and ours has stood on testimonies such as the Ciceronian one above. However, it ignored others, such as the one, a few lines earlier in the same work, in which Cicero had already said that all things in history should turn on truth (*ad veritatem referantur*) and, in the *De oratore* (2.62–4), stated that the first rule of history is that it should say nothing but the truth.[10] In short, history as written by the Romans, although more similar to what was expected in the nineteenth century, was also criticized by the moderns due to their alleged lack of precision, for adding fables and legends, for presenting the speeches of long-dead characters, among other requests for the standards of modern historiography loaded onto texts written two thousand years ago or more. And if the works written in prose presenting themselves as histories suffered under such judgment, Latin works that are usually ascribed to other formats or genres were marginalized even further.

The superspecialization of the historiographical genre of writing is, nonetheless, a characteristic of History as a discipline, developed in Western Europe. Therefore, it is not a fundamental requisite or a natural trait of narratives about the past. Rao, Shulman, and Subrahmanyam[11] defend that this kind of specialization did not occur in most parts of the world, having developed due to specific European professional and institutional reasons, and not due to an intrinsic necessity of factual reports—as such, then, the writing of history is not necessarily the monopoly of one category or type of text. Antiquity offered testimony that this question was already up for debate: the Greeks, according to Hartog,[12] did not invent history, but invented the historian as the one that writes. This individual who writes history determines and defines themselves at each moment, as Marincola[13] has shown, sometimes as the negative of another: they are not a philosopher, they are not a rhetorician, they are not a poet. This constant need for affirmation, however, seems to indicate that there was some confusion in the field, and Aristotle has left us this debate, by registering that "[t]he difference between a historian and a poet is not that one writes in prose and the other in verse—indeed the writings of Herodotus could be put into verse and yet would still be a kind of history, whether written in meter or not.[14] When Aristotle discusses the competence and genre of the historiographer, comparing them to others that do not seem, to our modern eyes, to compete at all with history, such as tragedy or epic, we can perceive, as the necessary background against which Aristotle argues, an opposite argument, that elides and blends these elements that our modern authors would clearly want to separate.[15]

Scholarship in the last decades have seen an impetus for reevaluating documentation assumed as non-valid for the writing of history. In this vein, we would like to consider the case for poetic texts, which were for a long time deemed unworthy of credit as historiographical work, relegated to second rank or as source of general information, when compared to prose works—a tradition that has been established since the nineteenth century. We advocate the use of poetry not only for studying the political history of societies from the past,[16] but also as self-proposed and self-conscious texts of historiographical flavor and value.

There are, of course, marked differences between an epic poem and the text of a self-proclaimed historian, such as Livy; but they do have many similarities as well, and this might be unnoticed to the untrained eyes of a modern reader. For instance, interpreting the construction of a historiographical Roman text demands the understanding that rhetoric was fundamental in the educational path traveled by all Latin authors, regardless of genre. Therefore, it is fundamental to inquire how rhetorical effects mark the writing of Roman history on multiple levels.[17] Indeed, writing in any genre in ancient Rome was only possible based on the knowledge of the rhetorical devices learned from manuals, from the observation of the practice in the forum and the Senate House, from the distinguished models of the past or from the learned and valuable contemporaries.

In the case of certain subjects, the use of commonplaces and stock characters were the accepted usage, known by all from their common rhetorical training.

That is for instance the case of the tyrant, a *topos* particularly remarkable in Aristotle.[18] However, when this commonplace is used by authors such as Tacitus, Pliny the Younger, or Suetonius to conform the representation of Roman leaders and Emperors such as Domitian—or, even before them by Sallust, Livy, and Cicero, or after them, by Cassius Dio, Velleius Paterculus, or Aurelius Victor, to name but a few—they were very often taken as face value by the modern historiographical tradition, and the subjects of their *vituperatio* passed on as evil or madmen in positions of power. Such was the fate of (for example) Tiberius, Caligula, Nero, Galba, Domitian, Commodus, and Elagabalus; and this transparent and naive reading of rhetorical elements still lingers,[19] in spite of studies such as those by Dunkle,[20] Tabacco,[21] Habinek,[22] and Johansson,[23] which debate the creation and usage of the rhetorical device of the tyrant in Roman environments.

Ancient rhetorical manuals invited writers of prose or poetry to use *topoi* and other devices everywhere in the invention, disposition, and enunciation of texts; every use of language was at the service of an argument with a persuasive goal, and prescribed the amplification or deamplification of attributes, the addition of color to narratives or speeches, the molding of the figure one wished to condemn or to praise with the use of strategies that would communicate a certain version of a historical figure or fact.[24] That was as true of "literary" poetry as it was true of "historiographical" prose narrative.

Under these conditions, one might ask, if both historiographers and poets manipulate the rhetorical machinery when creating their texts, would then the difference between them be an argumentative construction, prone to be doubted? Or rather, if it is necessary to constantly reaffirm that a poet is not a historiographer, would it be possible to perceive when and how, in constructing his own *ethos*, the author would be causing this kind of confusion?

Lucan, the first-century CE Roman poet whose only work to have come down to us is the *Bellum Civile* or *Pharsalia*, is a good author for us to ask these questions. By choosing the civil war between Julius Caesar and Pompey as the theme for his epic poem, he firmly planted his feet both in the most traditional of the forms of poetry and in a favorite historiographical theme. Indeed, he seems to have been considered more than a poet even during the Roman period. As Frederick Ahl[25] convincingly points out, Quintilian's comments on Lucan are praise indeed, when we consider his famous passage that marks Lucan as *oratoribus magis quam poetis imitandus* ("more worthy of being imitated by orators than by poets": *Inst. Or.* 10.1.90), together with other passages in which poets were more likely to be disparaged than rhetoricians. On the other hand, we must also remember that Quintilian "cannot mean that Lucan's work is too 'rhetorical' to be good poetry since he is himself writing a guide for instructors of rhetoric in their teaching and does not use 'rhetoric' and 'rhetorical' as terms of disparagement as nineteenth and twentieth century critics often did."[26]

The *Pharsalia* seems to have characteristics that were considered typical of historiography, not only by the Romans themselves, but even by nineteenth-century Western European readers. One example of such would be the commitment to natural—as opposed to supernatural—explanations of phenomena. The absence of deities in the *Bellum Civile* is often cited as one of its most marked characteristics,[27] and at odds with what is expected from an epic poem; that is not, however, out of sync with the work of a historian. The most canonical Roman historians are precisely those who are closer to this ideal, and Livy has been at the center of discussions about his skepticism in all that refers to the supernatural or prodigies, which he reports but tends to mark as doubtful or spurious.[28] Therefore, what surprises in Lucan's poetry would be an expected element in a work of historiographical nature. We shall now look at some examples, comparing Lucan's poem and elements of Roman historiography, to try and observe how Lucan seems to be much closer to the historiographical discourse than perhaps other poets. However, despite the ample possibilities, we shall confine ourselves to looking at elements of *elocutio*, leaving a closer investigation of other equally important aspects of Lucan's discursive construction (such as his *inventio*) to a future occasion.

For the sake of example, let us look at one episode referred to by both Livy and Lucan, as well as by other Roman authors:[29] the appearance of the shield of Numa. As Ovid recounts,[30] Numa Pompilius, second king of Rome, with the help of the minor gods Picus and Faunus, managed to request and be granted an audience with Jupiter himself. The god taught Numa how to avoid an imminent flood, the prospect of which terrified the population, and promised the king that early the next day there would be public proof of his power. As dawn broke, and the whole population gathered at Numa's door, thunder rolled three times, three lightning strikes were seen, and a shield fell from the sky. As the crowd exclaimed, Numa picked it up off the ground, and ordered that exact copies be made, all of which were put under the care of the Salian priests.

In Ovid, this narrative takes up almost 150 lines, and it is very detailed, as befits the work. Livy (1.20), on the other hand, does not mention the legend of the shield having fallen from the sky as he tells Numa's story: he mentions the shields only as part of the duties of the Salii, as they carry the heavenly weapons (*caelestia arma*) called *ancilia* in their procession, nodding to what would have been general knowledge through the use of the adjective *caelestia*. This lack of detail around supernatural elements is explained immediately prior to this passage, in a point in the narrative in which general skepticism was established in relation to portents during Numa's reign that were passed down by tradition. In 1.19, Livy points to the reason why Numa used legends and mysticism as a political device: "he [Numa] thought the very first thing to do, as being the most efficacious with a populace which was ignorant and, in those early days, uncivilized, was to imbue them with the fear of Heaven."[31] This is the usual pattern found throughout Livy's work when portraying the supernatural. Slightly later, in Book 5, during the episode of the war against the Gauls, Camillus gives a speech in which the shield that fell from heaven is again listed among other presages and portents as absurdities from a legendary past: "Here is the Capitol, where men were told, when of old they discovered there a human head, that in that place should be the head of the world and the seat of empire; [...] here are Vesta's fires, here the shields that were sent down from heaven, here are all the gods propitious, if you remain."[32] The doubtful episodes are used by Camillus not because they are truthful, or even credible, but as instruments of persuasion, to convince the credulous. Livy again clearly points it out immediately after: "The speech of Camillus is said to have moved them, particularly where he touched upon religion."[33]

Lucan mentions the shield of Numa in Book 9 of his poem, in a signally difficult point in the narrative: Pompey dies in Book 8, leaving behind a headless (that is, leaderless) army. At the beginning of Book 9, Pompey's soul floats through the heavens and ends up descending onto Cato's heart, which then makes him assume leadership of Pompey's legions. Cato decides to regroup the armed forces, bringing together his own dilapidated army and King Juba's, and, in order to do so, the soldiers must cross a part of Africa, passing by the fearful Sirtes, a coastal area in which the sandbanks are numerous and mutable, making navigation very dangerous. Lucan describes the Sirtes as areas left by nature midway between ocean and dry land (*in dubio pelagi terraeque*: 9.304), and brings up possibilities that one might now call scientific for their peculiarities, citing even the Stoic theory of the tides.[34]

What follows is what Paolo Asso[35] classified as a paradox: the description of a sea storm in a space that, as Lucan himself wrote, was *not* a sea; and a storm which is not really a storm, but rather a maritime obstacle which is constant only in its inconstancy. Pompey's followers end up shipwrecked by the Sirtes and, in this passage, there is mention of the strong winds that rip sails off masts and leave ships without ropes. Some of the ships get lost in the Sirtes, but others manage to find their way to Lake Tritonis. Cato decides then to continue on foot, marching through the desert to avoid the winter gales, known to be dangerous for navigation.

The narrator then proceeds in a scientific tone, explaining, on the basis of geographical theories, that the region close to the Sirtes, even on land, is treacherous and dangerous, not only because of the presence of quicksand, similar to the sandbanks on the sea; nor only because of the desert itself, scorching and inappropriate for human life,[36] but because the storms are also common on land, pushed by the southern wind through the Sirtes. The wind raises the desert sands in dust storms, more destructive than fire, carrying houses in their wake, creating chaos.[37] This wind takes the soldiers' weapons and, in a distant land, *creates false prodigies*. This is how Lucan describes it:

> [...] The wind, with violent blows, took away men's helmets and shields and javelins and carried them off fiercely through the empty sky. Perhaps they were a prodigy in some remote and distant land, and people there fear the weapons fallen from heavens thinking that what was taken from men's arms was sent by the gods. That is how those shield, which chosen patricians carry on their shoulders, fell for Numa as he performed sacrifice. The Auster and the Boreas stole them and brought them to us.[38]
>
> Luc. 9.471–80

In an almost casual manner (notice the use of *forsan*, "maybe"), here Lucan discredits one of the oldest Roman traditions, proposing, in turn, a rationalization of the myth of Numa's shield. He suggests that the mythical knowledge, traditionally passed from generation to generation, or that the memory of Rome's sacred past might be just an erroneous interpretation of a meteorological phenomenon, minimizing or relegating to discredit all supernatural explanations.[39] This diction seems to be similar to Livy's, when explaining Numa's or Camillus' use of superstition with the goal of attaining political power, containing the population through fear, or convincing people of going to war. In textual terms, the supernatural has a more rational explanation, which is made explicit by the historian, who is not fooled by such tales.

Therefore, Lucan, the epic poet, stands closer to well-established historiographical devices: both poet and historian are bent on removing divine agency from their narratives. We can also point to the constant demythification of fantastic or legendary places in Lucan' poem: the Hesperides, where once Hercules stood, and Lake Tritonis, where Athena was born, are visited by Pompey's soldiers in the same Book 9, and even though the narrator reminds us that these places are cited in myths, they have nothing of the unreal or supernatural, and nothing exotic or epic happens to the wearied soldiers there. Later in the poem, Caesar's visit to Troy is another warning that the mythical and supernatural elements of such places cannot be part of reality; in Lucan, they are not full of wonder, but burned, sterile, dry, and sad:

> He (Caesar) walks around the burnt Troy, of memorable name and searches for the lofty remains of the wall of Apollo. Now empty woods and rotting wooden trunks take hold of Assaracus' palace, and the idle roots grab the temples of the gods, and all of Pergamon is covered with thorns: even the ruins have disappeared. He sees Hesione's cliffs and, in the woods, the hidden chambers of Anchises, and in which cave Paris was judge, and the spot from which the boy was snatched to the sky; he sees the peak where the Naiad Oenone lamented. There is not a nameless stone. Unknowingly he crosses a stream running through dry dust: it was the Xanthus. He was walking with sure step through the tall grass, a local inhabitant stopped him from stepping on Hector's tomb. A pile of rocks was scattered, with no appearance of sacredness: "You do not respect" says the guide "the altar of Zeus?"[40]
>
> Luc. 9.964–79

Caesar has to search for the walls of Phoebus, which in the epic story are always the tallest: in Lucan's world, they are crumbling ruins. Pergamon is no longer golden, but covered in vegetation; the River Xanthus, an important boundary cited so many times in the *Iliad*, is a narrow and unimportant creek running through dusty ground; and not even Hector's burial mound is distinguishable from the rocks laid around it. The contrast with the descriptions of these places in the epic poems in the Trojan cycle does not need to be explained; Lucan is looking to imprint a factual texture to his poem that reinforces its historiographical character.

At the same time, elements marked as non-historic in nineteenth-century Europe could be understood as historic in first-century Rome, further underlining the authority of Lucan as a historian for his contemporaries, but not to modern-day scholars. One aspect of the *Pharsalia* that has been singled out as something not expected either from a historiographer or an epic poet is the prominence of the narrator's voice. Reed[41] mentions how Lucan's voice is passionate, interested, Roman, when contrasted with the more colorless voice of Vergil. Indeed, quite often Lucan abandons the position of an impartial narrator and clearly expresses his preferences, opinions, and suffering with regard to the facts he narrates: civil war, freedom, empire, the destiny of the Romans, as for example in 7.385–459. Bartsch[42] notices that, in many instances, one hears a tone of hatred or vengeance in the narrator's voice, a first person that breaks the wall between speaker and listener, asking Julius Caesar, for example, if he is not ashamed to wage a war disapproved of by his own soldiers, and if he is not tired of committing crimes.[43] This narrator's voice, categorized by Bartsch[44] as pro-Pompey, or even Republican, is unusual but not completely unheard of in epic, while it seems quite unacceptable for historiography. These are qualities pointed out by Quintilian (10.1.90) as characteristic of Lucan, that is, to be *ardens et concitatus*, vehement and vertiginous, and are in sharp contrast with writing *sine ira et studio*, without anger or interests, an ideal set up by Tacitus (*Ann.* 1.1).

However, in spite of Tacitus' opinion and the constant repetition of the *topos* of the impartiality of the historiographer, described by Marincola[45] as a need to seem objective, we have among the historians of the first century one that not only does not follow that standard, but actually has similarities with what we see in Lucan, including the partial and opinionated narrator. The two books of the *Historia Romana* by Velleius Paterculus, which unfortunately comes to us in a fragmentary state and missing the beginning of Book 1, are clear historiographical prose. What is left of it covers the period between the battle of Pydna in 168 BCE up to 30 CE, a period of particular historical interest. Velleius, as Lucan, dialogues with his own characters, who have been dead for decades or centuries; he expresses his sadness or horror towards the facts he narrates; he praises the actions of those with whom he agrees—usually Tiberius. Bartsch[46] chooses as the most notable of these moments in which the narrator's voice breaks through the facts of the narrative the censure to Mark Antony after the death of Caesar, reproduced below as one among the many examples found in the work:[47]

> But you accomplished nothing, Mark Antony—for the indignation that surges in my breast compels me to exceed the bounds I have set for my narrative—you accomplished nothing, I say, by offering a reward for the sealing of those divine lips and the severing of that illustrious head, and by encompassing with a death-fee the murder of so great a consul and of the man who once had saved the state. You took from Marcus Cicero a few anxious days, a few senile years, a life which would have been more wretched under your domination than was his death in your triumvirate; but you did not rob him of his fame, the glory of his deeds and words, nay you but enhanced them. He lives and will continue to live in the memory of the ages, and so long as this universe shall endure—this universe which, whether created by chance, or by divine providence, or by whatever cause, he, almost alone of all the Romans, saw with the eye of his mind, grasped with his intellect, illumined with his eloquence—so long shall it be accompanied throughout the ages by the fame of Cicero. All posterity will admire the speeches that he wrote against you, while your deed to him will call forth their execrations,

> and the race of man shall sooner pass from the world than the name of Cicero be forgotten.
>
> Vell. Pat. 2.66.35 (trans. Shipley 1924)[48]

Velleius Paterculus openly chooses one side in the events he narrates: he is against Mark Antony and, consequently, not only in favor of Cicero, but also in favor of Octavian, to whom Mark Antony will shortly afterwards be opposed, and to whom he will lose another important battle, at Philippi, also brought into play by Lucan in comparison to Pharsalus.[49] The interpellation to the characters is marked by Velleius as something perhaps not expected for the genre (*cogit enim excedere propositi formam operis erumpens animo ac pectore indignatio*, "for the indignation that surges in my breast compels me to exceed the bounds I have set for my narrative"), but not so damaging that it should be left out. It is also quite similar to what we see in Lucan when he confronts Pompey in 7.207–213: a passage that ends with *attonitique omnes ueluti uenientia fata, / non transmissa, legent et adhuc tibi, Magne, fauebunt*, "all will read, astonished, as if the fates were yet to come, and not already passed; and they will still favour your cause, Pompey."

There are still other elements of the texture of Velleius' narrative that have similarities to Lucan's style, and both works contain elements that we could classify as appropriate to texts considered historiographical in antiquity, such as the constant relation between present and past, which Hartog[50] demonstrates in Cicero, Dionysius of Halicarnassus, Livy, and Tacitus;[51] and elements that can be considered unusual for historiography, such as the expression of doubt about the future. Even if uncharacteristic of history in general, they were present, and therefore characteristic, of Velleius.

The interpellation of characters appears in yet another historiographer left to the margins of canon, like Velleius: Flavius Josephus. Even if less passionate than Velleius, Josephus also makes an observation about the inadequacy of his expressions of compassion towards the suffering of the Jews that appear here and there throughout his works.[52] And perhaps one could ask why these authors seem to be less famous as ancient historiographers, and how this erasure hinders a vision of works by authors doubtlessly accepted in antiquity as belonging to the genre of history.[53] Both Velleius and Josephus are closer chronologically to Lucan than Livy, and Lucan seems to be adding to his text elements that would make the audience recognize in him the factuality and authority of a historiographer.

Nonetheless, Lucan's attempt at establishing his own authority as a historiographer seems to have attained little success. That he was indeed attempting to do so seems clear. As Marincola[54] observes, the poet's claim for authority stems from the Muse, the historian builds his own authority from other sources; moreover, the difference between historiography and epic is that the former "contains commentary on the narrative" and the historian "employs an 'artificial authority' by which he interprets the events of his work for the reader".[55] All of these, as we have shown, can be found in Lucan, who seemed to be aiming for the kind of historiography written around his own times, as we have seen in comparing him to Velleius and Josephus. Yet, he is not listed by the ancients among the historians: Quintilian, who organized his list of recommended authors by genre, makes the aforementioned remarks about Lucan in his Roman poets section (*Inst. Or.* 10.1.85–96), and not in his list of Roman historians (which comes later, at 10.1.101–104). He did not make it, but we have at least one testimony from the ancients, which seems to confirm this attempt: in Servius' commentary on the *Aeneid* (1.382), we find the well-known statement: *Lucanus videtur historiam composuisse, non poema* ("Lucan seems to have composed history, and not a poem"). Perhaps it was the strength of the meter, in spite of Aristotle's defense of subject over meter; perhaps his style just fell out of favor, as one can see from Suetonius' brief *Life of Lucan* or in Fronto's letters, in which he classifies both Lucan and his uncle Seneca as authors of the worst type, and with bad vocabulary (Fr., *Orat.* 2–7; *Fer. Als.* 3.2).

Lucan fared no better in modern times: he is completely absent from the "Chronological list of the historians of Rome" in *The Cambridge Companion to the Roman Historians*,[56] and while there is a chapter on "The *Bellum Civile* as a Roman Epic," as well as chapters on connections between the *Pharsalia* and elegy, *silvae*, and Dante in the *Brill Companion to Lucan*, there is no chapter that discusses him as a historian. However, considering Lucan as a historian in his own merits could be a very productive field, and may open up new understandings of the *Bellum Civile*.

Notes

1   We can for instance mention Hardie (1997), Lowrie (2001), Harries (2009), Arthur (2020), to cover a space of two decades of study of authority in Ovid alone.
2   Vieira (2013).
3   Discursive field is a concept derived from the theory of fields by Bourdieu (1984), also used by Maingueneau (2021) in discourse analysis. We understand a discursive field as a set of discursive positions and discursive identities that occur dynamically

in the same space and time. The literary field is this set of positions connected to ancient Roman *litterae,* or to what we now refer to as literature: cf. Charaudeau and Maingueneau (2002).
4 Conte (1994: 112).
5 Rao, Shulman, and Subrahamnyam (2001: 2).
6 A discussion carried out by Hartog (1999).
7 Marincola (1997).
8 Laird (2009: 199–200)
9 Batstone (2009: 27).
10 Cic. *De or.* 2.62: *nam quis nescit primam esse historiae legem, ne quid falsi dicere audeat? Deinde ne quid veri non audeat?* […] This passage from the *De Oratore* has taken many scholars to support, on the other hand, a general notion that conceptions of historiography have changed relatively little over the ages (see Laird 2009: 200).
11 Rao, Shulman, Subrahmanyam (2001: 15).
12 Hartog (1999: 12).
13 Marincola (1997: 128–74).
14 Arist. *Poet.* 9.1451b: ὁ γὰρ ἱστορικὸς καὶ ὁ ποιητὴς οὐ τῷ ἢ ἔμμετρα λέγειν ἢ ἄμετρα διαφέρουσιν· εἴη γὰρ ἂν τὰ Ἡροδότου εἰς μέτρα τεθῆναι καὶ οὐδὲν ἧττον ἂν εἴη ἱστορία τις μετὰ μέτρου ἢ ἄνευ μέτρων.
15 And also Polybius, *Hist.* 2.56.11, perhaps responding to Aristotle.
16 Laird (2009: 197–8).
17 Laird (2009: 209).
18 Aristotle, *Pol.* 1311a2–6; 1313b–1314a.
19 Such is the case of Frazer Jr. (1966), Southern (1997), and Saller (2000), to name a few.
20 Dunkle (1967; 1971).
21 Tabacco (1985).
22 Habinek (2005: 8–15).
23 Johansson (2013: 7–8).
24 Wiseman (1979: 80–1); Johansson (2013: 8–9).
25 Ahl (2010).
26 Ahl (2010: 2).
27 Bartsch (1997: 63).
28 One of the most-cited excerpts in this discussion is Livy 27.23.2. A lengthy explanation on the theme is in Levene (1993), esp. 16–20. See also Davies (2004: 27–45) for a more complex and nuanced approach to the issue of belief of skepticism in Livy, building upon Levene (1993).
29 Besides Livy (1.20) and Lucan, the episode also appears in Ov. *Fast.* 3.259–398; Verg. *Aen.* 8.664.
30 *Fasti* 3.259–398.

31 Livy 1.19. [...] *omnium primum, rem ad multitudinem imperitam et illis saeculis rudem efficacissimam, deorum metum iniciendum ratus est.* Trans. B.O. Foster.
32 Livy 5.54.7: *hic Capitolium est, ubi quondam capite humano invento responsum est eo loco caput rerum summamque imperii fore;* [...]; *hic Vestae ignes, hic ancilia caelo demissa, hic omnes propitii manentibus vobis di.*
33 Livy 5.55.1: *movisse eos Camillus cum alia oratione, tum ea quae ad religiones pertinebat maxime dicitur.*
34 Luc. 9.303–14, cf. Asso (2011: 387–88).
35 Asso (2011: 388).
36 Luc. 9.411–35.
37 Luc. 9.445–53.
38 [...] *galeas et scuta uirorum / pilaque contorsit uiolento spiritus actu / intentusque tulit magni per inania caeli. / illud in extrema forsan longeque remota / prodigium tellure fuit, delapsaque caelo / arma timent gentes hominumque erepta lacertis / a superis demissa putant. sic illa profecto / sacrifico cecidere Numae, quae lecta iuuentus / patricia ceruice mouet: spoliauerat Auster / aut Boreas populos ancilia nostra ferentes.*
39 Asso (2011: 384–5).
40 *circumit exustae nomen memorabile Troiae / magnaque Phoebei quaerit uestigia muri. / iam siluae steriles et putres robore trunci / Assaraci pressere domos et templa deorum / iam lassa radice tenent, ac tota teguntur / Pergama dumetis: etiam periere ruinae. / aspicit Hesiones scopulos siluaque latentis Anchisae thalamos; quo iudex sederit antro, / unde puer raptus caelo, quo uertice Nais / luxerit Oenone: nullum est sine nomine saxum. / inscius in sicco serpentem puluere riuum / transierat, qui Xanthus erat. securus in alto / gramine ponebat gressus: Phryx incola manes / Hectoreos calcare uetat. discussa iacebant saxa nec ullius faciem seruantia sacri:/ "Herceas" monstrator ait "non respicis aras?"*
41 Reed (2011: 24–5).
42 Bartsch (2011: 203–4).
43 Luc. 5.310–16. The same kind of direct conversation with characters happens frequently in other moments, such as Luc. 7.168–71 and Luc. 9.1046–62.
44 Bartsch (2011: 79).
45 Marincola (1997: 55–7).
46 Bartsch (2011: 313–14).
47 Such as Vell. Pat. 2.52–3; 2.75.2.
48 *nihil tamen egisti, M. Antoni, (cogit enim excedere propositi formam operis erumpens animo ac pectore indignatio) nihil, inquam, egisti mercedem caelestissimi oris et clarissimi capitis abscisi numerando auctoramentoque funebri ad conservatoris quondam rei publicae tantique consulis inritando necem. rapuisti tu M. Ciceroni lucem sollicitam et aetatem senilem et vitam miseriorem te principe quam sub te triumviro*

mortem, famam vero gloriamque factorum atque dictorum adeo non abstulisti, ut auxeris. vivit vivetque per omnem saeculorum memoriam, dumque hoc vel forte vel providentia vel utcumque constitutum rerum naturae corpus, quod ille paene solus Romanorum animo vidit, ingenio complexus est, eloquentia inluminavit, manebit incolume, comitem aevi sui laudem Ciceronis trahet omnisque posteritas illius in te scripta mirabitur, tuum in eum factum execrabitur citiusque e mundo genus hominum quam Ciceronis nomen cedet huius. (Vell. Pat. 2.66.3–5).

49 In 1.694, in which the matron affirms *vidi iam Philippos*; but also the reference to *Emathios campos* at the opening of the poem.
50 Hartog (1999: 143–216).
51 Cf. Bartsch (2011: 316).
52 Jos. *BJ* 1.11–12.
53 Diodorus Siculus is also a precedent in his lament for Corinth (32.26.1), probably written way before the other works treated here. However, the lack of information on the place and time of composition of his work prevents comparisons. There are also some such digressions in Tacitus (*Ann.* 4.32–33; 16.16) that, even if less partial or politic than Lucan's or Velleius', are worth noticing as interruptions by the narrative voice, expressed in the first person.
54 Marincola (1997: 3–4).
55 Marincola (1997: 6).
56 Feldherr (2009: 407–54).

3

Truth and Authority

Roger Chartier

Speaking the truth. No historian can evade this injunction, especially in a time when historical falsifications, false information, and the willingness to give credit to the most absurd theories proliferate. A reflection on the conditions of possibility of truth, which are all together and sometimes contradictorily epistemological and discursive, is therefore urgent. Hence the need to understand, in their articulation and difference, the regimes of truth that pertain to fable, history, and memory.

The Will to Truth

In *The Order of Discourse*, Michel Foucault offers a first formulation of the tension between truth as discursive property and truth as production of knowledge.[1] The "will to truth" is one of the three "exclusionary procedures" designed to limit the proliferation of discourse. It is undoubtedly the most fundamental, since it justifies the other two, both the interdiction of prohibited discourse and the rejection of the madman's words. The will to truth is thus a "prodigious machinery designed to exclude. All those who, from time to time in our history, have tried to dodge this will to truth and to put it into question against truth, at that very point where truth undertakes to justify the prohibition, and to define madness, all of them, from Nietzsche to Artaud and Bataille, must now serve as the (no doubt lofty) signs for our daily work."[2] The will to truth "tends to exert a sort of pressure and something like a power of constraint on other discourses." This constraint has weighed on literature, which "for centuries sought to ground itself on the natural, the 'vraisemblable', on sincerity," on "science as well—in short, on 'true' discourse," but also on economic practices or the penal system.[3]

Foucault situates in "the great Platonic division" the decisive rupture that displaces the place of truth from "the ritualised, efficacious and just act of enunciation, towards the utterance itself, its meaning, its form, its object, its relation to its reference."[4] Such a displacement was traced by Marcel Detienne in *The Masters of Truth in Archaic Greece*, when the inspired word of the poet, the seer, or the king who has access to the beyond, to the invisible, to the eternal, is replaced by the "truth" inscribed in the discourses themselves.[5] Jean-Pierre Vernant, in his review of that book, describes this substitution as follows: "It is about establishing how the character of the philosopher took shape, both in keeping and at odds with the tradition of the masters of truth; how the magical-religious speech, effective and anchored in reality, has been replaced by another kind of speech, one of secular character, engaged in dialogue and argument, no longer aimed at slotting into the being, but to act upon the spirit of others."[6] Detienne refers to this shift as the substitution of the secularized "speech-dialogue" for the "magical-religious speech," inseparable from symbolic behaviors and values: "As the city comes into being, the word-dialogue takes up the leading role. It is the 'political tool' *par excellence,*" the privileged instrument of social relations. It is through speech that men act within assemblies, that they command and exert their dominion over others. Speech is no longer caught up in a symbolic-religious network; it gains autonomy, constituting its own world in the game of dialogue that defines a kind of space, a closed field where both discourses confront each other. Through its political function, the *logos* becomes an autonomous reality, subject to its own laws.[7] "Truth" is, therefore, closely linked to the uses of language. Two paths are open as a result: that of the philosophical sects that regard *logos* as a means of knowing the Being, and that of the Sophists, who, as Vernant writes, consider rhetoric as "a mere tool of persuasion, a delusional imitation of reality, a beautiful lie, a means of tricking others."[8] In this case, truth is a property of discourse, which does not imply that it adequately states what is or what was. Hence the observation by Foucault: "It was just as if, starting from the great Platonic division, the will to truth had its own history, which is not that of constraining truths."[9]

In his inaugural lecture, Foucault encounters "constraining truths" when he acknowledges his debt to "the work of the historians of science, especially Georges Canguilhem." Defined as "a set of theoretical models and conceptual instruments which is both coherent and transformable," science takes its place in the two histories distinguished by Foucault: that of the will to truth but also that of the history of scientific truths.[10] In the tradition of historical epistemology, identifying the historicity of the concepts and instruments that produce knowledge about the natural world or the human creature is not to deny their capacity to produce a rational knowledge of their objects. This is the meaning of the distinction between "scientific ideology" and "science" proposed by Georges Canguilhem in his last book, *Ideology and Rationality in the History of the Life Sciences*.[11] The expression "scientific ideology" can thus designate "discursive structures claiming to be theories, the whole variety of more or less consistent representations of interphenomenal relations, and the whole spectrum of more or less permanent structures in terms of which men have interpreted their everyday experience. In short, it is a useful way of denoting those pseudosciences whose falsity is revealed solely by the fact that a genuine science has been established to refute their claims."[12] Scientific ideologies belong, in Foucauldian language, to the history of the will to truth. But they are "non-sciences": "A scientific ideology comes to an end when the place that it occupied in the encyclopaedia of knowledge is taken over by a discipline that operationally demonstrates the validity of its claim to scientific status, its 'norms of scientificity.' At that point a certain form of nonscience is excluded from the domain of science."[13] Science is not, however, the knowledge of the eternal Being: "scientific laws [do not] simply tell a truth permanently inscribed in, objects or intellect. Truth is simply what science speaks. How, then, do we recognize that a statement is scientific? By the fact that scientific truth never springs fully blown from the head of its creator. A science is a discourse governed by critical correction."[14] If every historian of science "is necessarily a historiographer of truth," according to Bachelard's formula, historical epistemology must at the same time separate and interconnect the scientific ideologies and the sciences that are understood as a "purification governed by norms of verification."[15]

It is the same perspective that characterizes "science studies," whose methodological relativism should not be understood as sceptical relativism. The distinction is strongly affirmed by David Bloor[16] as well as by Steven Shapin.[17] Michel de Certeau attributes the same capacity to produce "scientific" statements to the writing of history, if we understand "scientific" as "the possibility of conceiving an ensemble of *rules* allowing control of operations adapted to the production of specific objects or ends."[18] These are the operations and rules that allow us to reject the suspicion of relativism, or scepticism, born from the use of rhetorical tropes or narrative formulas that historical writing shares with fictional narratives.

Rhetoric and Evidence

This observation has led to a reflection on the relationship between rhetoric and truth. Carlo Ginzburg characterizes in the following terms the linguistic, or more precisely, rhetorical turn that seduced some historians from the 1970s onwards: "both historians and rhetoricians attempt to convince their audience; the historian's work creates, as a novel does, a self-contained textual world, whose relationship with extratextual realities cannot be submitted to a rigorous examination; both historical and fictional texts are self-referential in so far as they share a common rhetorical dimension."[19] Ginzburg identifies the modern matrix of these assertions as two fundamental ideas expressed by Nietzsche in his posthumous essay *On Truth and Lie in an Extra-Moral Sense*. The first is that language is intrinsically poetic and therefore powerless to designate reality. The second idea asserts that truth is "[a] movable host of metaphors, metonymies, anthropomorphisms: in short, a sum of human relations which have been poetically and rhetorically intensified, transferred, and embellished, and which, after long usage, seem to a people to be fixed, canonical, and binding. Truths are illusions which we have forgotten are illusions; they are metaphors that have become worn out and have been drained of sensuous force, coins which have lost their embossing and are now considered as metal and no longer as coins."[20]

Rhetoric can therefore only be self-referential. It is a technique of persuasion that reduces truth to a set of tropes designed to arouse the emotions. Its history begins with the Sophists denounced by Socrates in the *Gorgias*: "Well then, I call it flattery, and I say this sort of thing is shameful, Polus, since I'm saying this to you because it guesses at the pleasant without the best. And I say it is not a craft, but a knack, because it has no rational account (*logos*) by which it applies the things it applies, to say what they are by nature, so that it cannot say what is the explanation of each thing; and I don't call anything a craft which is unreasoning (*alogon*)."[21] The Sophists who, as Socrates says, teach rhetoric—"that is, about everything, so as to be persuasive in a mob: not teaching, but persuading"[22]—had many heirs in early modernity.

The perils of their rhetorical skill were denounced in eighteenth-century France by the *Philosophes* who opposed the rational reflection permitted by the circulation of the written word to the dangerous enthusiasms unleashed by persuasive words. For Condorcet, it was the printing press that made it possible to replace the passions aroused by rhetorical arguments with the evidence of demonstrations based on reason. With the invention of Gutenberg, "a new sort of tribunal had come into existence in which less lively, but deeper impressions were communicated; which no longer allowed the same tyrannical empire to be exercised over men's passions, but ensured a more certain and more durable power over their minds; a situation in which the advantages are all on the side of truth, since what the art of communication loses in the power to seduce, it gains in the power to enlighten."²³ Thus, "the instruction that every man is free to receive from books in silence and solitude"²⁴ opposes the coldness of reasoning, critical examination, and enlightened judgment to the erroneous convictions imposed by the trappings of speech. For Kant, the public use of reason by private individuals is also based on the circulation of the written word, and not on listening to the spoken word, that of conversations or that of deliberation in common: "by the public use of one's own reason I understand that use which someone makes of it as a scholar before the entire public of the world of readers."²⁵ "As a scholar," i.e. as a member of "universal civil society"; "before the entire world of readers," i.e. before a public that is not defined by its membership of a particular social "family," united by a word of authority or sociability. For Kant, as for Condorcet, the reasoning permitted by the exchange of writings must protect against the deceptive seductions of the spoken word.

Ginzburg opposes Aristotle's definition of rhetoric to the sophistic and Nietzschean one, which has been taken up by postmodern thinkers (Paul de Man, Barthes, Derrida): "Aristotle's approach, focusing on proof as the rational core of rhetoric, utterly contradicts the current self-referential image of rhetoric, based on the assumption that rhetoric and proof are basically incompatible."²⁶ This reading of Aristotle's *Rhetoric* insists on a double refusal, which is also that of Ginzburg: "Aristotle rejects both the attitude of the sophists, who had praised rhetoric as a technique aiming to convince through the motion of affects, and the attitude of Plato, who in his *Gorgias* had condemned rhetoric for the same reason. Contrary to both of them, Aristotle detects a rational core within rhetoric: proof, or rather, proofs."²⁷

At the beginning of Book I, Aristotle states, in the French translation by Médéric Dufour (1991): "Jusqu'aujourd'hui ceux qui compilaient les Techniques des discours n'en ont fourni qu'une petite partie; car seules les preuves sont techniques; tout le reste n'est qu'accessoires."²⁸ The text as quoted by Ginzburg in the Italian version of his book is different, avoiding the adjective "technical": "le prove soltanto sono un elemento costitutivo, tutti gli altri elementi sono accessori."²⁹ The difference between these two renditions is important because Aristotle then introduces a fundamental distinction between "technical" proofs, which are the resources proper to the art of discourse, and "non-technical" proofs, which mobilize documents prior to the discourse, capable of attesting to the facts:

> Entre les preuves, les unes sont extra-techniques, les autres techniques: j'entends par extra-techniques celles qui n'ont pas été fournies par nos moyens personnels,

> mais étaient préalablement données, par exemple, les témoignages, les aveux sous la torture, les écrits, et autres du même genre; par techniques, celles qui peuvent être fournies par la méthode et nos moyens personnels; il faut par conséquent utiliser les premières, mais inventer les secondes.[30]

Aristotle takes up and analyses in the last part of Book I these "atechnic" proofs, independent of the art of speech: "Celles-ci sont particulières aux discours judiciaires. Il y en a cinq: textes de lois, dépositions de témoins, conventions, déclarations sous la torture, serments des parties".[31]

The Greek word that is translated in the French edition by Méderic Dufour as "preuves techniques," and by Carlo Ginzburg as "prove," is *pisteis*. This translation must not hide, as Ginzburg remarks, that "our concept of 'proof' is very different from Aristotle's",[32] since for Aristotle it means all the "proofs" produced by the figures of speech, i.e. examples and enthymemes—which are syllogisms whose premise is not stated because it is self-evident—and the proofs based on references to written documents outside the speech itself. However, the use of the word, which ignores the difference in English between "proof" and "evidence" (which is perhaps, according to Ginzburg, the one designated by the Aristotelian distinction between "technical evidence" and "extra- technical evidence"[33]), prompts us to give a central role to "non-technical evidence," the one that makes it possible to challenge the purely self-referential conception of rhetoric. But if the translation does not choose translate *"pisteis"* with "proof," the emphasis is shifted to the persuasive devices internal to the discourse, without reference to an external textual reality.

In English, J. H. Freese's translation, published in 1924, opts for "proofs": "Proofs are the only things in it [the art of rhetoric] that come within the province of art; everything else is merely accessory". W. Rhys Roberts' version, published in 1924, prefers "modes of persuasion": "The modes of persuasion are the only true constituents of art: everything else is merely accessory." A note makes clear that *pistis* "can also be translated as 'belief', 'faith', 'confidence' or 'credit'."[34] In 1991 George Kennedy retained the Greek word: "As things are now, those who have composed *Arts of Speech* have worked on a small part of subject: for only the *pisteis* are artistic (other things are supplementary").[35] The translator indicates that *"pistis* (pl. *pisteis*) has different meanings in different contexts: proof, means of persuasion, belief, etc. Aristotle distinguishes between '*pisteis*' which depend on art and those which do not, and he divides the former between means of persuasion based on character, logical argumentation, and emotional arousal."[36] In his recent English translation of the *Rhetoric*, C. D. C. Reeve chooses "means of persuasion": "only the means of persuasion are within the province of craft;

the others are appendages" because "these can take the form of argument, but do not need to (a piece of evidence persuades us of something), are at their best demonstrative, bu can be inductive, and are productive of conviction."

In Portuguese, Edson Bini translates *"pisteis"* as "meios de persuasão," "means of persuasion". He justifies his decision by implicitly referring to Aristotle's exclusively judicial definition of "extra-technical evidence": "We consider the broad and generic sense of the word, not its strict and specific sense of judicial evidence, since Aristotle distinguishes (and to some extent privileges) public, political rhetoric over judicial rhetoric; moreover, the broad sense does not exclude, but on the contrary, includes the strict one."[37] In another Portuguese translation, the three translators, Manuel Alexandre Júnior, Paulo Farmhouse Alberto and Abel do Nascimento Pena, translate the word *"pisteis"* in its first occurrence as *"argumentos retóricos,"* "rhetorical arguments." But in a note, they indicate: "The term *'pistis'* can have different meanings in different contexts: faith, means of persuasion, proof. In Aristotle it normally means 'proof', 'logical proof', 'argumentation', 'logical argument' or 'rhetorical argument'. From here on we simply translate it as 'proof'. Aristotle distinguishes between two categories of proofs—art-related and non-art-related—and he classifies the former into three categories: ethical proof, logical proof, and emotional or pathetic proof."

François Hartog proposes an alternative to the French translation as *"preuve"*: "Aristotle says *'pisteis'*, which might be better translated as probative reasons, since we are not in the domain of syllogism, but in that of enthymeme (a lower form of syllogism, which pertains to rhetoric)."[38] Recalling that *"pistis"* also means "conviction,"[39] Hartog concludes: "*Pistis*: is it conviction, according to the usual translations, or is it proof? Something like a probative reason leading to intimate conviction. At any rate, we are clearly on the side of the judge and of the 'proofs' that allow him to form a conviction."[40] The early translations of the *Rhetoric* attest the different meanings of *"pisteis"* at its first occurrence. A Latin translation of 1588 plumps for *"fides"*—"faith"—which is also the word used by two Italian translations of 1548 and 1549.[41] Two seventeenth-century French translations choose the term *"preuve"* and distinguish later in the text between "two kinds of proof," some "artificial," others "without artifice" (thus, in the second of these two translations, "witnesses, confessions made during questioning, writings, signatures and other similar things").[42] An English translation from the end of the seventeenth century retains neither "proof" nor "faith," but associates "credit," "belief," and "persuasion," thereby linking means and effects.[43]

At stake in contemporary debates is the role given to "extra-technical proofs" in rhetoric—and not only in Aristotle's *Rhetoric*. Do they constitute the "rational core," the most fundamental modality of proof from the point of view of knowledge and truth, or are they, in the end, only incidental to the other modes of proof (ethical, logical, pathetic) which are the result of the rhetorical art?

The challenge to the view that holds rhetoric to be a technique of persuasion in which the examination of extra-technical evidence, would have only a marginal role can be based on Quintilian's *Institutio oratoria*. In his Book V, *De probationibus inartificialibus*, Quintilian lists the proofs that are not produced by the speech, but based on documents that are prior and external to it. Six headings are thus distinguished: *De praejudiciis* (judicial precedents), *De rumore et fama* (public rumor), *De tormentis* (statements obtained under torture), *De tabulis* (contracts written on tablets), *De jurejurando* (oaths), and *De testibus* (witnesses).[44] As Ginzburg has pointed out, in the *Institutio oratoria* Quintilian, who takes up Aristotle's distinctions without perhaps having read him, was an essential reference for the link established in the Renaissance between the rhetorical form of speeches and the search for historical evidence. He recalls that Lorenzo Valla, who demonstrated that Constantine's Donation to Pope Sylvester was a patent forgery, possessed two ancient manuscripts of Quintilian's book and had annotated one of them.[45] His speech, which mobilized the forms and formulas of the rhetorical art (for example, the genre of the "*declamatio*" or the invention of imaginary dialogues), put forward the "inartificial proofs" mentioned by Quintilian which made it possible to highlight the historical and linguistic anachronisms of the supposed Donation. For Ginzburg, "Valla, on the contrary, regarded a word like *satrapis* as proof that the alleged date of the *constitutum Constantini* was untenable. The use of anachronisms as an instrument of historical analysis was a real turning point, which had an enormous long-term impact. Valla's approach led to Mabillon, Montfaucon, and the seventeenth-century scholars of the Congregation of St. Maur, which Marc Bloch regarded as the initiators of the historian's craft in the modern sense of the word."[46] This is a genealogy that is no longer that of self-referential rhetoric, which goes from the Sophists to the postmodernists via Nietzsche, but one that associates rhetorical discourse and historical proof.

Does the association hold when we move from the figures of rhetoric to the narrative procedures of history? Undoubtedly, but without necessarily inscribing this continuity in the reference to Aristotle. François Hartog points out that in the *Rhetoric*, historical inquiries (on constitutions and laws, on wars or on the revenues of cities) have the sole purpose of providing examples or premises for enthymemes.[47] They are, therefore, resources for arguments of the deliberative kind and, for this reason, belong to politics, not to rhetoric: "So it is clear that, in relation to legislation, reports of world travelers are useful (for there one can get hold of the laws of [foreign] nations), and in relation to political deliberations, the research of those writing about actions. All these are a function of politics, however, not of rhetoric."[48] In the Aristotelian typology of the three oratorical genres—deliberative, judicial, and epidictic—"history, as such, has no place. It has no place of its own."[49]

This is no longer the case in the order of modern discourse. The essential question concerns the compatibility between—or rather, the inseparability of—the membership of historical writing, whatever it may be, to the class of narratives and its capacity to produce knowledge held to be true because it is subject to the specific operations and criteria of proof of the discipline. The critical force of history is not limited to unmasking falsifications and impostures. It can and must submit the explanatory constructions of past realities to the categories of validation that distinguish between acceptable and unacceptable interpretations, without denying the possible plurality of scientifically acceptable interpretations.

These questions about the proper epistemological status of history have acquired particular importance in our time, threatened as they are by the strong seductions of imaginary histories intended to justify identities and ideologies. In this context, it becomes essential to articulate a reflection on the conditions that allow historical discourses to be considered as adequate representations and explanations of a past that was and no longer is in existence. This is possible if history makes its way between sceptical relativism and naive positivism, as Ginzburg suggests: "Sources are neither open windows, as the positivists believe, nor fences obstructing vision, as the skeptics hold: if anything, we could compare them to distorting mirrors. The analysis of the specific distortion of every specific source already implies a constructive element. But construction, as I attempt to demonstrate in the following pages, is not incompatible with proof; the projection of desire, without which there is no research, is not incompatible with the refutations inflicted by the principle of reality. Knowledge (even historical knowledge) is possible."[50]

Chronicles and "Histories"

However, historical knowledge has had to (and still must) coexist with other truths about the past: those offered by fables. The notion of "energy," which plays an essential role in the analytical perspective of "New Historicism," can help us understand how certain works of fiction have shaped collective representations of the past much more powerfully than the writings of historians.[51] The theatre in the sixteenth and seventeenth centuries, and then the novel in the nineteenth and twentieth centuries, took possession of the past by displacing historical events and characters onto the register of literary fiction and by bringing situations – whether real or presented as such – onto the stage or the page. When works are inhabited by a particular force, they acquire the capacity to "produce, shape, and organize collective physical and mental experience."[52] One such experience is the encounter with the past.

A possible example is that of Shakespeare's historical plays. When in 1623 John Heminges and Henry Condell (who, like Shakespeare himself, had been actors and shareholders in the King's Men) collected for the first time in a majestic Folio thirty-six of the bard's plays, they decided to divide them into three genres: "comedies," "histories," and "tragedies." While the first and third categories remained faithful to the distinction between the two genres of Aristotelian theatrical poetics, the second introduced a new genre, bringing together ten works in the process. These followed the chronological order of the reigns that unfolded in the history of England from King John to Henry VIII, thus excluding other "histories," those of Roman heroes or Danish or Scottish princes, which were placed in the category of "tragedies." The editors transformed plays written in an order that did not match the chronological order of the sovereigns' reigns into a dramatic and continuous chronicle of the English monarchy and nation, which were inextricably linked. They thus imposed a dramatic narrative organized according to a linear conception of time that had been shared by chroniclers such as Edward Hall, John Stow, Richard Grafton, and particularly Raphael Holinshed, who had provided Shakespeare with the historical material for his plays. Prior to the publication of the Folio, the "histories" (or at least some of them, especially *Henry IV* and *Henry V*) were among the most frequently performed and printed plays. It is therefore certain that they shaped for their viewers and readers stronger and more vivid representations and experiences of the national past than the history written in the chronicles.

But the history they show on stage is not the history of the chronicles. It is a history open to anachronisms, a history governed by a chronology that is properly theatrical, and not by the order of events in their succession. It is a history that offers the imagination or the memory of the viewers' ambiguous representations of the past, marked by uncertainties, contradictions, and the impossibility of assigning a certain, unique meaning to events. Thus, in his rewriting of the revolt of Jack Cade and the Kent craftsmen, as it appears in the second part of *Henry VI*, Shakespeare reinterprets the event by attributing to the rebels of 1450 a millenarian and egalitarian language and violent actions, destructive of all forms of written culture and all those who embody it, which the chroniclers associated, less radically, with the revolt of Tyler and Straw of 1381. The result is an ambivalent depiction of the 1450 revolt that recapitulates the formulas and gestures of popular revolts at the same time as it ridicules the rebel leader. Cade is cruel and manipulative, and intends to establish a carnivalesque world in reverse, without writing, without money, without differences; yet he is mocked by his own lieutenants. The performance is contradictory, unstable, and open to multiple interpretations.[53]

The time of dramatic "histories" is not, or not only, the time of events, of decisions and defeats, of desires and conflicts. It is also the time of Fortune, through which a fall inevitably follows a triumph, and misery follows glory. The unfortunate fates of the Duke of Buckingham, Queen Catherine, and Cardinal Wolsey in *Henry VIII* show, three times over, the illusions of those who believe they are submitting history to their will. They are victims of the inexorable movement of the wheel that lifts them to the heights of honor before plunging them down into misfortune. There is yet another time in "history": that of God's designs. Men must not and cannot decipher that time, except when they are invaded by a discourse of which they are only the interpreters. This is the case with the inspired prophets who foretell either disaster, like Bishop Carlisle in *Richard II*, or the Golden Age, like Cranmer in *Henry VIII*. The representation of the instability and opacity of the meaning of events is the singular strength of Shakespeare's historical plays. They offer their spectators and readers a stronger, more vivid relationship with the national past than that offered by the history written in chronicles.

Novel, Society, and Individuals

In the nineteenth century, the novel in turn seized the past. It did so in a new order of discourse characterized by the invention of "literature" as we understand it today. From the second half of the eighteenth century onwards, the term moved away from the meaning which, in the previous century, identified it with scholarship. In Furetière's *Dictionnaire* of 1690, the word is defined as follows: "Literature, deep knowledge of letters. Scaliger, Lipsius and other Critics, were people of great Literature, of surprising Erudition."[54] Even when literature is synonymous with "*belles-lettres*", as in Richelet's *Dictionnaire* of 1680, the definition does not distinguish between aesthetic creations and works of knowledge: "The *belles-lettres* are the knowledge of Orators, Poets, and Historians." It was not until the eighteenth century that a separation was made. In 1762, the *Dictionnaire* of the Académie indicates: "On entend par Belles-Lettres la Grammaire, l'Éloquence, la Poésie." Erudition and history are no longer "literature."

This new definition of literature is based on three fundamental notions: the individualization of writing; the originality of works; and literary property. The combination of these three notions was completed at the end of the eighteenth century, at the time of the "sacredness of the writer," to use Paul Bénichou's formula.[55] This "sacredness" is expressed in the conservation and fetishization of autograph manuscripts, which became a guarantee of the authenticity of the author's writings,[56] the desire to meet him or correspond with him, pilgrimages to the places where he lived, and the erection of statues and monuments that glorify him.[57] In the nineteenth century, this set of gestures culminated in a major event: the construction of the figure of the national writer who expresses the very soul of his people.[58]

Literature defined in this way is opposed to an earlier economy of fiction writing, based on other practices: collaborative writing and the reuse of previously told stories, shared commonplaces, and continued works. Until the mid-eighteenth century, there was a strong awareness of the collective dimension of all textual productions and little recognition of the author as such. His works were not his property, his manuscripts were not preserved, his life did not warrant any biography but only collections of anecdotes. The situation is quite different when the affirmation of creative originality leads to the interweaving of writing and existence, to situating works in life experiences and to finding these in the works themselves; hence, following João Hansen, the necessary warning against an anachronistic use of subjective and psychological categories specific to the age of literature. They can only obscure the fundamental discontinuity that distinguishes the Romantic aesthetics of literature from the rhetorical and poetic regime that precedes it.[59] In the nineteenth century, once literature had been established in its modern definition, the truth claimed by literary writing is that of the whole of society, as it was and as it is. This truth is ignored by the historians of the time, fascinated by great events and great characters. The primary task of the novel is therefore to take on the true knowledge of the social world. As Manzoni indicates, hidden behind an imaginary interlocutor, in his work *Del romanzo storico* (*On the Historical Novel*) published in 1845 and quoted by Carlo Ginzburg, the novelist must "put before me, in a new and special form, a richer, more varied, more complete history than that found in works which more commonly go by this name, as if by *antonomasia*. The history we expect from you is not a chronological account of mere political and military events or, occasionally, some other kind of extraordinary happening, but a more general representation of the human condition, in a time and place naturally more circumscribed than that in which works of history, in the more usual sense of the word, ordinarily unfold."[60] The object of the novel, Manzoni continues, thinking of his own work, *I Promessi Sposi* (*The Betrothed*), whose first edition appeared in 1827, is to make known the "customs, opinions, whether they are generally accepted or peculiar to certain social classes; the private consequences of public events that are more properly called historical, or of the laws, or will of the powerful, however these are expressed—in short, all that a given society in a given time could claim as most characteristic of every way of life and of their interactions—this is what you sought to reveal."[61]

In this perspective, the novelist is the true historian who points out the different temporalities that run through the same society. This is what *Illusions perdues* shows with particular acuity. Balzac presents his novel in the last sentence of the first paragraph, as a "great and trivial story."[62] It is a small story, because it begins in a small printing shop in a small provincial town: "At the time when this story begins, the Stanhope press and inking-rollers were not yet in use in the small provincial printing-offices. Angoulême, although its paper-making industry kept it in contact with Parisian printing, was still using those wooden presses from which the now obsolete metaphor 'making the presses groan' originated." So a "small story", therefore, but in truth a "big story" because the contrast between the wooden presses of the Angoulême workshop and the mechanical presses of those in the capital is the expression of the hopes of all those who leave the old-fashioned province, now past its best, for the capital where illusions are consumed. During the Restoration years, Paris and Angoulême share the same calendar, but the two cities do not live in the same time: what has been superseded in the capital is still the status quo in the province.

When the history of historians gave up on its fascination with political facts and great figures to focus on the study of societies, literature privileged singularities. Writing about the unique lives of particular individuals became a favourite genre. Borges named one of its precursors in *Biblioteca personal*, a book published in 1985: "Around 1935 I wrote a candid book called *Universal History of Infamy*. One of its many sources, not yet mentioned by critics, was this book by Schwob." Borges is referring here to Marcel Schwob's *Vies imaginaires*, published in *Le Journal* between 1894 and 1896 and collected in a single volume by the publisher Charpentier in 1896. To write them, Schwob "invented a curious method. The protagonists are real; the facts can be fictional and often fantastic. The particular flavour of this book lies in this back-and-forth."[63]

Schwob's "curious method" involved radically separating singular from collective destinies, in privileging the "singular and inimitable breaks" of existences, in emancipating biographical writing from the mere historical truth.[64] For him, art, whether literature or painting, is defined in opposition to history: "Historical science leaves us uncertain about individuals. It reveals to us only the points where they were attached to general actions," whereas "art is the opposite of general ideas, describes only the individual, desires only the unique. It does not classify; it declassifies." The art of the biographer, like that of the Japanese painter Hosukaï, consists "in accomplishing the miraculous transformation of resemblance into diversity," "in making individual what is most general." The search for the "oddities" or "anomalies" of each individual in no way implies submission to reality: the biographer "does not have to worry about being true; he has to create in a chaos of human features [...] In the midst of this crude gathering, the biographer sorts out what to compose into a form that resembles no other. It is not necessary for it to resemble that which was once created by a superior god, provided that it is unique, like any other creation." The ostensibly most historical genre—biography—must move away from history to a deeper, more essential reality: to recount with the same concern "the unique lives of men, whether they were divine, mediocre, or criminal." Thus, the ideal of biography, and more generally of literature as a whole, consists in an "infinite differentiation"; the truth that literature achieves is not constrained by the principle of reality; it emerges with greater force from the fable itself.

Following that path, twentieth-century literature took hold of what was ignored or obscured by the history of populations and economies, societies and mentalities, namely the truths of unique, obscure, fragile lives. In novels, this attention is focused on tiny lives or tiny stories, such as in the eight chapters of Pierre Michon's *Vies minuscules*, published in 1984,[65] or Pascal Quignard's *Les tablettes de bois d'Apronenia Avita*, published the same year.[66] But anonymous existences and ignored destinies do not only inhabit the imagination of writers. They can also be found in the archives themselves, particularly police and judicial archives. Treated as statistics by historians of crime and punishment, they preserve the brief, fragmented, mysterious traces of singular lives.

It was fragments of life such as these that Foucault wished to bring together in an "anthology of existences," presented in a 1977 essay conceived as a general introduction to a collection of documents from the seventeenth and eighteenth centuries entitled "The Life of Infamous Men" (*La vie des hommes infâmes*)—

infamous because they had no *fama*, no reputation, no glory: "Lives of a few lines or a few pages, countless misfortunes and adventures, gathered together in a handful of words. Brief lives, chanced upon in books and documents. [...] Singular lives, those which have become, through I know not what accidents, strange poems: that is what I wanted to gather in a sort of herbarium."[67] Reversing Schwob's procedure, Foucault situates "a certain effect of beauty and terror" in real existences, told in a few pages or a few sentences in police reports, internment registers, placets addressed to the king or lettres de cachet: "I wanted it to be always a question of real existences; that one should be able to ascribe a place and a date to them; that behind these names which no longer say anything, behind these rapid words which indeed may have been most of the time false, mendacious, unjust, excessive, there should have been men who lived and died, sufferings, wickednesses, jealousies, vociferations. Therefore I banished all that which that could be imagination or literature."[68]

In these lives known only by the brief and enigmatic features retained by the institutions, Foucault encountered lost existences, which would have been forever forgotten if it had not been for that moment when they collided with power, or tried to use it: "In short, I wanted to collect some rudiments together for a legend of obscure men, based on the discourses which in misfortune or in rage they exchanged with power."[69] The desire to get as close as possible to the truth of singular destinies, not from a fable but from a "kernel of reality," must confront an extreme situation, since "the existence of these men and women reduces itself exactly to what has been said about them; nothing subsists of who they were or what they did, except in a few sentences."[70] Foucault takes up the challenge and rejects the literature that makes fiction the very locus of the most intense truths about reality. In his project, the terms are reversed: "This pure verbal existence which turns these wretched men or these scoundrels into quasi-fictitious beings, is owed by them to their nearly exhaustive disappearance and to that chance or mischance which has allowed the survival, through the accident of rediscovered documents, of a few rare words which speak of them or which they themselves have spoken."[71] In the "legend of obscure men," there is thus "a certain equivocation of the fictitious and the real."[72]

Truth of Fiction, Poetry of Reality

Should historians choose between the truth of fiction and the poetry of reality? They can recognize, with Carlo Ginzburg, that there are many "forms taken on by fiction in the service of truth."[73] It is not a question of affirming that fiction and history produce the same truth, but of identifying the conditions under which a literary text, or its reading, produces knowledge of the realities of the past. In *Threads and Traces*, Ginzburg analyses three narrative devices that ensure such knowledge. The first is that of "estrangement," identified by the Russian formalists as "a literary process which transformed something familiar—an object, a behaviour, an institution—into something strange, senseless, ridiculous."[74] This is a "learned ignorance" that rejects the blind perception of the obvious, the automatic acceptance of customs, the submission to the order of things. The figures of the illiterate scholar, the wise savage, the astute peasant, or the animals of the fables embodied in writings and images this unveiling of hidden and ignored truths. A second process, specific to reading, consists in going back from a piece fiction to a piece of evidence; from aesthetic truth, which presupposes the suspension of disbelief, to the critical truth that relates "to an invisible past, through a series of opportune operations—marks scratched on paper or on parchment; coins; fragments of statues corroded by time; and so forth."[75] In this way, the approach of *New Historicism is* reversed. Its perspective draws attention to the aesthetic appropriation of the discourses and practices of the social world. The one proposed by Ginzburg, a reader of Chapelain, asserts that it is possible to discover historical truths in fables and thus "to build the truth on fiction (*fables*) and true history on the fictitious."[76] A third procedure that inscribes historical truth into fictional novels is the use of free direct speech, which is introduced into the third-person narrative, suspended for some time by the secret, intimate, silent thoughts of one of the protagonists. Ginzburg observes that "it is a process which seems to be unavailable for historians because free direct discourse by definition leaves no documentary traces. We are in territory that lies beyond historical knowledge, and is inaccessible to it." He adds, however, that "narrative processes act like magnetic fields: they provoke questions and potentially attract documents. In this sense, a procedure such as free direct discourse, which came into being to respond, on the terrain of fiction, to a number of historical questions, may be considered as an indirect challenge to historians."[77] Under certain conditions, "one day they may be able to confront it"—and certain attempts, such as the reconstruction of dreams in Jonathan Spence's book, *The Death of Woman Wang*, have already confronted it.[78]

It is about focusing on the historical truth of fiction, therefore, without erasing the difference between the art of the novelist and the profession of historians. This entails the question whether this profession is compatible with the party asserted by Foucault in his herbarium of singular lives: "This is in no way a history book. The selection that shall be found in it has conformed to nothing more important than my taste, my pleasure, an emotion, laughter, surprise, a certain fright or some other feeling"? Therefore, "this book will not satisfy historians, even less than did the others."[79] Is the beauty of these "strange poems" that are the existences of archives really forbidden to historians? In a book opened by a quote from Marcel Schwob ("Historical science leaves us uncertain about individuals") and inscribed in the reference to "The Lives of Infamous Men," Arlette Farge links sensitivity and knowledge, emotion and understanding. Her book, based on "shreds of archives," many unclassifiable relics where tattered existences can be read, affirms this certainty in its last sentence: "Let us dare to consider in their rightful place, affect and sensitivity as human universals, allowing us to be closer to the asperities of the reality of past centuries and to better grasp, in their most unexpected moments, these forgotten worlds; here, the shadows of the Age of Enlightenment."[80] As in Schwob, the object is the "unique," the irreducibly singular, but, unlike the "imaginary lives," those encountered in the archive fragments have indeed been lived, often in distress, sometimes in happiness. As in Foucault, emotion is born of the feeling of proximity to "the mystery, beauty and madness of life,"[81] but, unlike the "infamous lives," the book is indeed a book of history. It forces us to think about the shared constraints and common realities in which the most extravagant, unexpected and unusual experiences are embedded. Thus, if "the snippets of life are like the tiny details of much larger pictures," they have a place in the collective destinies where they insert their singularity. History takes over, since it is a question of "making perceptible, emotionally intelligible, the constant interplay of relations between power and subjects, social actors and daily practices."[82]

In the complex interplay between historical truth and literary truth, the appropriation of the techniques of history by fiction has paradoxically demonstrated the knowledge status of the discipline. This appropriation is like the inverted figure of the "reality effect" defined by Roland Barthes as one of the major modalities of "referential illusion."[83] In classical aesthetics, the category of the "plausible" ensured the kinship between historical narrative and imagined stories since, according to the definition given in Furetière's 1690 *Dictionnaire*, history is "description, narration of things, or actions as they happened or as they could happen." The term "history" therefore refers not only to "the continuous and linked narration of several memorable events that occurred in one or more nations, in one or more centuries," but also to "fabulous but plausible narrations, which are faked by an author." The division is therefore not between history and fable, but between plausible accounts, whether or not they refer to reality, and those that are not. Understood in this way, history was radically separated from the critical demands of antiquarian scholarship and detached from the reference to reality as a guarantee of its discourse.

By abandoning the plausible, the fable has tied up its relationship with reality by multiplying concrete notations that are intended to weigh down the fiction with the burden of reality and to produce a referential illusion. In this, it imitated history, for which the presence of references to reality is even more essential: "Resistance of the 'real' (in its written form, of course) to structure is very limited in the fictive account, constructed by definition on a model which, for its main outlines, has no other constraints than those of intelligibility; but this same 'reality' becomes the essential reference in historical narrative, which is supposed to report 'what really happened.'" History has thus been the model proposed to literature: "it is logical that literary realism should have been—give or take a few decades—contemporary with the regnum of 'objective' history."[84] The certainty of historians that "the *'having-been-there'* of things is a sufficient principle of speech" could be reinforced only by "the contemporary development of techniques, of works and institutions based on the incessant need to authenticate the 'real': the photograph (immediate witness to 'what was here'), reportage, exhibitions of ancient objects (the success of the Tutankhamen show makes this quite clear), the tourism of monuments and historical places. All this shows that the 'real' is supposed to be self- sufficient."[85]

This "having-been-there," this "concrete reality," the guarantor of the truth of history, must be introduced into the historical discourse if we are to accredit it as authentic knowledge. This is the role assigned to quotations, references, and documents that summon the past into the historian's writing while demonstrating its authority. For Michel de Certeau, unlike other narratives, the writing of history is duplicated, layered: "[the] discourse that can 'include' its other—chronicle, archive, document—in other words, discourse that is organized in a *laminated* text in which one continuous half is based on another disseminated half. The former is thus allowed to state what the latter is unknowingly signifying. Through 'quotations', references, notes, and the whole mechanism of permanent references to a prime language, [historiographical discourse] is constructed as a *knowledge of the other.*"[86] Thus, the historian's divided writing has the triple task of inscribing the past in a discourse in the present, showing the competence of the researcher, master of the sources, and winning the reader's conviction.

Should we, therefore, situate history and literature as two modalities of "a new verisimilitude, which is precisely *realism* (by which we mean any discourse which accepts 'speech-acts' justified by their referent alone)"?[87] Ginzburg, by affirming that "knowledge is possible, even in the field of history," and de Certeau, by indicating that the historical operation is a "scientific" practice that implies rules and controls, provide the epistemological rationale to refuse such a conclusion. There is another way of doing this: putting the "reality effects" at the service of a discourse that presents itself as historical while denying its condition of being true. This is the case with the biography of the painter Jusep Torres Campalans, published in Mexico in 1958.[88]

The book puts all the techniques of accreditation of historical discourse at the service of this biography: two photographs that show the painter and his friends in the company of Picasso; articles from two French newspapers, *L'Intransigeant* and *Le Figaro illustré*, which published statements from Campalans made in 1912 and 1914 before leaving Paris for Mexico; the edition of *Cuaderno Verde* in which he wrote about remarks, aphorisms, and quotations made between 1906 and 1914; the catalogue of his works compiled by a young Irish critic, Henry Richard Town, who was preparing an exhibition of the paintings of Campalans in London in 1942, but died in a German bombing raid; the transcription of the conversations Max Aub had with Campalans when he met him in San Cristobal de Las Casas in 1955; and, finally, the reproductions of the works themselves (which were exhibited in Mexico City in 1958, and then at the Bodley Gallery in New York in 1962, when the English translation of the book was presented).[89] The book thus exhibits all the techniques and institutions mentioned by Barthes: photographs, reports, exhibitions.

But Jusep Torres Campalans never existed. Max Aub, a Spanish socialist who was exiled in France after the defeat of the Republic and took refuge in Mexico to escape the persecution of the Vichy regime, invented this imaginary painter to make fun of the categories most dear to art historians. His targets are the explanation of works by the artist's biography, the elucidation of the hidden meaning of paintings, the arbitrariness of attribution and dating techniques, or the use of the contradictory and yet always associated notions of influence and precursor. Campalans, who was influenced by Matisse, Picasso, Kandinsky, and Mondrian, was nevertheless, as the dates of his works show, the inventor of cubism, Negro art, expressionism, and abstract painting.

Today, Aub's book can be read in a different manner. By mobilizing the modes of authentication of reality shared by historical writing and literary invention, he shows, in the manner of Barthes, the kinship that links them. But he also multiplies the ironic warnings that must awaken the reader's vigilance. It is not by chance that Aub meets Campalans at a symposium celebrating the 350th anniversary of the publication of *Don Quixote*, or that the book's "Indispensable Prologue" ends with a reference to the "best" of all prologues, precisely that of *Don Quixote*.[90] One of the epigraphs of the book attributes to a certain Santiago de Alvarado, author of a book entitled *Nuevo mundo caduco y alegrias de la mocedad de los años de 1781 hasta 1792* (a work that could be included in the "Museum" of imaginary texts collected by Borges in *The Author*)[91] the sentence: "¿Cómo puede haber verdad sin mentira?" ("How can there be truth without lie?").[92] Thus, literary deception itself recalls the gap that separates true knowledge and fable, the reality that was and the illusory referents. In this way, it accompanies, in a parodic way, the works devoted to historical falsifications—always possible, increasingly subtle, but also unmasked by critical work.[93] It thus shows the radical difference between the enchantments of fiction and the operations proper to historical knowledge.

* * *

This knowledge is the condition of possibility of an "equitable memory," as Ricoeur writes—"equitable," because it obliges particular memories to confront a representation of the past situated in the order of a universally acceptable knowledge.[94] It is thus affirmed that the regime of truth of memory, individual or collective, internal or instituted, is different from that of history. In *Memory, History, Forgetting*, Ricoeur establishes the fundamental differences that characterize these two forms of the presence of the past, which are the work of memory and the historiographic operation. The first difference is that between testimony and document. While the former is inseparable from the witness and presupposes that his or her words are believed, the latter gives access to "numerous reputedly historical events [which] were never anyone's memories."[95] Instead of accepting (or challenging) the credibility of the word that testifies, a critical exercise is carried out that subjects traces of the past to the regime of truth and falsity, of the refutable and the verifiable. The circumstantial nature of the document is opposed to the testimony, whose credibility is based on the trust placed in the witness. A second difference opposes the immediacy of reminiscence to the explanatory construction of historical phenomena, whatever the scale of their analysis and whatever the model of their intelligibility, which can privilege either the determinations ignored by the actors, or their explicit reasons and strategies. Hence the third distinction, between the recognition of the past and the representation of the past. "Memory's aim of faithfulness" is opposed to "history's project of truth,"[96] based on the critical analysis of documents, which are the many traces of what was and no longer is, and on the operations that produce understanding.

"Presumed truth of the historical representation" and "presumed trustworthiness of mnemonic representation":[97] both claims deserve examination. For Ricoeur, memory has two modalities adequately designated by the Aristotelian lexicon.

Memory is "*mneme*," the emergence of remembrance, and it is also "*anamnesis*," the work of recollection. In both forms of memory, forgetting is the condition of its possibility. Ricoeur thus comments on Heidegger's formula according to which "remembering is possible only on the basis of forgetting, and not the other way around."[98] "No one can make it the case that what is no longer has not been. The forgetting which, according to Heidegger, conditions remembering is related to the past as having-been. We comprehend the apparent paradox if, by forgetting, we understand an immemorial resource and not an inexorable destruction."[99]

There are therefore two forms of forgetting: "profound forgetting," which is loss, destruction, erasure of traces; and the "reserve of forgetting", which preserves and is a resource for memory. Of this second, which tends towards the unforgettable, Ricoeur indicates: "Forgetting has also an active side linked to the process of recollecting, as a search aiming at the recovery of lost memories, of memories that are not actually blurred out, but only made unavailable."[100] The processes of recollection take different forms, such as the psychoanalytic cure, the politics of memory, and the historical reappropriation of the past.

Under what conditions can the latter be held as objective? For Ricoeur, "the idea of historical objectivity deserves to be vindicated against some forms of relativism which would deprive historiography of its main claim, namely that of offering a reliable representation of the past. This claim must be reasserted, not only against a rhetorical treatment of historical knowledge, but also against some alleged claims on the part of some supported communitarian memories. If there were no truth claim in historical knowledge, history would not play its role in the confrontation between history and memory."[101] This representation, which Ricoeur designates with the term "re- presenting," understood as "the expectation attached to the historical knowledge of constructions constituting reconstructions of the course of past events"[102]—does it produce a truth? Certainly, if we understand this truth as an approximation by replacement, as a modality of knowledge given in a narrative which intends to show events "as they actually happened," according to Ranke's famous formula, while knowing that "a narrative does not resemble the event it recounts."[103] The procedures of the historiographical operation, which combine criticism, proof, and control, protect historical writing from arbitrariness, sceptical relativism, and falsification. The representation it offers of the past is not, however, the past that has become a narrative; it is a knowledge situated at "the intertwining between reality and fiction, between truth and possibility."[104] In our present, the claims of personal and collective memories have opposed historical knowledge, considered cold and inert, preferring the intense and committed relationship with the past that the immediacy of reminiscence allows. In fact, history is challenged robustly when memory or literature takes charge of the true representation of the past and asserts the authority of memory or fable in the face of the "current general malaise" that Yosef Yerushalmi sees in modern historiography.[105] It is for this reason that history and, more generally, the human sciences, must reaffirm the specificity of their own regime of knowledge. By confirming the differences that distinguish them from literary and memorial discourses, by showing their capacity to unmask the falsifications of past or present realities, they take up their tasks: to denounce alternative truths, to destroy absurd certainties, to establish what happened. In this way, history can fully assume its critical and civic role and, perhaps, soothe the wounds inflicted by an unjust and cruel past.

One of the essential characteristics of the "illiberal" policies that have emerged and been theorized on both sides of the Atlantic in recent years is the desire to rewrite history in order to put it at the service of a mythical vision of the past, one that is capable of fortifying and justifying the actions of the present. Both memory and history are threatened by this: memory, because manipulated representations of the past are imposed on it; history, because the reality of what was is denied. In both cases, the truth is challenged, betrayed, and ignored. The ancient links woven between the use of reason and civic deliberation, between ethics and politics, are brutally unraveled. The danger is great. The responsibility of history is to confront it by opposing to it the act of speaking the truth.

Notes

1 Foucault (1981). Whenever possible, reference is made to the English translations of the works under discussion.
2 Foucault (1981: 56).
3 Foucault (1981: 55).
4 Foucault (1981: 54).
5 Detienne (1996). In a preface added to the 2006 French reprint of his book, Marcel Detienne ironically points out this kinship: "En 1970, dans L'Ordre du discours, sa 'leçon inaugurale au Collège de France', Foucault découvrait en Grèce archaïque le lieu du partage qui régit notre 'volonté de savoir' et, plus précisément, cette 'volonté de vérité'. Vraisemblablement, il se référait au paysage du vrai que j'avais dessiné en mon enquête" (Detienne (2006: 13).
6 Vernant (1969: 195); the translation is mine.
7 Detienne (2006: 118–19).

8   Vernant (1969: 196).
9   Foucault (1981: 55).
10 Foucault (1981: 73–4).
11 Canguilhem (2009).
12 Canguilhem (1988: 29).
13 Canguilhem (1988: 33).
14 Canguilhem (1988: 11).
15 Canguilhem (1988: 39).
16 Interview with David Bloor by François Briatte, 2007. Available online: https://halshs.archives-ouvertes.fr/halshs-01511329/file/InterviewDB_FBriatte2007.pdf (accessed December 1, 2021).
17 A conversation between Steven Shapin and Bernardo J. Oliveira, 2004. Available online: https://www.sbhc.org.br/arquivo/download?ID_ARQUIVO=149 (accessed December 1, 2021).
18 De Certeau (1988: 103 n. 5).
19 Ginzburg (1999: 39).
20 Quoted by Ginzburg (1999: 9).
21 Plato, *Gorgias* 465a (trans. T. Irwin): κολακείαν μὲν οὖν αὐτὸ καλῶ, καὶ αἰσχρόν φημι εἶναι τὸ τοιοῦτον, ὦ Πῶλε – τοῦτο γὰρ πρὸς σὲ λέγω – ὅτι τοῦ ἡδέος στοχάζεται ἄνευ τοῦ βελτίστου· τέχνην δὲ αὐτὴν οὔ φημι εἶναι ἀλλ᾽ ἐμπειρίαν, ὅτι οὐκ ἔχει λόγον οὐδένα ὧν προσφέρει, ὁποῖ᾽ ἄττα τὴν φύσιν ἐστίν, ὥστε τὴν αἰτίαν ἑκάστου μὴ ἔχειν εἰπεῖν. ἐγὼ δὲ τέχνην οὐ καλῶ, ὃ ἂν ᾖ ἄλογον πρᾶγμα.
22 Plato, *Gorgias* 459a: περὶ πάντων ὥστ᾽ ἐν ὄχλῳ πιθανὸν εἶναι, οὐ διδάσκοντα ἀλλὰ πείθοντα.
23 Condorcet (2012: 71).
24 Condorcet (2012: 73).
25 Kant (1996: 18).
26 Ginzburg (1999: 62).
27 Ginzburg (1999: 44).
28 Ar. *Rhet.* 1354a: Νῦν μὲν οὖν οἱ τὰς τέχνας τῶν λόγων συντιθέντες ὀλίγον πεπονήκασιν αὐτῆς μόριον· αἱ γὰρ πίστεις ἔντεχνόν ἐστι μόνον, τὰ δ᾽ ἄλλα προσθῆκαι.
29 Ginzburg (2000: 52). In a note Ginzburg makes clear: "Uso, modificandola in alcuni punti sostanziali, la traduzione di A. Plebe (Aristotele, *Opere*, a cura di G. Giannantoni, Vol. X, Bari, 1973, p. 3)". Silvia Gastaldi, on the other hand, translates "pisteis" as *"mezzi di persuasione"*, in Aristotele, *Retorica*, ed. S. Gastaldi (2014: 41).
30 Ar. *Rhet.* 1355b: Τῶν δὲ πίστεων αἱ μὲν ἄτεχνοί εἰσιν αἱ δ᾽ ἔντεχνοι. ἄτεχνα δὲ λέγω ὅσα μὴ δι᾽ ἡμῶν πεπόρισται ἀλλὰ προϋπῆρχεν, οἷον μάρτυρες βάσανοι συγγραφαὶ καὶ ὅσα τοιαῦτα, ἔντεχνα δὲ ὅσα διὰ τῆς μεθόδου καὶ δι᾽ ἡμῶν κατασκευασθῆναι δυνατόν. ὥστε δεῖ τούτων τοῖς μὲν χρήσασθαι τὰ δὲ εὑρεῖν.

31 Ar. *Rhet.* 1375a: ἴδιαι γὰρ αὗται τῶν δικανικῶν. εἰσὶ δὲ πέντε τὸν ἀριθμόν, νόμοι μάρτυρες συνθῆκαι βάσανοι ὅρκος.
32 Ginzburg (2000: 44).
33 *Ibid.* In a "Nota all'edizione italiana", Ginzburg writes: "la distinzione tra prove "tecniche" e "non tecniche", che in sostanza corrisponde a quella tra *proof* e *evidence*, venne introdotta da Aristotele nella *Retorica* per reagire all'indeterminatezza della parola *pistis* (prova)": Ginzburg (2000: 11).
34 Roberts (1924: 96).
35 Kennedy (1991: 30).
36 Kennedy (1991: 31 n. 11): "*Pistis* (pl. *pisteis*) has a number of different meanings in different contexts: 'proof, means of persuasion, belief,' etc. In 1.2.2-3 Aristotle will distinguish between artistic and non- artistic *pisteis* and divide the former into three means of persuasion based on character, logical argument, and arousing emotion."
37 Bini (2013: 9 n. 1): "*pisteis* – contemplamos aqui e na sequência o sentido lato e genérico da palavra, e não o estrito e específico de prova judicial, uma vez que Aristóteles distingue (e até uma medida, privilegia) uma retórica pública, politica, além da retórica judiciaria; de resto, o sentido lato não exclui, mas inclui o sentido estrito."
38 Hartog (2013 : 138 n. 1): "Aristote dit '*pisteis*' qu'il vaudrait peut-être mieux traduire par raisons probantes, puisqu'on n'est pas dans le domaine du syllogisme, mais de l'enthymème (syllogisme inférieur propre à la rhétorique)."
39 Detienne (1996 : 76) recalls that in the religious thought of the diviners and inspired poets, *pistis* is "la confiance qui va de l'homme à un dieu ou à la role d'un dieu; elle est confiance dans les Muses, foi dans l'oracle, mais la notion de *Pistis* est aussi fréquemment liée au serment."
40 Hartog (2013 : 140).
41 Riccoboni (1588: 2): "*Fides enim artificiosa est solum*"; *Traddottione Antica de la Retorica de Aristotile* (1548 : "la principale e artificiosa opera de la ditta arte é di dar fede"); *Retorica e Poetica d'Aristotile* (1549: 2, "l'acquistari fede per via degli argumenti é propio di questa arte.")
42 *La Rhétorique d'Aristote en Français*, (1654 : 2: "toute l'adresse de cet art est renfermé dans la Preuve"); *La Rhétorique royale d'Aristote*, Traduit par M. Bauduin de la Neufville, (1669: 3: "pour faire bonne preuve il faut avoir recours au moyen que l'art nous fournit", and 13: "il faut savoir que pour persuader nous devons nous servir de sortes de preuves dont l'une est appelée artificielle et l'autre sans artifice.")
43 *Aristotle's Rhetoric; Or the true Grounds and Principles of Oratory* (1686: 2. "only Art prevails to gain Credit and Belief by Persuasion.")
44 Quintilian, *Institutionum Oratorum Libri XII* (1522: 78–81).
45 Ginzburg (2000: 61).
46 Ginzburg (2000: 64).
47 Hartog (2013: 141–2).

48 Arist. *Rhet.* 1360a: ὥστε δῆλον ὅτι πρὸς μὲν τὴν νομοθεσίαν αἱ τῆς γῆς περίοδοι χρήσιμοι (ἐντεῦθεν γὰρ λαβεῖν ἔστι τοὺς τῶν ἐθνῶν νόμους), πρὸς δὲ τὰς πολιτικὰς συμβουλὰς αἱ τῶν περὶ τὰς πράξεις γραφόντων ἱστορίαι· ἅπαντα δὲ ταῦτα πολιτικῆς ἀλλ᾽ οὐ ῥητορικῆς ἔργον ἐστίν.
49 Hartog (2013: 145).
50 Ginzburg (2000: 25).
51 Greenblatt (1988: 1–20).
52 Greenblatt (1988: 6).
53 Chartier (2006).
54 "Littérature, connaissance profonde des lettres. Scaliger, Lipse et autres Critiques, étaient des gens de grande Littérature, d'une érudition surprenante."
55 Bénichou (1996).
56 Chartier (2015.
57 Lilti (2014).
58 Thiesse (2019).
59 Hansen (2001, 2004, and 2019).
60 Quoted in Ginzburg (2012: 63).
61 Ibid.
62 Balzac (1971).
63 Borges (1988: 70).
64 Schwob ([1898] 2004). All quotations in this paragraph are taken from Marcel Schwob's "Preface," pp. 53–60.
65 Michon (2008).
66 Quignard (2019).
67 Foucault (1979: 76).
68 Foucault (1979: 78).
69 Foucault (1979: 80).
70 Ibid.
71 Ibid.
72 Foucault (1994: 241).
73 Ginzburg (2012: 4).
74 Ginzburg (2012: 99). In a note added to the French edition, the translator Martin Rueff recalls his hesitations regarding the translation of the Russian term "*ostranenie*": "*étrangisation*", *singularisation*," or "*estrangement*", which he uses (142 n. 2).
75 Ginzburg (2012: 82).
76 Ibid.
77 Ginzburg (2012: 150).
78 Spence (1978).
79 Foucault (1994: 237, 239).
80 Farge (2019: 293–4).

81 Farge (2019: 7).
82 Farge (2019: 99–100).
83 Barthes (1989).
84 Barthes (1989: 146).
85 Barthes (1989: 146–7).
86 De Certeau (1988: 94).
87 Barthes (1989: 147).
88 Aub (1999) (or. ed. 1958). The book was "adapted from [the] Spanish" by Alice and Pierre Gascar (1961). For the French reception of this "adaptation," see Malgat (1999).
89 Aub (1962). The exhibition catalogue was included in the *Catalogue Jusep Torres Campalans. The First New York Exhibition. Bodley Gallery, 223 East Sixtieth Street*; see also the exhibition catalogue *Jusep Torres Campalans. Ingenio dela vanguardia española*, Madrid, Museo Nacional Centro de Arte de la Reina Sofía, June 13–August 23, 2003.
90 Aub (1999: 22).
91 Borges (1985: 90–2).
92 Aub (1999: 13).
93 Vidal-Naquet (1993); Grafton (1990); Caro Baroja (1992); Ginzburg (1999: 54–70).
94 Ricoeur (2004: 500): "there is a privilege that cannot be refused to history; it consists not only in expanding collective memory beyond any actual memory but in correcting, criticizing, even refuting the memory of a determined community, when it folds back upon itself and encloses itself within its own sufferings to the point of rendering itself blind and deaf to the suffering of other communities. It is along the path of critical history that memory encounters the sense of justice. What would a happy memory be that was not also an equitable memory?"
95 Ricoeur (2004: 497).
96 Ibid.
97 Ricoeur (2004: 278).
98 Quoted in Ricoeur (2004: 442).
99 Ricoeur (2004: 442–3).
100 Ricoeur (2015: 155).
101 Ricoeur (2015: 153).
102 Ricoeur (2004: 274–5).
103 Ricoeur (2004: 279). Ricoeur's formulation is reminiscent of that of Pascal Quignard, quoted recently in Arlette Farge's *Vies oubliées* (2019): "Is it legitimate to claim to report reality by recounting the past—Certainly not. For to the question: 'How did things happen in reality', one can answer with certainty: 'In reality things did not happen in a narrative.'"
104 Ginzburg (2012: 70).
105 Yerushalmi (1982: 88).

4

The Time of Restitution of All Things: Past as Future in Michael Servetus

Elaine C. Sartorelli

It was only in the sixteenth century that Vasari described the long process of recovering lost treasures from antiquity as a *rinascita*: "The word, then, waited almost two centuries after the *idea* had emerged."[1] It demonstrates that humanists had been elaborating their relationship with the ancients and the *recentiores* for a very long time, and, by doing so, they invented a notion of time and past in a deliberate and intentional move, shaping "their conceptual vocabularies and modes of experiencing the world."[2]

As a Christian humanist, Erasmus looked at the pagan Greco-Roman authors with admiration, but also with the awareness of their lack of the Advent of Jesus that gave human history a sense. He definitively did not think of the past as a place to return to. Maybe more than anyone else, he considered himself as being at the edge of the best possible world during the years from 1510–20. He had then "such a primacy and authority" like "no one else in the spiritual history of the western world,"[3] and believed that his educational project would increase both knowledge and faith. A purer religion would follow a deeper understanding of the scriptures, but never without Horace, Terence, and Lucian of Samosata.[4] And such an achievement would never have been possible until Erasmus's own time.

But his ideal collapsed completely with the Reformation.[5] His cosmopolitism, which, according to Teichman,[6] reflects the idea of a universal church, shattered in a kaleidoscope of interpretations. And every tiny piece of it claimed him as its predecessor, only to end up accusing him as a traitor and a coward, since he, faithful to his motto *concedo nulli* ("I yield to none"), had never conceded or agreed to anyone involved in schisms. His position was marvelously exposed in a letter to Martin Bucer, of 1532:[7]

> Even if I had less aversion for your dogmas, there is something else that would prevent me from giving my name to them: once enrolled in your militia, I would never be free to abandon my adherence to you. Obviously the fame by which I am weighed down stands in the way. And new dogmas continue to appear, to which I would have to subscribe, willing or not, once I had given my name.[8]

Averse to divisions, Erasmus had been, however, sowing the seeds of something that would soon turn against him. Guided by philology, like his predecessor and model Lorenzo Valla, Erasmus and other Christian humanists "rediscovered the Gospel as they did the *Iliad*" and submitted it to the *ex fontibus* criteria of investigation.[9] It is not, therefore, untouchable.

Thus, Erasmus, producing a work of outstanding philological craft, published in 1516 his first edition of the *Novum Instrumentum*. Drawn from *vetustissimis simul et emendatissimis* ('the most ancient and the most correct') codices in Greek and in Latin, his version was printed in columns, side by side. When he found inconsistencies in the Vulgata, he pointed them out and dared to correct Jerome.

For instance, having not found the excerpt 1 Jn 5, 7–8 in the oldest codices, he excluded it. But those verses, known as *comma Johanneum* (the Johannine Comma), happen to be practically the only mention to the Trinity in the Scriptures. Accused of Arianism and Pelagianism,[10] Erasmus gave in and reinserted them into his 1522 version out of prudence rather than conviction.[11] But he had already taught others how to investigate and where.

Another time bomb was "the great commission" of Matthew 28: "go and make disciples in all nations, baptizing them."[12] If baptism occurred after instruction on faith precepts, it was for adults only, as it is in the Acts of Apostles. Erasmus proposes diplomatically in his *Paraphrases* to Matthew an intermediary solution: that children, once they reached the age of reason, should be asked to declare whether they agree (*interrogentur ratumne habeant*) with that promise made in their name when they were baptized.

In both cases, however, he had inoculated a new "drop of poison" from old heretical doctrines. If the philological method could demonstrate that the basis of some dogmas was not scripturistic, then it certainly contributed to the erosion of a structure built on authoritative foundations. It was also the first time in history when it was possible and affordable to buy a copy of the Bible and read it, both in *koine* and Latin. The Roman Church no longer had the monopoly on literacy, and some would notice very soon that the *corpus christianum* maybe was not scripturistic either, after all.

If the ministerial Reformation did not touch fundamental dogmas such as Trinity and pedobaptism, before long a movement emerged in Reformed countries that not only confronted Papist legitimacy in all matters and levels but also refused any authority not validated by the Scriptures, even Augustine or Jerome. Since Williams' magisterial 1962 study,[13] its consecrated name is Radical Reformation. In my opinion, it should be Restitution, because such a word contains the aim, the ideal, and the interpretation of human history of that movement. And, at the same time, if, due to both its millenarist expectations and its taste for prophetic mysticism, the Radical Reformation could seem to be closer to the illiterate movements of the Middle Ages, in my opinion. Its very emergence at that time is a consequence and a radicalization of humanism, to the extent of becoming its nemesis. In that sense, the Radical interpretation is precisely the one that would not have been possible before the sixteenth century. Despite their radicalism, its proponents claimed they were the heirs of Erasmus too.

Restitutio

The Radical Reformation encompasses a multiplicity of different groups, spread throughout many newly Reformed regions and under the influence of several preachers and "prophets." Despite their differences, however, Anabaptists, Spiritualists, and Evangelical rationalists shared the fundamental ideal of a *restitutio*.[14] They sought to restore Christianity through the restoration of each word in the scriptures, by deleting the interpolations attached by tradition. The whole movement thus emerged from the return to the sources and depended on the reading of the Bible. Unlike the Christian humanists, however, they had no interest in any literature or philosophy *other than* the Scriptures.

Restoring the primitive church was in their view the condition for the second advent of Jesus Christ, the human contribution to it. The true visible community of saints will be the whole world and cannot coexist with the church of the Antichrist. This cannot be reformed. It must disappear.

For them, the true church of Christ had been corrupted and destroyed by its union with the temporal power that occurred under Constantine. Since Nicaea, the Antichrist had been sitting on Christ's throne. Therefore, all the events, saints, and doctrines that appeared after the year 325 were evil.

The *restitutio* starts from Acts of Apostles, 3:21, where Peter mentions the return of Christ, "whom the heaven must receive until the time of restitution of all things." Restitution and millennium are thus indissolubly linked.

Calendarizers, who "treat the Bible like a box of jigsaw puzzle pieces" and "take the pieces out one by one and gradually fit them into a picture,"[15] had calculated the "end times" from various starting points, and each of those systems had its own intrinsic logic. If the Reformation accepted the Augustinian hermeneutic, according to which 1,000 is nothing but a perfect number indicating the fullness of time (*ut perfecto numero notaretur ipsa temporis plenitudo*: *City of God* 20.7), the Radical Reformation is a Millenarist movement that meets all the conditions described by Norman Cohn:[16]

1. collective (to be enjoyed by the faithful as a collectivity);
2. terrestrial (to be realized on this earth);
3. imminent (about to come both soon and suddenly);
4. total (to transform life on earth, after which the status will be perfection);
5. miraculous (to be accomplished by or with the help of supernatural agencies).

On the Radical side, the future millennium would bring terrestrial happiness for all the righteous and transform the whole world into the visible church, with the intervention of Jesus Christ and the saints. These are also the martyrs, who are compelled to act because the time has come.

Thus the idea of a *completum tempus* ("time fulfilled") is not a figure of speech, but a revealed secret: a "history of the future," as the Portuguese-Brazilian millenarist Antonio Vieira would say.[17] It is conceived of as a reality that is imminent, but nevertheless concrete because it is inherent to the very nature of all things, although they have been deviated from God due to the action of evil. And, once everything in the world is ruined, the *restitutio* could occur only through a great battle, for which the heavenly armies are already mobilized. Meanwhile, here on earth, man must do his part and "fight the good fight" (2 Tim. 4,7). In that combination of eschatology and expectation for the new Jerusalem here and now, those who die fighting for it will be resurrected first, or may not even experience death at all. In this war of divine proportions, the heroes are the martyrs. In the early modern period, martyrdom, encouraged by sermons and praised in song, became art—the art of dying, an *ars moriendi*.[18]

Servetus

Born in 1511, Michael Servetus left Spain, newly unified under the Catholic monarchs Ferdinand and Isabella, to become synonymous with dissent, in what would be regarded as a case of total heresy.[19] Antitrinitarian,[20] antipedobaptist, millenarist, and psychopannichist, he was also an astrologer (taken to court for practising judicial astrology), a medical doctor who became involved in the polemics between the Galenists and Arabists, an anatomist who discovered that blood circulates through the lungs for oxygenation, and much more. Having written his arch-heretical masterpiece secretly in a French episcopal palace, Servetus, who had been condemned to the stake by Catholics, became in 1553 the first person burned for heresy in a Reformed city—in this case, Geneva. His duel with Calvin, before dying on a pyre of green firewood, inspired Sebastien Castellión to write the first manifesto for freedom of conscience and religious tolerance, 235 years before *La déclaration des droits de l'homme* (*Declaration of the Rights of Man*). With such a rich and captivating biography, and since only three copies of the original and clandestine edition of the *Christianismi Restitutio* (*The Restitution of Christianity*) were not destroyed, Servetus was turned into a martyr of freedom against tyranny, or a humanist against ignorance. As a result, many have ignored the cause for which he believed he was dying. To understand his motivations, one needs to find in his work the same coherence displayed in his life. Moreover, one has to understand that his death was the signature, so to speak, with which he attested his doctrine.

His arch-heretic career began in 1531, with the publication of *De Trinitatis erroribus libri septem* (*Seven Books on the Errors of the Trinity*). Servetus was so sure about his interpretation that he not only put his true name on the cover of such a book but also tried to publish it in Basel, where he went to in 1530, intending no less than to meet Erasmus himself. Having lost a lot of his prestige, however, the former prince of the humanists had left the town in a rush, when Oecolampadius arrived, and churches were vandalized. Servetus would have followed Erasmus to Freiburg, but the Dutchman refused to see the Young Spaniard.[21] The *Errors of Trinity* would have caused Erasmus deep disappointment, to the extent that he preferred to avoid its author.[22]

Erasmus certainly knew about the *libellus de tribus personis* ("booklet about the three persons"), whose publication he complains about in a letter of 1532,[23] and it is very likely that he, already a sexagenarian and the greatest name of Christian humanism, had had in his hands a letter from the teen Servetus trying to entangle him in the Trinitarian controversy revival. Erasmus would have replied with the same glacial silence addressed to all those who were willing to sacrifice *concordia* to prove a point at any price. But, if he was supposed to subscribe to an idea, it is precisely because it was presented as an heir of one of his own.

Servetus soon published another book, *Dialogorum de Trinitate libri duo* ("Dialogues on the Trinity"), however. The dialogical format, largely practiced by humanists, especially by Erasmus, was the standard method for didactic treatises. We are thus entitled to suppose that a twenty-year-old Servetus is introducing himself as a *magister* teaching the true Trinity.[24] As for the promised recantation after the scandal caused by his first book, his only regret was for his bad and juvenile Latin, *imperitiae meae et typographi incuriae* ("due to both my lack of qualification and the typographer's negligence").

After the controversy created by those two books, he was forced to change his name. More than twenty years later, the Inquisition found him in Vienne as Cardinal Palmier's medical doctor, using the pseudonym of Michel de Villeneuve. Over two decades he had been devoted to secretly writing the *Christianismi Restitutio*, "a masterpiece of heretical writing."[25] The printing presses had been brought to the region by his order and installed quietly nearby, and the book's 734 pages were typeset one by one, and the originals then burned. Servetus's name was no longer written in full on the cover, but its contents now included a set of letters that he had sent from Vienne to Calvin, who had saved them for years. Calvin denounced the sender of the letters as the author of the newly released heretical book and supplied the evidence for his claim, sending the handwritten letters to the Roman Catholic authorities. Arrested and interrogated, Servetus was sentenced to death, but, having somehow escaped from prison, he was burned in effigy, with all books written by him that the inquisitors were able to find. Four months later, though, he was seen in Geneva, and arrested immediately. During his long interrogations, Calvin appeared in person in court to question him on doctrinal points and, after a very long trial, Servetus was sentenced to be burned at the stake, a penalty never applied in a Reformed city before. His execution went ahead in Champel, near Geneva, on October 27, 1553, only a few months after the release of the *Restitutio*.[26]

The book has a monumental, completely coherent system, with implacable inner logic. It is also a clear and certainly scary example of radicalization by a scholar and humanist who could undoubtedly be called a true Renaissance man. But he did not belong to the first decades of the century, when Erasmus's *Folly* was admired and appreciated for satirizing the religious orders; instead, he was part of the world in which Erasmus himself no longer had a place. If Erasmus had never encouraged dissidence and rupture, Servetus, on the other hand, eschewed both Catholic and Reformed churches (and, indeed, did not seem to be entirely affiliated to any Radical group either) because he was at war with all sides. Although his battle was spiritual, and in his view fought alongside the angels, its aim was to annihilate everything introduced into Christianity after 325.

His theology will not be analyzed here. It is enough to mention that, for him, there was no essential or real distinction between the persons of the Trinity. The distinction was by mode or dispensation, and *persona* is never substantial, but rather aspectual or, so to speak, functional.

Servetus's modalistic Trinity underpins his conception of history, divided into progressive phases of divine revelation. The Father, ineffable and unmeasurable, manifested Himself in His historical Son and communicated Himself through His Spirit after the Son ascended to heaven. Manifestation and communication, Son and Spirit, are like "the two hands of God," not two different entities. Christianity and history are thus, as Friedman puts it, "a string of very independent and separate acts of divine self-disclosure."[27]

The Father is *immensitas inaccessibilis, incomprehensibilis, lux inuisibilis* (inaccessible immensity, incomprehensible, invisible light), and, therefore, under the Law of the Old Testament, there were *vmbrae* (shadows). *Shadow* is the prefiguration of something future (*quasi rei futurae praefigurationem*): "For in the Law the types of things that will be were anticipated, and those types can be called shadows" (*nam praecesserunt in lege futurorum typi, quos possumus et umbras uocare*).[28] The "law of the letter" has been abrogated by the "law of the spirit." His typological exegesis allows him to interpret prophetic texts as foreshadowing. Therefore, he could (literally) take his presuppositions to the last consequences in order, as promised: *ad hanc vero rem ab ipsis principiis ordine deducendam.*[29]

In the past, Adam's original sin caused a downfall of humankind; Jesus restored it. But soon after his departure, the Church began to deteriorate due to "inventions" (*figmenta*), that, however, "had already been decreed by Jewish laws" (*Iudaicis legibus iam tunc decreta*).[30]

> It degenerated seditiously, the same way as it did before, when we first departed from Egypt, when we first passed by twelve springs of water and seventy palm trees, when the first leaders were absent to us. After the apostles and disciples, the church was like this, deprived of the truth and empty of its defenders (...). Paul knew it prophetically: that, after his departure, the wolves would enter immediately, and the Antichrist would be placed in the temple of God very soon.[31]

In addition to the Trinity of real personal distinctions, another monstrosity was introduced into the church by the Antichrist: pedobaptism, a practice never mentioned in the primitive church. Erasmus, who had noticed the same, preferred to preserve tradition rather than to cause another scandal. Servetus, with the Anabaptists, argued for the abrogation of the baptism of babies, given by priests who are in fact servants of the Antichrist. No concession, no agreement, no peace.

The Servetan ecclesiology expands the Radical topics with his own interpretation, in a unique category entirely dependent on its own intrinsic premises. First, there is the belief in the superiority of the Church in the apostolical period, followed by the downfall and consequent doom of true Christianity following its assimilation by the Rome; according to him, in line with the Radical Reformation in general, the Council of Nicaea had been the crucial stage. Second is his doctrine of the *ecclesia fugata*—that is, the conviction that the true church of Christ had been chased away by the Antichrist's kingdom, the Roman papacy; third, the belief that the true church, visible, present here on earth, should be restored; and finally, the anxious expectation for that time, the puzzle piece that explains and gives sense to the whole prophetic scheme, derived from his periodization of history, in which the future is waiting for the restoration of the past. In this sense, Friedman affirms that Servetus's interpretation did not lie "in a vision of the future, but in a systematic presentation of the past," to the extent that it might be called "the pre-history of the millennium."[32]

Since Nicaea, the true Church of Christ, after being forced to flee to the desert, is *fugata*, chased away, persecuted and fugitive (*vera Christi ecclesia tunc in solitudine fugata secessit, apoc. 12. Christianismi Restitutio*, 399). And it absolutely must be rescued, with the utmost urgency, because the time of the restitution of all things must be fulfilled. Servetus could not be clearer than this: "all things must be restored after 1,260 years. The restoration of all things ought necessarily to be done now" (*post annos 1260 esse omnia nunc restituenda. Necessario debet nunc fieri eorum omnium restitutio*).[33]

The urgency is due to the number 1,260, a traditional mystical cipher and a key to solving biblical mysteries, from Daniel to the Apocalypse. 1,260 is the answer to different formulations of time, such as "three and a half years," "forty-two generations," and the enigmatic "a time, two times, and a half time." In Servetus, it is the number for his apocalyptical mathematics:

> But "day" is to be understood in the prophetical way as "year". The prophets teach us all the time that, from the time of Constantine and Sylvester, the true Antichrist reigned for one thousand two hundred and sixty years.[34]

Servetus also included in the *Restitutio* a little treatise, or rather a catalogue, called *Sixty signs of the Antichrist*. The haste with which it seems to have been written fits with the subject: brief, direct, hyperbolical; in short, apocalyptical. Two signs are especially relevant here:

> Seventeenth sign: the 1,250-year duration of the reign, in which Daniel and John coincide beautifully. Although the mystery of the Antichrist began soon after Christ, his kingdom only truly manifested itself and was established at the time of Sylvester and Constantine. At that time, in an ecumenical council, immediately the son of God was taken from us, the church ran away from us, and all abominations were enacted laws. Since then time and times and a half time have passed: one thousand two hundred and sixty years.[35]
>
> Thirtieth sign: The battle of Michael and the angels (Dn 12 and Apc 12). At the time of the Kingdom of the Antichrist, says Daniel, after a thousand, two hundred and sixty years of his reign, Michael will rise up, fighting in defense of the children of God's people, and those will be times of the greatest anguish. John saw this heavenly battle that will take place after a thousand, two hundred and sixty years. The heavenly and earthly armies are already moving against the Dragon, the Antichrist. The noblest saints will then fight, Daniel says.[36]

By adding 1,260 to 325, the year of the Antichrist's victory, one arrives at a date very close to that on which Servetus was living. Therefore, he must act, because, when the deadline runs out, the battle will begin. Servetus expresses this with great precision, employing both a perfect and a future tense whose connection is the adverb "now": "The kingdom of the Antichrist lasted (*durauit*) for one thousand two hundred and sixty years, at the end of which now (*nunc*) there will be (*erit*) a heavenly battle."[37] A similar construction is seen in "John saw (*vidit*) that this heavenly battle will take place (*futuram*) after one thousand two hundred and sixty years."[38]

Friedman[39] correctly suggests that there is no evidence that Servetus "shared even a mild interest in Thomas Muntzer," or anyone "who sought some measure of social and economic reorganization in the coming of the Kingdom of the Saints." The chiliastic speculation had been an obsession throughout the later Middle Ages and Reformation period, but Servetus seems to have considered only Daniel, John, and Revelation. And in those books a cosmic battle is mentioned, the *pugna* ("battle") fought by the Archangel Michael. Therefore, the *Restitutio* begins with a *vocatio*, when soldiers are ordered to go to war. Its cover features a phrase in Greek—"and there was war in heaven"—from Revelation 12:7, which finishes with the sentence "Michael and his angels fought against the dragon," as well as one in Hebrew: "and Michael appeared in heaven." Servetus also exhorts the reader to think about the meaning of Michael's forthcoming and his fight after the 1,260 years of desolation (*cogita, lector, quid apud Danielem et Ioannem significet ille Michaëlis futurus aduentus, et pugna post annos desolationis mille ducentos sexaginta*).[40]

Servetus is thus expecting the battle of Michael against the Antichrist and his church. His task is therefore to be the voice crying in the wilderness, the prophet, and the martyr. It is a central theme in Servetan historiography: he believes himself to be living at the edge of a cosmic event, in which he would play the leading role.

Michael

A prophet's speech necessarily has to be presented as the expression of the truth. The speaker does not speak in his own name or by his own volition, but because he was charged with a mission. His speech is validated by proxy, and the *nuntius* is nothing but an instrument. But the prophet must build his credibility as a herald before the prophecy he brings comes true. Berger theorizes on the *apostolikon*, the envoy's self-presentation that is also a self-testimony and a self-recommendation, in which "the apostle gives his name, explains his function, summarizes his message and reproduces his self-image."[41]

His words, that make sense only in a period of crisis and danger, fit in a scheme of revelation,[42] consisting of the following elements:

1. a hidden secret;
2. since the beginning of Creation;
3. it is time for its revelation;
4. which has been revealed to the apostles, apostles, who will transmit them to others;
5. that secret is the reason for so many persecutions.

Servetus believed he was the emissary of a secret manifested to him and him alone; he must tell the world, immediately, simply because "the time is fulfilled" and the final battle was about to begin. Michael and his angels would fight in heaven, and he, Michael, would lead the true Christians on earth. Servetus specifically presents himself as a soldier associated to Michael, the warrior archangel whose feast day, September 29, is also Servetus's birthday and the date he chose for the printing of the first page of the *Restitutio*.

An outraged Calvin protests in his *Commentary on Daniel*:[43]

> That foul hypocrite, Servetus, has dared to appropriate this passage to himself; for he has inscribed it as a frontispiece on his horrible comments, because he was called Michael! We observe what diabolic fury has seized him, as he dared to claim as his own what is here said of the singular aid afforded by Christ to his church. He was a man of the most impure feelings, as we have already sufficiently made known. But this was a proof of his impudence and sacrilegious madness— to adorn himself with this epithet of Christ without blushing, and to elevate himself into Christ's place, by boasting himself to be Michael, the guardian of the church, and the mighty prince of the people! This fact is well known, for I have the book at hand should any one distrust my word.[44]

Servetus himself had written it explicitly in a letter to Calvin:

> I work incessantly for the restoration of this church, and you take offense that I mingle in this fight of Michael and desire that all Godly men should do so. But read this step carefully and you will see that there will be men who will fight then, exposing their lives to death, in blood and in the testimony of Jesus Christ, as John teaches there openly. Men who will be called angels, as stated in the scriptures.[45]

The circle completes with martyrdom, since the cause of Truth is a war against a world over which the Antichrist prevailed. The restitution is therefore a mission in which many will die, as he interprets the fifth seal of Apocalypse 6: 12–17 (*in quinto sigillo interfectorum martyrum ingens numerus, Christianismi Restitutio*, 410). But the angels would not be able to win without the martyrs.

> If we are vanquished, they (the angels) are also vanquished, being deprived of the function and power to serve us properly. They fight for us, as our servants, and if we win, they win. Even more: these struggles of the angels anticipate and figure ours and culminate in ours, as it is clearly seen in Daniel, chapters 10 and 12, and in the Apocalypse, chapter 12.[46]

Christian history and imagery have always been fed with martyrs' narratives, in which the most excruciating penalties were, in fact, the strongest proof against the executioners.

In my opinion, the answer to Bainton's "Why Geneva?" question[47] seems to be found in this grandiose sense of a mission. Identified with a messianic archetype, Servetus had already announced in the prologue of his *Restitutio* that its content "is imposed on us" (*quid nobis ponitur*). It is thus a task, a commission. Addressing Christ, he affirms that "thine is the cause (...) which was ordered to me by a certain divine impulse, so that I, who was worried about the truth, could defend it" (*causa haec tua est... quae diuino quodam impulse tractanda sese mihi obtulit, cum essem de tua veritate sollicitus*).[48] He also quotes the parable of light (Matthew 5, Mark 4, and Luke 8 and 11): "thou hath taught us that the light cannot be hidden, thence, woe is me if I do not evangelize!" (*lucernam non esse abscondendam, tu nos docuisti, ut vae mihi sit, nisi euangelizem*).[49] He needed to act, so he wrote the *Restitutio*. Since the Roman Catholic Inquisition had found and burned practically every copy of it, we are entitled to think that he felt compelled to find another way to "put the light on a high stand." In fact, in Geneva he could speak more freely than ever before, and not only are all interrogations of him are recorded[50] but he was also allowed to establish from prison a widely distributed correspondence with his accusers. He never gave in, recanted, or regretted his doctrine. Bainton[51] thinks that "he may have been awaiting help, not from Perrin and Vandel, but from the archangel Michael." If he did not wish for martyrdom, he certainly faced it as an act that would become evidence, in a legal sense, that he was on the side of the Truth. Facing the flames, in his last moments he could have chosen decapitation instead, by pronouncing the formula "the eternal Son of God" instead of "the Son of the eternal God." But he refused to.

In his book *Discipline and Punish*, Michel Foucault says that the tortures inflicted on people that seem barbaric or simply unthinkable to us, were, in fact, "inexplicable, perhaps, but certainly neither irregular nor primitive."[52] *Supplice* is indeed the guarantee of a hierarchical order, validated by "the dissymmetry between the subject who has dared to violate the law and the all-powerful sovereign who displays his strength."[53] The king *displays* it, meaning it existed previously and it is already lawful. The tortured body is thus a speech by the king, an "orator" whose *fides* comes from an absolute and exclusive power. In the intrinsic logic of messianic world views, which is, in a broader sense, the vision of Christianity as a whole, one can think, on the other hand, that martyrdom was also a kind of speech performed by the martyr.

Klassen says that the existence of men "like even Servetus" who "could think of themselves as actors in the drama of the end-time, indicates primarily the common powerful certainty of living at the end of time" and "demonstrates again that the sense of being oneself a fulfillment of biblical and subsequent prophecy was not limited to the people often regarded as the lunatic fringe in Reformation times."[54]

I would argue that it happened because Servetus was a humanist, but a humanist who took the *ex fontibus* interpretation to its ultimate conclusion, a man of unbreakable logic committed to a system entirely coherent in itself but which was necessarily at war against reality. But far from intending to foster empty polemics or to invent new interpretations, Servetus was in dialogue with primitive Christianity, and followed a totally rational train of thought from the premise that the Church should be restored in order to make possible the Babylonic Dragon's defeat. He built his authority by himself; an authority which legitimated his interpretation, inside his scheme. It is not chaotic, illogical, or unmotivated absurdity; it is not the "beastly stupidity" (*beluina stupiditas*) Calvin accused it of being: rather it is a perfectly organized system, which exposed the inconsistencies and incongruities of many dogmas validated by the Church, but with no scriptural foundation. Nowadays Servetus is acknowledged as the sixteenth-century medical doctor who discovered that blood, not air, flows from the heart to the lungs. This is considered to be the first appearance of blood circulation in Western culture. But it had to be discovered again, not long after, in 1628, by William Harvey. Servetus, who was dissecting veins to look for the soul in the blood, as in the Book of Leviticus 17, hid that passage in a few pages of the *Christianismi Restitutio*. Rushing ahead of the final battle, perhaps he did not even notice the importance of his finding. Collecting signs, reading prophecies, and preparing for the heavenly conflict, he did not care for posterity. There was time for nothing but eternity, and Michael was ready.

Notes

1 Hay (1965: 1).
2 Gowens (1998: 56).
3 Telle (1974: 95): "Personne dans l'histoire spirituelle du monde occidental, n'a joui d'une primauté et d'une autorité telles."
4 For Erasmus's method of education and the ancient authors recommended by him, see Chomarat (1981).
5 Cf. Barral-Baron (2014).
6 Teichman (1986: 7).
7 Erasmus (2018: 341).
8 Erasmus (1938: 482): *Iam si minus abhorrerem a vestris dogmatibus, est aliud quod deterreret a dando nomine. Mihi semel asscripto in vestram militiam nunquam esset integrum a vobis desciscere. Nimirum obstat fama, qua degrauor. At apud vos subindex prodeunt noua dogmata; quibus velim nolim subscribendum esset, si semel dedissem nomen.*

9   Hilar (2002: 72).
10 By Diego López Zúñiga, for example, who, in 1520, published the *Annotationes contra Erasmum Roterodamum in defensionem translationis Novi Testamenti*. In 1522, he published in Rome the pamphet *Erasmi Roterodami blasphemiae et impietates nunc primum propalatae ac próprio volumine alias redargutae*.
11 Levine (1999: 43).
12 Cf. Friesen (1998).
13 Williams (1962).
14 Williams and Mergal (1957: 19–20).
15 Klassen (1992: 23).
16 Cohn (1970: 13).
17 Antonio Vieira (1608–97), famous preacher and rhetorician, author of *História do Futuro*. He believed in the myth of the King Sebastian of Portugal, and expected a Christian and Portuguese Fifth Empire, which would extend its dominions throughout the world.
18 Gregory (2001: 52).
19 Friedman (1978).
20 Servetus was not an antitrinitarian, in fact, but rather against the Nicene Trinity. He explains his conception of a Trinity of dispensations in all his theological books, from 1531 to 1553.
21 Bietenholz (2008: 35–9).
22 Biagioni (2012: 119).
23 Erasmus (1938: 453).
24 In his introductory study to the Spanish translation of the *Restitutio*, Ángel Alcalá (1980: 64) proposes that Servetus took this kind of exposition from the *Scrutinium Scripturarum*, by Paul of Burgos (Solomon Ha-Levi), or from the *Dialogi in quibus impiae Judaeorum opiniones confutantur*, by Petrus Alphonsi (Moses Sephardi). Both of them were converted Jews.
25 Friedman (1978: 13).
26 *Hunted Heretic: The Life and Death of Michael Servetus, 1511–1553*, by Roland H. Bainton, whose first edition was released in 1553, is still the first and main reference on Servetus's biography.
27 Friedman (1978: 463).
28 *Christianismi Restitutio*, 202.
29 Ibid., 355.
30 Ibid., 671.
31 *Seditiose degeneratum est, sicut et olim, cum primum exiuimus de Aegypto, cum primum transiuimus duodecim fontes aquarum, et septuaginta palmas, cum primum defuerunt primi duces. ita post apostolos et discipulos fuisse ecclesiam defensoribus veritatem destitutam, et vacuam (. . .). Id prophetice nouit Paulus, post ipsius discessum*

ingressuros confestim lupos, et Antichristum in templo Dei mox collocandum (*Christianismi Restitutio*, 672).

32 Friedman (1978: 39).

33 *Christianismi Restitutio*, 401.

34 *Diem vero prophetico more pro anno esse sumendum, passim nos docent prophetae, vt a Constantini, et Syluestri tempore iam annos mille ducentos sexaginta regnauerit Papa, verus Antichristus* (ibid., 396).

35 *Decimum septimum signum, Tempus regni annorum mille ducentorum sexaginta, in quo pulchre conueniunt Daniel et Ioannes. Quamuis post Christum mox coepit Antichristi mysterium: vere tamen emicuit, est stabilitum est regnum, tempore Syluestri et Constantini. Quo tempore est mox oecumenico concilio a nobis ereptus filius Dei, fugata ecclesia, et abominationes omnes legibus decretae. Hinc transierunt tempus et tempora et dimidium temporis, anni mille ducenti sexaginta* (*Christianismi Restitutio*, 666).

36 *Tricesimum signum, Michaëlis et angelorum pugna, Dani. 12. et apoc. 12. In tempore illo regni Antichristi, ait Daniel, post anos mille ducentos sexaginta regni eius, consurget Michaël stans pro filiis populi Dei, et erit tempus maximae angustiae. Vidit Ioannes futuram post anos mille ducentos sexaginta, hanc caelestem pugnam. Caelestia et terrestria contra draconem, et Antichristum iam mouentur. Santos altissimos hic pugnaturos ait Daniel* (Ibid., 667–8).

37 *Annos mille ducentos sexaginta durauit regnum Antichristi, quibus finitis erit nunc caelestis pugna* (ibid., 395).

38 *Vidit Ioannes futuram post annos mille ducentos sexaginta, hanc caelestem pugnam* (ibid., 668).

39 Friedman (1978: 36).

40 *Christianismi Restitutio*, 395.

41 Berger (2005: § 82).

42 Ibid.

43 Calvin (1853).

44 *Ausus est ille foedissimus nebulo Servetus ad se trahere hunc locum. Nam quasi elogium commendationis inscripsit suis horrendis commentis, quia scilicet vocatus fuit Michael. Et videmus ut diabolicus furor abriupuerit illam bestiam, quoniam quod hic dicitur de singulari Christi auxilio erga ecclesiam, ausus est sibi arrogare. Erat enim impurissimus canis, quemadmodum satis nobis copertum fuit. Sed hoc fuit documentum impudiciae ipsius, et sacrilegae etiam amentiae, quod non erubuit, quum se ornaret hoc Christi elogio, et statueret se quasi in locum ipsius, dicere et iactare se illum esse Michaelem ecclesiae custodem, et principem magnum populi. Res satis nota est. Liber enim apud me exstat si quis mihi non habeat fidem* (*Praelectionum in Danielem Prophetam*, Cap. XII–1, 286–7).

45 *In huius ecclesiae restitutione ego iugiter laboro, et ob id tu mihi succenses, quod pugnae illi Michaelis me immisceam, et pios omnes misceri desiderem. Sed locum illum diligenter expende, et videbis, homines fore, qui ibi pugnabunt, animas suas morti expondendo, in sanguine et testimonio Iesu Christi, vt aperte docet ibi Ioannes. Angelos veros dici, obuium est in scripturis* (*Epistola Vicesima ad Calvinum, Christianismi Restitutio*, 628). He repeats the same in a letter addressed to Abel Poupin, translated by Bainton, *Hunted Heretic*, 99: "Perhaps it will offend you that I meddle in this fight of Michael and wish to involve you. Study that passage carefully and you will see that they are men who will fight there, giving their souls to death in blood and for a testimony to Jesus Christ. Before the fight there will be a seduction of the world. The fight then follows, and the time is at hand . . . I know that I will certainly die on this account, but I do not falter that I may be a disciple like the Master. (. . .) Goodbye, and do not expect to hear from me again. I will stand above my watch. I will consider. I will see what He is about to say, for He will come. He will certainly come. He will not tarry."

46 *Nobis victis, illi vincuntur, spoliati munere et potestate nobis rite ministrandi. Illi pro nobis pugnant, quasi ministri, et nobis vincentibus illi vincunt. Imo illae angelorum pugnae nostras pugnas designant, et figurant, ac in nobis illae complentur, vt manifeste apparet Dani. 10. 12. et apoc. 12* (*Christianismi Restitutio*, 389).

47 Bainton (1953: 168).

48 *Christianismi Restitutio*, 4.

49 Ibid.

50 Kingdon (1962).

51 Bainton (1953: 120).

52 Foucault (1995: 31).

53 Foucault (1995: 48–9).

54 Klassen (1992: 82).

Part Two

Modern Questions

5

Classics and Western Civilization: The Troubling History of an Authoritative Narrative

Rebecca Futo Kennedy

Introduction

Western civilization is a story. It is a story about the evolution of human societies. It is a story about how history works. It is a story about our relationship to the past. It is a story of race and ethnicity, of ideals and prejudices, of ownership and identity. A fabulist in the Western civilization tradition story can shape their tale with desirable elements set against whatever they oppose. One fabulist emphasizes the rhetoric of "freedom, private property, reasoned debate, and democracy." Another spins a tale about Christendom or the ancient Greeks and Romans. Still another chronicles canons and academics. Whatever the explicit aims of the story of Western civilization, it remains a story about Whiteness and White supremacism, even when it conceals and disguises a direct, straightforward reference to the concept of a White race. As Alastair Bonnett has argued: "The term 'western' remained and remains racially coded, burdened with the expectation that the world will never be 'free', 'open' and 'democratic' until it is Europeanized'."[1]

Western civilization is not a single story, but a multifarious and at times ambiguous tale that flitters in and out of our intellectual, political, and economic discussions. It structures conflicts, alliances, global capitalist conglomerates, history, and identities. This fundamental ambiguity is in fact the source of its power and authority. Russia can be both the biggest threat to Western civilization and its savior, depending on the fabulist.[2] Ukraine can be both a part of "the West" and "relatively civilized," but not quite a Western country, as numerous reporters have stumbled over during the early stages of the Russian invasion of Ukraine in early 2022.[3]

Western civilization is also an idea premised on a world divided into cultural (but really bioracial) groups that, as most famously formulated by Samuel Huntington, clash and must be ranked against each other.[4] Amartya Sen has described the mechanism well: "Theories of civilizational clash have often provided allegedly sophisticated foundations of crude and coarse popular belief. Cultivated theory can bolster uncomplicated bigotry."[5] We can take Sen even further. It is not just models of civilizational clash but the concept of civilization itself, especially the idea of Western civilization, that bolster bigotry, both complicated and uncomplicated.

It is odd to assert baldly that "there is no such thing as Western Civilization."[6] The idea exists and continues to exert power. What I challenge is the claim that Western civilization is a neutral, universal, or eternal idea or identity. It is a modern charter myth (only really about 100 or so years old) for a specific definition of technological and social development that is mobilized historically within models of racial, cultural, or civilizational hierarchy. There is no definition of Western civilization that does not assume its exceptionalism, or present it (falsely) as a universal value when it is in fact "rooted in the experiences and expectations of a narrow social strata."[7] In this way, the concept is, despite many valiant efforts to claim otherwise, a dangerous charter myth for a racialized and White supremacist world.

This chapter explores various manifestations of the Western civilization narrative, considering how it is defined, what it encompasses and how it has been popularized and naturalized. The chapter illustrates in particular the story's frequent grounding in the ancient Greek and Roman pasts and ardent defenses of it by ancient historians as an important analytical category. My perspective is as an insider, one who has been raised within "the West" and encouraged to believe in the value of "Western civilization." I write this, therefore, as something akin to the navel-gazing exercise of a "Westerner," but in recognition that there are other versions of "the West", stories told by those excluded from belonging to "the West." I consider three main questions: (1) What forms historically have the story of Western civilization taken, with emphasis variably on the "Western" or the "civilization" parts? (2) How has yoking ancient Greece in particular to this authoritative narrative as the "foundation of Western civilization" shaped the way the ancient world has been interpreted? (3) How has this Western civilization narrative, grounded in an ancient Greek past, been a dangerous story we tell ourselves to justify war, capitalist exploitation, and even genocide?

The Western in Western Civilization

Some scholars fervently wish there to be nothing inherently racial or racist about the idea of a "West" or "Western civilization."[8] They construct a "West" linked to geography, seeking to preserve "Western civilization" as a neutral category of analysis, hoping against hope to avoid falling into racist tropes. Ian Morris' *Why the West Rules – For Now* (2010) is a prominent example. Morris brings together many of the most common aspects of the geographic approach to Western civilization. For him, the "West" is:

> ... simply a geographic term, referring to those societies that descended from the westernmost Eurasian core of domestication, in the Hilly Flanks. It makes no sense to talk about "the West" as a distinctive region before about 11,000 BCE, when cultivation began making the Hilly Flanks unusual; and the concept starts to become an important analytical tool only after 8,000 BCE, when other agricultural cores started appearing. By 4500 BCE, the West had expanded to include most of Europe, and in the last five hundred years colonists have taken it to the Americas, the Antipodes, and Siberia. "The East", naturally enough, simply means those societies that descended from the easternmost core of domestication that began developing in China by 7500 BCE. We can also speak of comparable New World, South Asian, New Guinean, and African traditions.
>
> Morris 2010: 117

Hilly Flanks refers to the foothills regions alongside the so-called Fertile Crescent, the region that ranges across modern Iraq, Iran, Syria, Lebanon, Israel, Palestine, Jordan, eastern Egypt, and the southeastern tip of Turkey. This is where Morris situates the origins of the "West" and what will become "Western civilization." But this definition is not quite so simply geographic as Morris asserts, a fact that shadows every definition of "West" that purports to be about geography and not values.

Morris identifies seven "core" regions for the development of civilizations: Hilly Flanks, Yellow-Yangzi Valleys, Indus Valley, eastern Sahara, New Guinea, Oaxaca, and Peru. He elects to use the civilization he designates as "the westernmost Eurasian core of domestication" and call that "the West." From there, he builds his theory of social development and the place of geography in it. But this designation of what begins the "West" is not neutral. It lays claims to very specific types of technologies and pace of utilizations that he considers as types of progress. For Morris, Western civilization rests on a theory of geographic determinism, not a geographic designation.

Morris's theory differs from other geographic determinists, like Jared Diamond in *Guns, Germs, and Steel* (1997), however, for two reasons. First, he proposes that any of the cores could, with proper exploitation of resources and the right timing, "rule." And second, he explicitly works to naturalize his definition of "West" with appeals to deep history, which other Western civilization advocates like Niall Ferguson reject. And yet his theory remains a defense of a concept of "Western exceptionalism" because he defines both "social development" and the "West" through an anachronistic lens premised on a history of human social evolution as a history of exploitation and domination (of land, resources, and people) and then provides a geographic pattern of transmission of the designated values that support the modern status quo. The theory is an example of *petitio principii*. We never get an explanation of why Hilly Flanks is the only viable place to locate the "birth of the West".[9] Why not consider the eastern Sahara (Nile valley), Oaxaca, or Peruvian cores? These are all certainly further "west" from the standpoint of the center of Eurasia. And why are we measuring what constitutes "simply a geographic term" from the center of Eurasia? This question is never even posed, let alone answered, an indication that even Morris, a committed geographic determinist,[10] cannot make geography define "the West". Instead, we are given a tale of how, over the course of approximately 12,000 years, those whom he has designated (through "common sense") as the "West" ("those societies that descended from the westernmost Eurasian core of domestication") "rule" because they were the "earliest" domesticators, had the most resources to exploit, used this to expand into and dominate Europe and the Mediterranean Basin and then, after a relatively short period of "decline," expanded to the Americas and Australasia to also soon dominate the entire globe.[11] Hilly Flanks becomes "West" based on a theory of priority.

The simple geographic term, then, is actually a values-laden moniker that obscures the force of a very ideological work his notions of the "West" (as "earliest" and eventually European) and, especially, of "civilization" perform. The simple geography appears, almost as if by coincidence, to coincide with the history of Euro-American imperialism.

Despite his carefully erected edifice of geographic determinism, Morris tells a values-driven story of Western civilization. The values become obvious in his definitions of "social development" and "civilization." He defines civilization as the domestication of plants, gender divisions in labor and reproduction, concerns for ancestry and inheritance, and the creation of institutional and household hierarchies.[12] Morris defines "social development" as "... societies' ability to get things done—to shape their physical, economic, social, and intellectual environments to their own ends".[13] Although vague, these definitions are clearly teleological. They embed the expectation that the modern, industrialized, global capitalist state is the goal.[14] Western civilization has nothing to do with geography. The "Western" part serves simply as a mechanism for laying claim to the idea of "civilization."

The Civilization in Western Civilization

The functional ambiguity of the stories of Western civilization owes much to the ambiguity of the term "civilization." When Morris lists technological and social advances that must occur before a people reaches the level of "civilization," he gestures at what Lucien Febvre, one of the initiators of the Annales school of history, considers the first usage of the term:

> In the first case, civilization simply refers to all features that can be observed in the collective life of one human group, embracing their material, intellectual, moral, and political life and, there is unfortunately no other word for it, their social life. It has been suggested that this should be called the 'ethnographical' conception of civilization. It does not imply any value judgment on the detail or overall pattern of facts examined.
>
> Febvre 1973 [1929]: 220

Since there are almost no peoples today who do not share these basic structures of society, such a concept of civilization does not seem to imply any notion of superiority or inferiority. Once these social structures are placed within a framework of development or "ruling," the implications change. Such definitions of Western civilization rest on Febvre's second usage:

> When we are talking about the progress, failures, greatness and weakness of civilizations we do have a value judgment in mind. We have the idea that the civilization we are talking about—ours—is in itself something great and beautiful; something too which is nobler, more comfortable, better, both morally and materially speaking, than anything outside it – savagery, barbarity, or semi-civilization. Finally, we are confident that such civilization, in which we participate, which we propagate, benefit from and popularize, bestows on us all a certain value, prestige, and dignity. For it is a collective asset enjoyed by all civilized societies. It is also an individual privilege which each of us boasts that he possesses.
>
> Febvre 1973 [1929]: 220

Febvre recognized in 1929 that linking "civilization" to a concept of progress or development turns it into a value and these values are treated as superior. Morris is tepid on ranking; he sees it more like a horse race where any group can surge ahead given the right confluence of circumstances. Ferguson, however, not only does not shy away from ranking societies, he believes it is absurd not to rank them:

> There are those who dispute that, claiming that all civilizations are in some sense equal, and that the West cannot claim superiority over, say, the East of Eurasia. But such relativism is demonstrably absurd.
>
> Ferguson 2011: 5

Ferguson explicitly states that empire and colonialism are fundamental to Western civilization. He repeatedly makes clear that the West is a superior culture, that its rise was "the single most important historical phenomenon of the second half of the second millennium after Christ",[15] and that the proof of this is in the pervasiveness of a "Western way of life":

> For some reason, beginning in the late 15th century, the little states of Western Europe, with their bastardized linguistic borrowings from Latin (and a little Greek), their religion derived from the teachings of a Jew from Nazareth and their intellectual debts to Oriental mathematics, astronomy, and technology, produced a civilization capable not only of conquering the great Oriental empires and subjugating Africa, the Americas and Australia, but also of converting peoples all over the world to the Western way of life—*a conversion achieved ultimately more by the word than by the sword.*
>
> Ferguson 2011: 4–5; emphasis mine

In this story of Western civilization, an accident ("for some reason") produced a superior society, a superiority that dominated less by violence than by the force of its values. It is easy to see how the fabulists of Western civilization end up treating their protagonist (Western civilization) as coterminous with civilization itself. Morris works very hard to obscure this move, insisting on "West" as a simple geographic term. Yet the values-based civilization story remains central even to his project, the guiding light of his narrative, even as he appeals to Hilly Flanks. In stories of Western civilization, west has little to do with geography and civilization has little relation to the descriptive ethnographical term Febvre mentions. Instead, Western civilization stands for "Civilization" through a specifically capitalist, imperialist, and colonialist lens, a civilization assumed greater, morally and materially, to anything else.

Race and Western Civilization

Ferguson is not the only fabulist to combine globalized capitalism with the idea of civilization. This story has roots in eighteenth- and nineteenth-century imperialism and colonialism. Some would place it earlier, connecting its emergence to the trans-Atlantic slave trade. At the turn of the twentieth century, "Western civilization" was an emerging term that would come to denote what in other contexts was called either simply "civilization" or "White civilization." There are those who assume that Western civilization is coterminous with White civilization, both those who defend the idea of an exceptional Western civilization and those who argue that the Western civilization narrative is embedded in White supremacism. As Alastair Bonnett[16] has detailed, however, the concept of Western civilization as we understand it today, at least in the Anglophone world, as denoting a law-governed and socially and technologically advanced society, emerged only in the last century and did so in part because of the failures of the idea of White civilization as a world idea.[17] Western civilization and White civilization are not identical, but they are intertwined and, in most ways, impossible to disentangle from each other in no small part because they are both viewed as either coterminous with civilization itself, as its culmination, or as its most exceptional manifestation. Where in the past, White sat in opposition to Black, now terms like "multiculturalism" are used in opposition to Western, or Western sits uncomfortably in ranked order above the so-called Third World based on relationships to social development and capitalism. Today, many defenders of the concept of Western civilization spare no effort in asserting that Western civilization has no connection to race, imperialism, and global capitalism, though these forces are themselves inextricably bound to racism. In the end, every story of Western civilization features race as a primary protagonist, always there even when unmentioned.

It is impossible to disentangle Western civilization (or, perhaps, any civilizational discourse)[18] from race because race is inherently a matter of hierarchy, not biology. Since the nineteenth century, many have understood "race" through imagined categories of peoples, categories based sometimes on specific physical features like skin color or sometimes on supposed geographic origins. In reality, those categories are not "race" but are the signifiers for the system that is race. Race is the political technology used to craft and maintain institutional structures that enforce hierarchies and oppressions.[19] When scholars or political pundits explain that their idea of Western civilization is unconnected to "race" because the theory of race as a biologically grounded reality has been disproven scientifically,[20] they are practicing a sleight of hand, ignoring that race was *never* about biology, but rather about socio-political population management. Any imperialist system and any concept of civilizational progress, which *de facto* ranks cultural, kinship, or geographic groups along evolutionary or developmental lines, will be inherently racial, as Levbre argued long ago. The question that serves as the title for Morris' book, "Why does the West rule?", is inevitably racial, whether you discuss it in terms of environmental adaption, technological or economic development, political systems, or military capacity. As Alastair Bonnett remarks, "the idea of the West cannot be understood in isolation from other ways of dividing up humanity."[21]

A Western civilization narrative appeals to many because it is a triumphal story of Euro-American exceptionalism that its proponents imagine can overcome the "broken logic" of race: "race is fixed, but culture is fluid: whiteness cannot be acquired, but 'Westernness' can".[22] But the logic of race and Whiteness leaves its traces. It is, perhaps not surprisingly, difficult to distinguish advocates for Western exceptionalism from explicitly White supremacist definitions. The following discussion of civilization is a good example:

> Civilization is complex. It involves the existence of human communities characterized by political and social organization; dominating and utilizing natural forces; adapting themselves to the new man-made environment thereby created; possessing knowledge, refinement, arts, and sciences; and (last, but emphatically not least) composed of individuals capable of sustaining this elaborate complex and of handing it on to a capable posterity...
>
> For the last eight or ten thousand years civilizations have been appearing all the way from Eastern Asia to Europe and North Africa. At first these civilizations were local—mere points of light in a vast night of barbarism and savagery. They were also isolated; the civilizations of Egypt, Chaldea, India, and China developing separately, with slight influence upon each other. But gradually civilizations spread, met, interacted, synthesized. Finally, in Europe, a great civilizing tide set in, first displaying itself in the "Classic" civilization of Greece and Rome, and persisting down to the "Western Civilization" of our own days.

This discussion would not be out of place in a book by Morris, Ferguson, Victor Davis Hanson, Samuel Huntington, Jared Diamond or any number of other authors, journalists, politicians, or scholars who discuss the preeminence of the West. The author, however, is Lothrop Stoddard, from his 1922 book, *The Revolt Against Civilization: The Menace of the Under-man*. Stoddard is, perhaps, best-known for his debate with W. E. B. Du Bois on race in America and his other book, *The Rising Tide of Color Against White World Supremacy* (1920).[23] Stoddard was a Harvard trained historian, journalist, and prominent member of the mainstream American eugenics movement. He wrote apologist articles on Hitler and the Nazi movement in Germany for various US media outlets and wrote a memoir in 1940 that praised the Nazi social engineering projects that were "weeding out" those deemed by the Nazi government to be inferior Germans.[24]

The reason why Stoddard's views on Western civilization don't seem that extreme, however, is because I removed the text in between the ellipses that would have set his views apart from those of an Ian Morris, Niall Ferguson or others. Let me restore it:

Not all the branches of the human species attained the threshold of civilization. Some, indeed, never reached even the limits of savagery. Existing survivals of low-type savage man, such as the Bushmen of South Africa and the Australian "Black fellows," have vegetated for countless ages in primeval squalor and seem incapable of rising even to the level of barbarism, much less to that of civilization. It is fortunate for the future of mankind that most of these survivals from the remote past are to-day on the verge of extinction. Their persistence and possible incorporation into higher stocks would produce the most depressive and retrogressive results. Much more serious is the problem presented by those far more numerous stocks which, while transcending the plane of mere savagery, have stopped at some level of barbarism. Not only have these stocks never originated a civilization themselves, but they also seem constitutionally incapable of assimilating the civilization of others. Deceptive veneers of civilization may be acquired, but reversion to congenital barbarism ultimately takes place. To such barbarian stocks belong many of the peoples of Asia, the American Indians, and the African negroes.

This paragraph rests between Stoddard's definition of civilization and his reference to the Greco-Roman foundations of modern Western civilization. Many Western civilization fabulists today want desperately to pretend it is not there, that simply removing that paragraph preserves the value of the ideas that came before and after, that the legacy of White supremacism is not intricately and intimately connected to the discourse of the evolution or progress of the development of human cultures. Stoddard's central paragraph, however, still echoes in the ears of many when they hear the fabulists of Western civilization, Western exceptionalism, or the West.

Classics and Western Civilization

In reference to Donna Zuckerberg's *Eidolon* editorial, "How to be a Good Classicist Under a Bad Emperor,"[25] John Bloxham[26] suggested that it is hyperbolic to connect White supremacists and fabulists of Classics as the foundation of Western civilization.[27] Bloxham's assessment results from misunderstanding White supremacism. It is not only men donning white hoods and burning crosses, or painting swastikas on Jewish businesses, or colleagues explicitly stating that people only have their jobs because they are not White. As discussed above, White supremacism also includes the stories told since the nineteenth century about social and cultural development and the rising, falling, and relative status of various world civilizations. It is not only a story of Whiteness, but a story of the intertwined nature of Whiteness and Westernness. In the academic world, however, the development of an academic curriculum of defining Western civilization through a canon of books descended from them as a "Golden Nugget" (to use Appiah's phrase) has functioned in much the same way as the term Western itself—to obscure the centering of a specific nineteenth-century notion of Whiteness with curricula and paper over the broken logic of White supremacy in order to maintain a status quo in higher education in the face so called "advocates of multiculturalism."

The story-tellers of Western civilization, like those of White civilization, frequently appeal to Greco-Roman antiquities, the so-called "Classics". This chapter closes with a brief exploration of the American University Culture Wars in the 1980s and 1990s, a period that continues to shape some contemporary discourse both around the discipline and higher education generally. Throughout the Culture Wars, many classicists, both reactionary/conservative and liberal, appealed to Western civilization in their battles against contemporary trends in scholarship or teaching. In the process, they frequently misrepresented the ancient past they claimed to champion while accusing their opponents of doing the same. The sheer volume of works written by ancient historians and classicists about Western civilization since the 1980s makes it impossible to do it justice, especially the proliferation of essays and articles in the last five to ten years. Instead, I will highlight some obvious (and not so obvious) ways this story has been told that show the continuities between the general problems of Western civilization and its use within the discipline called Classics.

For over two decades at the end of the last century, American universities were a central site of what has been called the Culture Wars, a period of contestation and dispute about the role of higher education and, especially, the humanities in American society.[28] Western Civilization was often at the center. Self-styled traditionalists claimed to be fighting for ancient Greece as the foundation for Western civilization. They defended this position by aligning ancient Greece with a modern, White European, Christian, militaristic, patriarchal conception of "the West".[29] They set themselves in opposition to "advocates of multiculturalism and militant feminists".[30] They accused these militant feminists and multiculturalists of highlining only the negative aspects of antiquity (slavery, patriarchy, imperialism), of devaluing the so-called Greek Miracle, a supposedly unique cultural and artistic flowering among the ancient Greek peoples that gave rise to modern European (i.e. Western) civilization.[31] They felt the need to preserve the uniqueness of the ancient Greeks in the face of feminist criticisms of patriarchy and against suggestions of cultural borrowing and integration in the broader Mediterranean world.

Martin Bernal's *Black Athena* (1987) fell like gunpowder into this fire. Without getting into the merits of Bernal's thesis, he challenged the uniqueness of the Greeks and undercut any simple narrative of Western civilization as European. Indeed, Bernal tied such stories to racist ideas. Bernard Knox, perhaps one of the best-known classicists of his era, entered into all these debates with his own defense of Classics, *The Oldest Dead White European Males* (1993). Knox asserted the value of the study of Classics and Western civilization in the face of adversarial "advocates of multiculturalism," a catch-all term that included anyone, from strict Afrocentrists to archaeologists who recognized the importance of the broader Mediterranean in shaping ancient Greek cultures. Knox defended the Western civilization narrative against the charge of being White supremacist by asserting "racism in our sense was not a problem of the Greeks; their homogenous population afforded no soil on which that weed could easily grow".[32] Even leaving aside the factual inaccuracy of ancient Greek homogeneity, several problems with this defense remain. The Western civilization narrative is a modern creation; ancient Greek racism is not relevant.

Knox's understanding of "race" is, not surprisingly, unsophisticated. He treats race as biological difference, asserting not only that the ancient Greeks were free from racism but also that they were all "undoubtedly white".[33] He likewise assumes that racism occurs in societies with biological (and cultural—he conflates them) diversity. Knox's understanding of race structures his understanding of the ancient world, making it hard for him to recognize and value cultural exchange and difference. Thus Knox ends up, probably despite his intentions, positioning the ancient Greeks as the origins of White civilization. He never calls it *White* civilization, of course, but the ambiguity of Western civilization allows him to universalize and neutralize and ignore what is actually a racial narrative.

Knox writes that it is feminists and multiculturalists who have forced his ancient Greeks into the category of "Oldest Dead White European Males." Knox prefers to embrace the proposition of Percy Shelley (1822) that "We are all Greeks." And yet, throughout his essay Knox constrains the Greeks within the confines of Europe (even remarking multiple times how the Greeks "invented" the idea of Europe). He also cites (with two exceptions) only male Euro-American scholars.[34] And he does this in defense of ancient Greece being the "inventor" of a whole list of areas of study and inquiry that only one ignorant of what was happening simultaneously in antiquity and even earlier in Asia and Africa could lay claim to. Whether he intended to or not, Knox's own scholarly practice reinforced and embraced the very identity he claims was forced upon the Greeks by "modern multicultural and radical feminist criticism" as foundational to

Western values. The only way we can all be Greeks is by assimilating ourselves to an unmarked universal Western man.

Knox's commitment to a narrative of Western civilization led him to some strange places. Countering the radicals of his day with his radical, revolutionary, or subversive ancient Greeks, he deploys a historical argument that links the discovery of Greek classics to the age of colonization:

> In this respect as in others, the study of the newly discovered Greek classics was one of the key elements of the Renaissance, that age of renewed intellectual and scientific inquiry, of exploration and colonization, the beginning of the process in which the old, stable civilizations of Asian, Africa, and the Americas were confronted with the dynamics of change introduced by the West.
>
> 1993: 17

The power of the ambiguous Western civilization narrative allows Knox to gesture at historical connections without stooping to argument or explanations. But the logic of Western Civilization also leads him to describe modern histories of genocide in the American, mass enslavement of Africans, and forced Christianization and opening of Asia as "dynamics of change." Niall Ferguson will, as we have seen, claim that it was "achieved ultimately more by the word than by the sword." But it is a history of violence nonetheless presented as mild (and inevitable) interventions.

As we have come to suspect, Western civilization narratives also bring hierarchies with them. Knox, fighting against multiculturalist "academic radicals," defends his canon of works as superior to others:

> As for the multicultural curriculum that is the ideal of today's academic radicals, there can be no valid objection to the inclusion of new material that gives the student a wider view. But that new material will have to compete with the old, and if not up to the same high level it will sooner or later be rejected with disdain by students themselves; only a totalitarian regime can enforce the continued study of second-rate texts or out-worn philosophies.
>
> 1993: 21

This sense of superiority is expressed repeatedly, especially in the insistence on the Greeks being "first" in the "invention" of various things from biology to theater to rhetoric, "in startling contrast to the magnificent but static civilizations of the great Eastern river valleys—Tigris, Euphrates, and Nile...".[35] The Nile is perhaps better described as south and almost all of the scientific theories and many literary genres Knox praises as inventions of the Greeks emerged in places where Greeks lived and worked side by side with "Easterners." The language of invention and priority is unnecessary to appreciating the value of Greek culture, unless the value is in the priority itself. Knox insists that the legacy of the Greeks rests in a set of values: its spirit of innovation and "impatient rhythm of competition." Even if he does not state it explicitly, Knox justifies and explains "Why the West Rules" by reference to values derived from a narrowly tailored vision of the Greek past.

Victor Davis Hanson, a persistent advocate for a Western civilization narrative rooted in ancient Greece, maintains a blog and podcast titled "The Classicist." Hanson has long ceased to teach and write scholarship about the ancient world, having found his niche in political punditry and as a fellow of the Hoover Institute at Stanford University. His decision to focus his career around political punditry may be found in his disgruntlement both with the elitism of the academic discipline and with its "theoretical turn" during the Culture Wars of the 1980s and 1990s, which he explicates so forcefully in his co-authored book *Who Killed Homer? The Demise of Classical Education and the Recovery of Greek Wisdom* (1998).[36]

Beginning with *Western Way of War* (1989), Hanson's work brims with efforts to ground what he defines as the best of the modern world, i.e. Western civilization, in the ancient Greek past. Hanson was first and foremost a military historian and his Western civilization narrative is heavily militaristic, defined by ideals of warfare. He imagines a "*spirit* of Hellenic warfare"[37] where the ancient Greek-style infantryman stands for ideals of masculinity, ideals set in direct contrast to "Eastern" and "Middle Eastern" styles of guerilla warfare. This military violence and dominance is the backbone of his vision of Western civilization—dominance through violence without regret or apology. "Great Battles" not "Great Books" is his mantra.[38] Although most observers note that Hanson's views took on an increasingly anti-Islamic position after 9/11,[39] elements of it already exist in *Western Way of War* and in *Who Killed Homer?* (1998). The West, for Hanson (and Heath, it seems), is the source of all that is good and possible in the world. For example:

> By the same token the remedies for all such ecological, biological, social, and political catastrophes looming on the horizon will also, most likely, be found only in the West. Alternative motor fuels are unlikely to be developed in the Arab world. Indigenous African culture is not going to craft the medicine to stop the AIDS virus. The Orient, to the degree that it resists the Occident, will not forge new methods of international cooperation. Nonpolluting vehicles that run on renewable and sustainable fuel will probably not come from the Caribbean basin. The United Nations has no plans to move to Colombia. The universities of Iraq and Iran cannot train the world's engineers of tomorrow. Despite propaganda to the contrary, other cultures will not offer an entirely different social paradigm

that ensures a similar standard of material comfort and safety without exploitation of the physical landscape. It is left to the Greeks either to destroy us or save us ... That is not to say that the world's great literature, religions, innovative music, food, and fashion cannot arise outside of the West. They do, very often. But the core of our evolving international culture – science, government, language and communications, agriculture, medicine, business, economic and military practice, social organization – will be largely determined by what happens in Europe, America, and the former commonwealth nations of the United Kingdom, whose cultural heritage is linked to the Greeks.

Hanson and Heath 1998: 75–6

There are, of course, no citations or evidence provided for these assertions. They are simply "facts" constructed from a belief that "West is Best." The powerful ideology allows them to shift from a list of technological innovations to the claim that the ancient Greeks will solve the problems of modernity. If one examines the societies that Hanson and Heath mention, one gets the sense that Western and White are the same. And like Knox before them, they make the ancient Greeks complicit in that conflation.

While Eric Adler remarks that "[f]rom his perch as a columnist for *National Review Online* ... Hanson defends the humanities from...the 'utilitarian right,'"[40] Hanson also has used that perch extensively to rail against multiculturalism, immigrants, feminism, and other aspects of the modern world he views as "anti-Western" or even "anti-civilizational", and to push what are historically White supremacist narratives. You can see some of the language he uses, for example, in this 2013 article in the *National Review* called "Western Cultural Suicide":[41]

> Multiculturalism—as opposed to the notion of a multiracial society united by a single culture—has become an abject contradiction in the modern Western world. Romance for a culture in the abstract that one has rejected in the concrete makes little sense. Multiculturalists talk grandly of Africa, Latin America, and Asia, usually in contrast to the core values of the United States and Europe. Certainly, in terms of food, fashion, music, art, and architecture, the Western paradigm is enriched from other cultures. But the reason that millions cross the Mediterranean to Europe or the Rio Grande to the United States is for something more that transcends the periphery and involves fundamental values—consensual government, free-market capitalism, the freedom of the individual, religious tolerance, equality between the sexes, rights of dissent, and a society governed by rationalism divorced from religious stricture. Somehow that obvious message has now been abandoned, as Western hosts lost confidence in the very society that gives us the wealth and leisure to ignore or caricature its foundations. The result is

that millions of immigrants flock to the West, enjoy its material security, and yet feel little need to bond with their adopted culture, given that their hosts themselves are ambiguous about what others desperately seek out.

The list of values Hanson gives for what define Western civilization are familiar, but they are surrounded by anti-immigrant language that rejects the notion of a multicultural world as in any way positive. There is a "Western paradigm" that can take from and be "enriched by" other cultures, but which ultimately non-Westerners must submit to. The insistence that Western civilization is fundamentally about free-market capitalism is strikingly at odds with the ancient Greek world he positions as its roots, but speaks directly to the anti-communist, anti-Russian positioning of the modern West since the Cold War, while also hinting at the association historically of Jewish and Black Americans with unionization and socialist parties in the United States.[42] The language of Western civilization has some of the racial elements of White supremacism under this Cold War rhetoric, but the anti-immigrant, anti- multiculturalism he states so explicitly makes it clear that race is fundamental to his vision of Western civilization.

For those of you (pleasantly) unfamiliar with the discourses on "suicide," it is a common White supremacist term for "miscegenation" and interracial marriage that one might have hoped had died in the 1960s but is still alive and well on many a website these days; a White person commits "race suicide" when they marry or "breed" with a non-White or Jewish person.[43] This idea was grounded in both anti-Semitism and Jim Crow in the United States and was a fundamental pillar for the eugenics movements of the early twentieth century whose purpose was to prevent the "interbreeding" of mixed "stock" for the preservation of Western civilization.[44] The mixing of cultures is viewed as inseparable from the mixing of bodies. We see in Hanson's rhetoric reflections of Lothrop Stoddard, quoted above; he flirts frequently with the language of explicit White supremacism by substituting the term "culture" for "race," and "Western" for "White," his dog whistle intact. The imagined homogenous classical past that gave birth to a mythically unicultural Western civilization are myths held up in opposition to the multiculturalist and nation-of-immigrants realities of both the past and present.

Does any of this make the study of ancient Greece and Rome itself or the academic discipline of Classics culpable in the White supremacist legacies of imperialism, colonialism, and global capitalism of Euro-American military and political powers? It is the persistent retort of those who either claim the term Western civilization is a neutral, quasi-geographic marker or those who make claims for Western exceptionalism rooted in ancient Greece that one cannot hold the ancient Greeks responsible for the sins of the later West. Morris's way of dodging this past with respect to the Greeks is by recognizing that the Greek Miracle was not, in fact, a "miracle." His chapters on the period covering the years that most scholars, especially Hanson, identify as the unique flowering of Western civilization in antiquity are recognized by Morris as the period when cultures from the Western Mediterranean to China were thriving, innovating, and interacting.[45] Morris' use of the Western civilization narrative is not structured around a Greek Miracle or imagining the ancient Greeks as a homogenous, isolated society, but is instead an investment in the modern evolutionary model of social development, which is itself a direct product of racist ideologies.

For Hanson and Heath's part, they recognize the sins of the nineteenth century when "the 'Grecians' were sometimes held up as little more than southern European Victorians, one-dimensional supermen who likewise had conquered darker people, built lavish buildings, written heroic poetry and made beautiful things".[46] They fail to see their own ways of repackaging the multicultural ancient Greek world as the foundation of an anti- multicultural, anti-immigrant, anti-Mediterranean (emphases original) world:

> First, *Greek wisdom is not Mediterranean but anti-Mediterranean; Hellenic culture—as idea not predicated on race—is not just different from, but entirely antithetical to any civilization of its own time or space.* The *polis* is neither African- nor Asian-inspired, but an institution of deliberate opposition to Eastern approaches to government, literature, religion, war, individual rights, citizenship, and science. Whatever Greece was, it was not Tyre, Sidon, Giza, or Persepolis, nor was it Germania, Britannia, or Gaul. The *core values* of classical Greece *are* unique, un-changing, and non-multicultural, and thus explain both the duration and dynamism of Western culture itself . . .
>
> 1998: xviii–xix

No one who has read any scholarship on the ancient Mediterranean world written in the last fifty years can assert such statements as the above without intentional ideological bias. Ian Morris' *Why the West Rules. . .For Now*, whatever issues one may take with his definitional strategies, cannot deny the evidence he presents for the multicultural and very Mediterranean nature of the ancient Greeks (and their wisdom). No scholar who engages earnestly and honestly in a study of the ancient evidence that remains to us, especially the archaeological record, could make these statements without willful misinterpretation.[47] What Hanson and Heath present isn't just a series of false statements, but it is an ideology steeped in a political agenda embraced by far right, "Occidentalist" and "Western chauvinist" extremist groups worldwide.[48] The ancient Greeks do not even present themselves in such opposition to those they lived and interacted with their world, not even the Persians at the height of their wars. The ancient Greeks are being used by Hanson to promote a modern ideology of Western and White supremacy that is out of step with the realities of antiquity itself, but is well within the scope of the history of the concept of Western civilization.

Conclusions

> Whether you claim it, as many in Europe and the Americas do, I think you should give up the very idea of Western civilization. It's at best the source of a great deal of confusion, at worst an obstacle to facing some of the great political challenges of our time. I hesitate to disagree with even the Gandhi of legend, but I believe Western civilization is not at all a good idea, and Western culture is no improvement.
>
> Appiah 2018: 191

When academic Classicists embrace the story of Western civilization as a story of antiquity and its legacy to the present, they are also promoting this modern ideology of White supremacism. This may seem an extreme position, as Bloxham points out, especially since some of the most fervent defenders of the ideas of Greek uniqueness and Western exceptionalism are, like Donald Kagan and Mary Lefkowitz, Jewish. Kagan was always explicit in his belief that:

> [T]he world has been more shaped by the experience of the West than by any other, and therefore the products of Western civilization are of broader consequence and significance than those other great civilizations.[49]

As Kagan makes clear in his course lectures on Greek history, ancient Greece and Rome (taken as a single entity) and the ancient Judeo-Christian traditions are the dual pillars of Western civilization.[50] But, Kagan, of course, obscures the reasons *why* the experience of the West has dominated the world—imperialism, colonials, global capitalist exploitation—and the anti-Semitic supersessionism of yoking Judaism to Christianity through a foundational narrative.[51] For Lefkowitz, acknowledging the "shortcomings" of Western civilization was good. But those doing so, she thought, were only focusing on the negatives of Western civilization, and that too was a problem:

> The students who chanted "Western Civ has got to go" were only considering the downside of Western Civ, which is pretty much the downside of human nature generally, anger, violence, self-aggrandizement, etc. Plato and Aristotle showed us

ways in which all people could lead more constructive lives, but their visions did little to address social issues, like oppression of certain people, such as slaves.[52]

In both cases, the ambiguous but powerful language of using "Western" as a description hides the deeply racial problems of the Western civilization narrative, allowing scholars who would have been (and still often are) excluded from the story to not only be part of it, but to become its staunchest defenders. The language of "Western" gets one out of the trap set by emphasis on race and can provide us with a civilizational discourse cleansed of its White supremacism while keeping its Whiteness and making it accessible to those whose Whiteness is conditional. It is not a mistake that much of the Culture War rhetoric surrounding Western civilization congealed around *Black Athena*; by homing in on the inaccurate pasts presented in Afrocentrist "myths," they could pass over their own participation in Western mythmaking. If Western civilization is a myth about our relationship to the past, what sort of relationship are we forging? The West as a concept has no real foundation in geography. It is an ideology defined either through a set of values or a set of technologies and social structures that move through space and time, embedded within racist evolutionary models of social development and connected most explicitly by the imperialist activities of modern European nations and the spread of global capitalism. If the West were a simple geographic term, it would not be as flexible and portable or as tied to the concept of "progress" as its history shows it to be. As Bonnett says of Western civilization, "Its continuing use reflects the maintenance of racial power relations and gives the lie to the idea that the rhetorical deracialization of public life means that racism no longer matters. White privilege is no less real today than it was 100 years ago." This was said in 2004, but is still true today.[53]

And yet, despite this truth, the narrative continues to shape our understanding of the ancient past. This is because its usefulness lies precisely in its ambiguity, its usefulness in obscuring the Whiteness, racism, imperialism, and genocide that underpin the power of modern European and North American nations. The ability to root this power in an imagined ancient past helps obscure that the current world status quo is precisely a product of such horrors. It shapes the view of the ancient Greeks especially as "The Oldest Dead White European Males" and authorizes a view of history that is not accurate to that past itself. The narrative of Western civilization, that "we are all Greeks" positions the story as an anti-nationalist story, where nationalism is understood as racial while Western civilization, itself a vestige of a White supremacist worldview that cannot accept the realities of a multicultural world, presents itself as if free of any racist implications entirely.

But this use of the ancient Greek past to support a modern ideology of Western civilization is itself a form of colonialism or crypto-colonialism that constructs an explicitly Western type of Greece. As Yannis Hamilakis remarks:

> Western Hellenism was the form that colonization took in the case of Greece, at first as a colonization of the ideal, and the vehicle that allowed the incorporation of that land and its people into the Western sphere of influence. Western Hellenism can be defined as the construction of a certain version of Hellas (which had only a tenuous connection to the social realities of ancient Greece as an eastern Mediterranean phenomenon) and its designation as the originary moment of Western civilization.
>
> Greenberg and Hamilakis 2022: 11

Imperialism, colonialism, civilization, and a fixation on the "Glory the *was* Greece"[54] are what underpin the Western civilization discourse and give ownership of that past a universal possibility. But they do so by reconstructing the past to look like the present from a very limited perspective, that of a modern idea we call "the West," a product of White racial anxiety, class conflict, and European and American capitalism and imperialism. Unless we want to continue to reproduce these old narratives of White supremacism and continue to invest them with authority, perhaps we should consider taking Appiah's advice and give up the notion altogether. It might require us to forge new stories about our relationship to the past. But revising our stories isn't always a bad thing; maybe those new stories will be better.

Notes

1 Bonnett (2004: 34).
2 The position of Russia in the discourse of Western civilization is complex. In one of the earliest uses of the phrase, Russia is the explicit enemy of Western civilization (see Kennedy 2019 for discussion); this was also a central feature of Cold War rhetoric. On some of the complexities, see for example Bova (2003). Far-right groups around the world today, however, see Russia as the savior of Western civilization. See, for example, "Extremists Turn to a Leader to Protect Western Values: Vladimir Putin," *New York Times* Dec. 3, 2016 (https://www.nytimes.com/2016/12/03/world/americas/alt-right-vladimir-putin.html; accessed March 28, 2022).
3 Media coverage of the Russian invasion of Ukraine has been filled with Western civilizational rhetoric. For discussion, see, for example "How the Ukraine war exposed Western media bias" *CNN Business* Mar. 4, 2022 (https://www.cnn.com/2022/03/04/media/mideast-summary-04-03-2022-intl/index.html; accessed March 28, 2022) and "Ukraine, Russia, and 'Western Civilization,'" *Society for US*

Intellectual History Blog Feb. 26, 2022 (https://s-usih.org/2022/02/ukraine-russia-and-western-civilization/; accessed March 28, 2022).

4 Huntington (1996).
5 Sen (2007: 44).
6 This is the title of a 2016 reprint in *The Guardian* of one of Kwame Anthony Appiah's BBC Reith Lectures. I do not know if Appiah was himself responsible for the headline/title. It is not uncommon for headlines to be written by editors and not authors (https://www.theguardian.com/world/2016/nov/09/western-civilisation-appiah-reith-lecture; accessed March 6, 2022). A fuller discussion by Appiah of his ideas around the idea of Western civilization can be found in Appiah (2018), ch. 6.
7 Bonnett (2004: 15).
8 A recent example is the four-part defense of the concept of Western civilization by ancient historian James Kierstead on the online publication *Quillette*, beginning with "The Future of Our Ancient Past," Jan. 10, 2019 (https://quillette.com/2019/01/10/the-future-of-our-ancient-past/; accessed March 28, 2022).
9 Morris (2010: 86).
10 Morris (2010: 29–35).
11 Morris (2010: 31).
12 Morris (2010: 104).
13 Morris (2010: 24).
14 For other examples, Hanson and Heath (1998: 25–6) and Ferguson (2011), *passim*. See Weller (2017) for discussion of Ferguson within the context of arguments similar to his own.
15 Ferguson (2011: 8).
16 Bonnett (2004).
17 On the ideas underlying an Anglo-American White empire before the Second World War and its failure as an idea, see Bell (2020).
18 Blouin (2018).
19 For race as technology, see Sheth (2009).
20 Morris states repeatedly throughout his book, but see pp. 50 and 61, especially. It also underlies the dismissal of discussing "race" in antiquity found in standard approaches to identity like that of McInerney (2014: 3–6 esp).
21 Bonnett (2004: 14).
22 Bonnett (2004: 27).
23 On the debate with Du Bois, see Taylor (1981). There was a report of the debate produced in 1929 by the Chicago Forum Council that sponsored the debate.
24 See Kühl (2002) for a full discussion of the connections between the Nazis and the American eugenics movement.
25 D. Zuckerberg (2016), "How to Be a Good Classicist Under a Bad Emperor," (https://eidolon.pub/how-to-be-a-good-classicist-under-a-bad-emperor-6b848df6e54a; November 21, 2016, accessed March 28, 2022).

26 Bloxham (2018).
27 Bloxham (2018: 235).
28 See Adler (2016) for a thorough discussion of some of the main battles within the discipline during the period.
29 See Greenberg and Hamalakis (2022) on the development of this package of Westerness in connection to Greece during and after the Greek War of Independence beginning in 1821.
30 Knox (1993: 12).
31 Hanson and Heath (1998) are, of course, the most famous, but we also see such tendencies in the much less contentious Lefkowitz (2008), who also misrepresents (from the first page) the terms of some of the disputes.
32 Knox (1993: 12).
33 Knox (1993: 26).
34 Froma Zeitlin is the only woman scholar named (57). He does mention *Reign of the Phallus* (1985) but refers to the author (Eva C. Keuls) only as a "female scholar" (52).
35 Knox (1993: 67).
36 On this book and Hanson's position within the Culture Wars, see Adler (2016: 173–212).
37 Hanson (1989: 225).
38 The core argument of *Why the West has Won: Carnage and Culture from Salamis to Vietnam* (2001).
39 Bloxham (2018: 198–203).
40 Adler (2016: 212).
41 Hanson, "Western Cultural Suicide," *National Review*, May 29, 2013 (https://www.nationalreview.com/2013/05/western-cultural-suicide-victor-davis-hanson/; accessed Mar. 28, 2022). I acknowledge that I could not bring myself to read *The Dying Citizen: How Progressive Elites, Tribalism, and Globalization Are Destroying the Idea of America* (2021), which provides a detailed progression of the ideas in this article after hearing Hanson speak and reading posts on his blog about the topic. It should be noted, however, that when Hanson says "globalization," he is not referring to global capitalism, but to an anti-Semitic trope that dates back to the nineteenth century and the so-called "Protocols of the Elders of Zion." "Progressive Elites" also serves as a similar anti-Semitic dog whistle. For non-academic (i.e. popular) discussions of the history, see R. R. Barenblat, "Ranting Against 'Globalism' Is Anti-Semitic," *Forward*, Oct. 24, 2018 (https://forward.com/scribe/412627/globalism-anti-semitism/; accessed Mar 28, 2022) and B. Zimmer, "The Origins of the 'Globalist' Slur," *The Atlantic*, Mar. 4, 2018 (https://www.theatlantic.com/politics/archive/2018/03/the-origins-of-the-globalist-slur/555479/; accessed Mar. 28, 2022).
42 These associations for Jewish Americans are often encompassed under the phrase "Cultural Marxism." See Berlatsky, "The Lethal Antisemitism of 'Cultural Marxism'," *Jewish Currents*, May 3, 2019 (https://jewishcurrents.org/the-lethal-antisemitism-of-cultural-marxism; accessed Mar 28, 2022) and Berkowitz, "'Cultural Marxism':

Catching On," *Southern Poverty Law Center,* Aug. 15, 2003 (https://www.splcenter.org/fighting-hate/intelligence-report/2003/cultural-marxism-catching; accessed Mar 28, 2022). Associations between communism and Black Americans emerged during the Great Depression when the Communist Party began anti-racist work in the American South; see R. Kelly (1990). *Hammer and Hoe: Alabama Communists during the Great Depression* (Chapel Hill: UNC Press). In the case of both groups, the Red Scare played a pivotal role in cementing negative associations in White supremacist propaganda between the two ethnic groups and communism in public discourse.

43 Talia Lavin details the contemporary resonances of much of this rhetoric in her 2021 book *Culture Warlords: My Journey into the Dark Web of White Supremacy.*

44 Stoddard remarks on this concept repeatedly throughout *Rising Tide* (1920), but it was also part of academic scientific debates. See, for example, W. S. Thompson (1917), "Race suicide in the United States," *The Scientific Monthly* 5: 22–35.

45 Morris discusses his discomfort with the Greek Miracle narrative in his introduction (2010: 22–3) and then in Chapter 5, especially.

46 Hanson and Heath (1998: 21–2).

47 One of the most important works of scholarship on this topic has been Horden and Purcell's *The Corrupting Sea* (2000).

48 For extensive documentation of the evidence of this, see the database at PHAROS: Doing Justice to the Classics (https://pharos.vassarspaces.net/; accessed March 17, 2022). See also Zuckerberg (2018: 21–39).

49 Kagan, in an interview with the *Chronicle of Higher Education* upon his retirement. "To the End, Donald Kagan Argues for the Primacy of the West," *The Chronicle of Higher Education,* May 13, 2013 (https://www.chronicle.com/article/to-the-end-donald-kagan-argues-for-the-primacy-of-the-west/; accessed Mar. 28, 2022).

50 As he states explicitly in Lecture 1 of his Yale Open Courses class (available at the Yale University webpage: https://oyc.yale.edu/classics/clcv-205; accessed Mar. 28, 2022).

51 On the anti-Semitism of Christian supersessionist uses of "Judeo-Christian," see for example Smith (2019), which includes analysis of the term's origins and Jewish dissent in its usage. The term emerged in anti-fascist contexts in the 1930s, which likely explains the use by Kagan.

52 From an interview with Lefkowitz in 2020. "A Conversation with Mary Lefkowitz," *The Postil Magazine.* May 1, 2020 (https://www.thepostil.com/a-conversation-with-mary-lefkowitz/', accessed March 28, 2022). For a detailed telling of her experience in the Culture Wars, see Lefkowitz (2008).

53 See also Weller (2017) for a detailed discussion of continued contemporary intersections between Western and White civilizational discourses.

54 From a line of Edgar Allan Poe's 1843 version of his poem "To Helen," which has been used repeatedly since then to refer to the ancient Greek world. It is even used at times as the title of college courses on ancient Greek history (for example, it is the title for the University of Florida's course numbered CLA 2100).

6

"The Society That Separates Its Scholars from Its Keyboard Warriors": Tracking Thucydides on Twitter

Neville Morley

Introduction

Over the last two centuries, Thucydides has been discussed and invoked in multiple fields of intellectual activity as a key ancient authority. In historiography, most obviously, he appears as one of the founders of the discipline, with an especially strong association with the values of truth and objectivity—leading lights of self-consciously critical historiography in the mid-nineteenth century identified him as the one classical writer who had anticipated their own approach, and this view has persisted.[1] In International Relations theory, he has had a still more important role as a founding figure—certainly he is far more regularly cited in contemporary disciplinary debates here than in history—seen as a thinker who sought to move beyond mere chronicles of events in order to understand their underlying dynamics and causes, and to establish normative principles of inter-state relations.[2] He has given his name to the most widely recognized theory of current global politics, originally applied to US–China relations and now extended to other rivalries, the Thucydides Trap (however arguable that the theory is as an actual representation of Thucydides' ideas).[3] In war studies and strategic studies, he is likewise identified as effectively a colleague, surprisingly contemporary in his views and approach, offering important accounts of individual battles and establishing general principles of strategy, as well as playing a crucial role in military education and in the commemoration of the war dead.[4]

These readings are clearly based on very different conceptions of Thucydides and different assumptions about the nature and basis of his authoritative status. Some emphasize his historical or political-theoretical methodology and the explicit statements offered in Book 1.20–2 (however these are interpreted), some focus more on his status as eye-witness to events and contemporary reporter, on his expertise and experience in war and (allegedly) politics, and even on claims about his character and the way his biography 'made' him a historian. One thing they have in common is a tendency to neglect much of the text, cherry-picking passages that are most readily assimilated to their specific modern perspective—note the frequent reliance on speeches rather than narrative sections, and the recurrence of a limited set of speeches—and to ignore critical aspects of it, above all its literary and rhetorical nature. Above all, there is the habit of attributing the statements and ideas of his characters to Thucydides himself, not least because, if one is looking for something that resembles a normative political principle in his text, that is for the most part where they can be found. Finally, we can note the way that the existence of contradictory interpretations of Thucydides—is he a theorist of a bipolar world or a multipolar one? a defender of superpower dominance or an advocate of justice and ethics? a determinist or someone whose worldview emphasizes chance and contingency?—never seems to put into question the idea that he is a figure of authority whose ideas can help us understand the present. Belief in Thucydides, founded to a great extent on accepting one or other of the established traditions of belief in Thucydides, then motivates the search for examples of his prescience and understanding.

This impression is not confined to academic discussions—or to the attempted popularisation and dissemination of those discussions by the academics concerned, as in the Thucydides Trap.[5] Thucydides appears in a range of other contexts in the modern world, again in the role of authority, sage and visionary: in discussions of politics and democracy (given credit for words that he puts in the mouth of Pericles), in accounts of plague (real and metaphorical), and in dark warnings about the rise of autocracy and war ("exiled Thucydides knew", as W. H. Auden's poem *1 September 1939* noted, a theme which has recurred with the renewed popularity of the poem after 9/11 and now the Russian invasion of Ukraine). Thucydides is quoted in video games, on T-shirts, and in newspaper articles; even more than in academic discussions, this involves a limited range of quotations, above all from the Funeral Oration and the Melian Dialogue, returning time and again to the same basic themes of politics and war; the persistent assumption is that this is a name one might be expected to know and respect, if you want to be taken seriously as a commentator on contemporary events—especially if you want to be taken seriously as someone who sees the world as it really is (Friedrich Nietzsche's reading of Thucydides as the anti-Plato and man without illusions has proved widely influential).

All this is both reflected in and reinforced in social media such as Twitter. Despite its apparent triviality, with the idea that its strict character limit is incompatible with any serious thought, over the last ten years such "microblogging" has become increasingly important as a space where perceptions of antiquity, including its contemporary relevance, are shaped and disseminated.[6] Sometimes this involves interaction between traditional forms of scholarly authority and wider publics—the expectation that academics should publicise their work, not only writing more popular pieces in non-academic publications but also disseminating these and engaging with non-academic readers—and even here we can see the emergence of new discursive styles, debates about the appropriate behavior and forms of interaction for an academic on Twitter, with which tweeting academics may not be wholly comfortable. Failure to recognize that this is a different sort of space, where academic authority is not necessarily discounted but might certainly be valued differently, and where expectations and norms continue to develop, regularly leads to pile-ons, complaints, and accusations.[7] That is to say, academic authority is still acknowledged in this sphere, at least partially, but there are questions about how it should be used, how those possessing it should behave, and what limits might be set on it, especially as this tends to intersect with issues of hierarchy, exclusion, gender, race, and power. Twitter, it is suggested, offers "an egalitarian format that creates equivalence, real or not," where every opinion is valid; this is not always a comfortable space for experts.[8] The invocation of Thucydides, but still more an insistence on a complex, ambiguous, or rhetorical Thucydides, is not always welcome.

But there are also many areas of social media where the academic voice is largely or entirely absent, and authority is constructed in different ways, arguably but not definitively more democratic and less hierarchical—or, at any rate, subject to different kinds of hierarchy and discursive power. This chapter explores Twitter references to and discussions of Thucydides as a case study, that reflects on issues of authority in relation to classical material in multiple ways. Many citations of Thucydides reflect existing assumptions about his authority; invocation of his name and (alleged) ideas gives credibility to claims and statements, as well as potentially lending weight to the poster as someone who possesses such knowledge and expertise. Some users even incorporate this into their own online identity, by using Thucydides' name as part of their own Twitter ID and/or name (e.g. "General Thucydides", @GeneralThucydides), using an image of him as their own avatar or as a background image, or including a quotation or alleged quotation as part of their Twitter biography. At the same time, the cumulative effect of such citations and discussions shapes the image of

Thucydides for those who have little or, most commonly, no prior knowledge of him and his work, which then in turn shapes the reception of future references to him. I seek to explore how Thucydides is used, for what purposes, what this implies about perceptions of him and his authority—and what happens when these discursive spaces encounter, or are invaded, by more traditional forms of academic authority, offering corrections to the "popular" image.

Patterns of Thucydides References

On average, Thucydides is mentioned in tweets about thirty to forty times a day (excluding those where the word occurs in a user's ID or name—which can lead to dramatic increases in the number of search results when one of those users gets into a discussion of argument).[9] This is a trivial amount compared with a topic like #BlackLivesMatter, #StopAsianHate, or #TaylorSwift, but comparable to Plato, Aristotle, or Herodotus. Typically, at least a quarter of these tweets are quotations or misattributed quotations without any further comment (somewhere between half and a third normally being falsely attributed to Thucydides), and a quarter of students discussing their studies or people talking about their reading of the text; the rest are made up of retweets of articles which mention Thucydides (most often relating to the Thucydides Trap), and jokes and discussions of different topics in which Thucydides is alleged to have something relevant to contribute, these latter two categories both implying (or being intended to imply) that the poster has some knowledge of Thucydides and his ideas. These topics are vary widely; every day, at least a few people—besides students and those with a professional interest—will attempt to relate Thucydides to contemporary events or issues, but there is little consistency in what events or issues will be considered. As discussed below, certain key events spark dramatic increases in the invocation of Thucydides and then dominate the conversation for weeks or months, many of which then die away again. However, a few topics do recur, featuring in at least one of the sampled weeks in every year since 2010: US–China relations, sport, finance, the ethnic identity of Macedonia, and the nature of democracy. If the sample had included the second week of November (this was avoided deliberately), it would also have observed an annual wave of Thucydides references, mixing quotes from the Funeral Oration and those commenting on military duty, related to Veterans Day, ANZAC Day, and Armistice Day. But one cannot predict the most likely theme for any other time of year.

The most predictable element is quotation: not just the proportion of tweets in any given week that are quotations, but the dominance of a limited selection of these. Between 2010 and 2017, at least half of all genuine quotations were the line from the Funeral Oration, "the secret of happiness is freedom and the secret of freedom is courage"; only from 2018 was this matched by "the strong do what they want, the weak suffer what they must" from the Melian Dialogue. In third place over this period is the misattributed W. F. Butler quotation, "the society that separates its scholars from its warriors...," though this became really popular only from 2013.[10] Otherwise the pattern is of a very long tail; there are twelve genuine quotations that feature at least once in the sampled weeks from every year, and three misattributed ones, then another eight genuine and six misattributed ones that appear at least once every three years. The majority of these quotations are presented with no other information, either comment or hashtags.

What lies behind this practice? One significant element is the construction of an online persona as a form of brand management. "Social media provides more than just a channel for disseminating personal brand content: it provides the content itself. In fact, it is possible to develop a social media presence without expressing a single original idea, simply by re-posting content created by others."[11] In the case of "social jukebox" apps and other paid-for means of having an online presence created for you, the result is simply a rolling program of "meaningful quotes" with no obvious relevance to the account's interests or business activities; these receive little engagement, except from other automated accounts, and one might seriously wonder whether it's worth the money. Other users either have paid more for a more bespoke service, or are actively managing their accounts to tweet and retweet relevant content; this can be seen most clearly in the close association of the "secret of happiness is freedom..." quote—usually also pasted into a stock image of people in sports clothing running, jumping, or standing on a rocky outcrop looking out across the landscape, sunsets, birds escaping from cages and the like—with individuals and businesses in the field of personal training, meditation, "wellness," and leadership development. The underlying process here is clearly the harvesting of quotation websites for lines tagged with terms like "freedom." Thucydides simply happens to be the author of one such inspirational line, rather than playing any role in its selection or the reception of the sentiment; there is no concern with context (let alone the tension between the original context, a call to arms, and the themes of peace and harmony). Similarly, the Melian Dialogue line seems to be taken from collections of "quotes about strength" without any concern for its original meaning.

Both these lines are commonly found in published collections of quotations; their prevalence on Twitter reflects a general tendency to reduce Thucydides to the Funeral Oration and the Melian Dialogue, associates him further with ideas of freedom and power, and perhaps introduces his name into unexpected new circles. More striking is the large number of quotes that appear only intermittently, a much larger range than features in any published collection, and still more the proliferation of misattributions; a few of the latter have a relatively long history, but the majority—especially "scholars and warriors"—are creatures of the internet. They have been nurtured by websites that gather content with no concern for quality control (the majority of which simply ignore requests to remove or relabel misattributed material); by the growth of user-generated content and the drive for engagement (Goodreads, which is treated as authoritative by many users, refuses in the majority of cases to relabel or delete any quotations that have been liked by enough people, and claim that "While we do have quotes on the site, we consider them to be community-owned content and therefore we have strict rules regarding removing them");[12] and by Twitter itself, as new misattributions can quickly take hold as they are liked and retweeted by real people as well as bots. The reposting of these fake quotations reinforces the idea that Thucydides wrote them, and hence promotes the idea of him as the sort of author who wrote such things—though at the same time, the majority of these misattributions seem plausible because they conform to the pre-existing image of Thucydides and his areas of expertise.

The most obvious and striking determinant of changes in this regular background of Thucydides reference is external events; things happen that cause a greater than usual number of people to think of Thucydides and his ideas. Some of these events are relatively minor and short term, but just happen to coincide with one of the sampled weeks (for example, the then Australian prime minister Malcolm Turnbull making a reference to Thucydides in a speech in January 2016); a full survey of a given year would doubtless identify more short-term bursts of activity. Others, however, reverberate and prompt Thucydides references throughout the year and beyond, and these are easily guessed: the 2014 Russian occupation of Crimea, the Brexit vote and election of Donald Trump in 2016 (both of these persisted for years), and Covid in 2020; the Russian attack on Ukraine in 2022 seems overwhelmingly likely to join them. There are three main facets to the response. First, newspaper and magazine articles which mention Thucydides in relation to current events are retweeted or quoted, often with no further comment; for example, a series of pieces on the 'Thucydides Trap', a January 2016 *Atlantic* article on "Trump and New York values," the July

2017 *Atlantic* piece by Kori Schake on misreadings of Thucydides in the White House, and a February 2022 *New York Times* essay suggesting that Putin's world was defined by Thucydides' "the strong do what they want." That is, Twitter amplifies an invocation of Thucydides as some kind of authority by a conventional pundit, often offering a very conventional view, rather than adding anything new.

However, there are plenty of examples of the second facet, where Twitter users invoke Thucydides in their own words to support a wide variety of positions on war, foreign affairs and politics. To offer just a small selection of examples: "T. predicted over 2500 years ago the future of the Eurozone; he would want out of the EU" (2016); "T. basically describing what is happening in America" (2017); "Under no circumstances should young people be exposed to T., or they might understand what's happening here" (2017, on US politics); "Reading T. with care: essential. Reducing T. to a bumper sticker: recipe for disaster" (2018); "History is just syndicated T. in perpetual re-runs" (2019). The nature of Thucydides' authority is rarely explained, but taken for granted, perhaps because the user assumes his audience will share this perspective; he is rarely identified as a particular sort of thinker, but simply presented as someone whose views are worth taking seriously. There is a recurrent emphasis on his absolute prescience, the fact that his work perfectly anticipates events 2,500 years later—this is a particular theme in discussions of politics, especially in the post-2016 United States, whereas comments on foreign policy tend rather to emphasize that he had correctly identified the universal and unchanging principles of state and/or human behavior. As with the use of Thucydides as an authority in academic discussions, there is no consensus about how those principles should be understood, or how one should respond to them. To take the most recent and powerful example: the first two months of 2022 saw a dramatic upsurge in references to the Melian Dialogue, but commentators were roughly evenly divided as to whether "the strong do what they must ..." is a true statement about the nature of the world, implying the need for the weak to acquiesce, or a characterization of the mentality of the powerful, demanding firm resistance.[13] Thucydides' authority is not questioned—just what it is used to support.

Third, there are the tweets that simply quote Thucydides with an appropriate hashtag to link it to current events. Sometimes, the meaning is obvious: "'The strong do what they want ...' #BlackLivesMatter" is straightforward to interpret. Sometime it is not; the same quote with the hashtag #Ukraine could be understood in either of the senses just discussed, and one must imagine that either the user thought it would be obvious, or they had no clear intent but felt that Thucydides nevertheless must have something to contribute to the conversation. This does raise the possibility that at least some quotes *without* hashtags, posted during such events, are also intended as interventions in the discussion and interpretation of events—that one might see them as a kind of subtweeting, a comment on current affairs that those in the know will recognize immediately even if the casual reader might fail to grasp. Given his established reputation, mentioning Thucydides without any context is itself a substantive statement.

Who Wants to Be Thucydides?

At last count (March 2022) there were nearly 200 individual Twitter accounts (not all of them active, and some currently suspended) that included some reference to Thucydides in their online identity, not including those who mention him in their biography (quotations, expression of interests) but do not in any way present themselves as Thucydides, and not including the limited number of accounts where the owner is clearly genuinely called Thucydides.[14] Just over fifty of these named him just in their Twitter ID, often with a lengthy number (@Thucydides12345); this is sometimes a sign of a bot or fake account, but can also indicate someone struggling to come up with a unique username; in the one case where the number might be interpreted as having political significance (e.g. the way "18" in the name of the neo-Nazi terrorist organization Combat 18 represents the first and eighth letters of the alphabet, A and H, meaning Adolf Hitler), the user insisted that this was not the case. Other than suggesting a certain awareness of "Thucydides" as a memorable name that might not be too common, it's not obvious that there is much to be inferred from this data. However, forty-five accounts include "Thucydides" in their username, a field which is more easily modified and where Twitter's requirement for uniqueness does not apply, and over 100 have it in both their ID and their name. A few of these accounts were set up explicitly to tweet Thucydides' history line by line, or with the apparent intention of tweeting in the voice of Thucydides (these experiments do not seem to have been followed through); the majority appear to be personal accounts, or set up as such, where the aim is apparently rather self-presentation through association with Thucydides. Some are humorous (variations on @ThucydidesTrapped), some purport to indicate location (e.g. @ThucydidesNYC) and a few incorporate political statements (e.g. @ThucydidesTrump). Just over forty accounts use a picture of Thucydides as their avatar, in the majority of cases an image of the bust that appears on the Wikipedia page and as the top search result on Google, occasionally modified with e.g. the addition of sunglasses. Ten or so include a Thucydides quote, or fake quote (the ubiquitous "scholars and warriors" line is most common) as part of their biography. Clearly the more ways in which an account has sought to evoke Thucydides, the more likely it us that he has some significance for them, and/or that his authority is in some way being borrowed.

In the absence of a full-scale investigation—the success of which will depend heavily on the willingness of those accounts that are still active to respond to questions—I can at best offer only tentative impressions, based on online exchanges over the years. None of the accounts claimed any great expertise; they had encountered the name of Thucydides on history podcasts, or in reading about international relations ("I wanted to focus on foreign policy and Thucydides is the father of foreign policy"), or in Bob Dylan's autobiography, or articles about the Thucydides Trap. Two emphasized the importance of Realism in their conception of him—"the strong do what they can . . ."—while another insisted on the need for the modern world to value philosophy and not forget great thinkers. In one case, it was clearly the association of Thucydides with opposition to compulsory vaccination during the Covid crisis that inspired the choice, combined with the quotation "The secret of happiness is freedom."

An alternative approach would be to analyse systematically the tweets of these accounts, or at any rate a sample of the most active ones, to seek to identify whether there are any consistent patterns. At this point in the research, the findings are again provisional and speculative. Where geographical location is indicated by subject matter, especially when this seems to be corroborated by the account's claimed location, the clear impression is that many of these accounts are based in the US. Some, as one might expect, are especially interested in foreign affairs and war, though I have seen no evidence so far that many of these accounts have a direct connection to military service, something which I must admit I had thought I would encounter. Several are heavily engaged in online debates about politics, but for the moment I detect no obvious patterns, if only because the sample size is so small: there are several unmistakable partisans of Donald Trump, but also at least one avowed liberal (in US terms) and a supporter of Jeremy Corbyn.

More systematic research may yield more significant results—but it is nevertheless still interesting to eliminate, or at any rate question, hypotheses such as the idea that Thucydides people might show a consistent tendency to adopt right-wing positions or insist on a hard-nosed Melian Dialogue Realism. For those who have responded to casual questions, Thucydides clearly is/was a relevant part of their online self-presentation and expression of values—though with none of the passion or vehemence sometimes encountered in those who identify strongly with particular sentiments attributed to Thucydides (see the next section). Is there a sense in which they are also borrowing his authority to support their own views? Certainly their names and/or avatars are sometimes perceived as relevant by people disagreeing with them, with the suggestion that their ideas or quality of argument are not worthy of Thucydides. For the moment, however, the overall impression is that the adoption of Thucydides as part of an online persona is a personal preference rather than a clear assertion of group membership or values, and that it reflects broader conceptions of him rather than making a distinct contribution.

Correcting Thucydiocies

In July 2015, the Thucydides Bot account (@Thucydiocy) was born, with the biography: "Historian, political theorist, philosopher, whatever. Stickler for accuracy. Did NOT say that thing you think I said." The account has since tweeted over 8,500 times and amassed 1,700 followers—somewhat surprisingly, given that the vast majority of those tweets are very similar: it corrects misattributed Thucydides quotes, and since just a couple of examples make up the vast majority of such misattributed quotes, it offers the same corrections time and again.[15] My original aim in creating this account was twofold: to dissuade other accounts from repeating such misattributions, in the forlorn hope of driving them off the internet, and to ensure that misattributions are respectively labeled as such, so that other readers are made aware that the quotation is not genuine even if the original account ignores or rejects corrections. This latter aim is especially relevant here because many of these accounts are bots or social jukebox accounts which take every response as evidence of engagement regardless of its nature or intention; they pay no attention to attempts at correction and, although many of their followers are also bot accounts, their sometimes high numbers of followers and retweets might persuade the Twitter algorithms to give them greater prominence in people's feeds.

Over time, as a result of the experience of engaging with other Twitter users about the authenticity of "Thucydides" quotations and of reading more widely in the scholarly literature on internet misinformation (that is: false information that is shared in good faith, rather than deliberately disseminated disinformation), I have justified the time spent every week on this activity through two additional aims. First, these interactions provide a certain amount of further evidence for popular perceptions of Thucydides (including early warning of the appearance of new misattributions) and, perhaps more importantly, personal engagement with him; at least for some people, it genuinely matters that a quotation is associated with this specific author. Second, perhaps optimistically, I hope to enhance the level of critical and historical understanding on Twitter through opening up discussions of the problems of misattribution and the dynamics of mis- and dis-information on social media.[16] In recent years, especially in the aftermath of the 2016 Brexit vote and US election which gave rise to widespread anxieties about "fake news," there has been extensive research into the heuristics of credibility and trust of information in digital networked environments, the question of why people believe and disseminate false information on social media and how (and how far) they can be persuaded to change their minds.[17] The Thucydiocy Bot is a means, within a very limited field, of attempting to motivate other users to evaluate information and sources of information, in part by highlighting the heuristics they may have been employing that led them to accept an inauthentic quote as genuine "Thucydides"; it seeks to promote "epistemic vigilance" more generally through concrete examples rather than vague exhortations.[18]

The account was conceived originally as a genuine bot, that would perform the task of correcting different misattributions automatically, inspired by examples such as @hegeltweets that engage with specific content (e.g. mentions of Hegel) by retweeting, liking, or responding. This task proved well beyond my coding abilities and supply of time to develop them, so the process is automated only to the extent that I have a permanent column within Tweetdeck searching for Thucydides references and a set of pre-written responses to all known misattributions that can simply be posted into reply tweets. The retention of "Bot" in the name was a deliberate decision, on the basis that people might be less alarmed or offended at a strange account muscling into their conversations if it appeared at first glance to be an automated response. Further, I was concerned that the immediate invocation of academic authority through using my personal account might set up precisely the wrong dynamic—the aim is to make the (entirely true) point that evaluating the authenticity of a quotation is generally not a matter of specialised academic knowledge but simply the application of basic critical thinking (asking the question whether this is actually Thucydides) and some simple research procedures (evaluating the source of information, looking for a specific reference to the text rather than just accepting a non-specific attribution). Only a few interlocutors have ever shown any interest in the

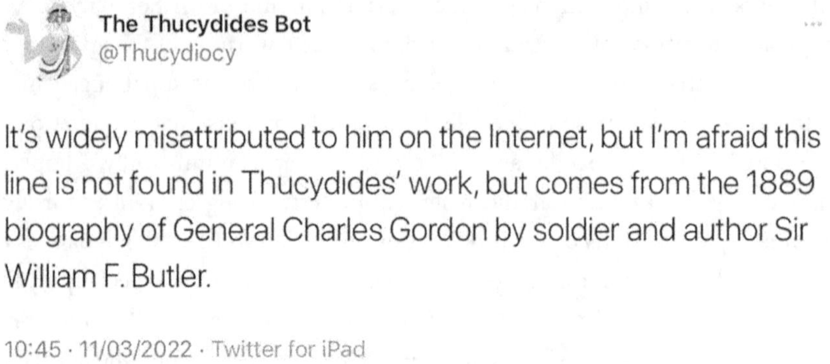

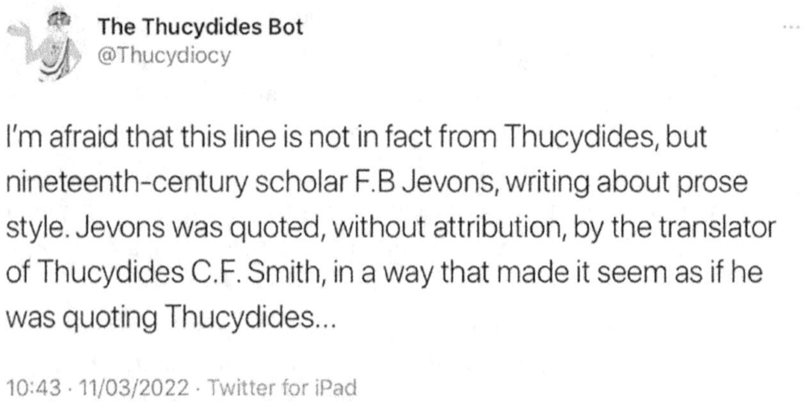

The Thucydides Bot
@Thucydiocy

It's widely misattributed to him on the Internet, but I'm afraid this line is not found in Thucydides' work, but comes from the 1889 biography of General Charles Gordon by soldier and author Sir William F. Butler.

10:45 · 11/03/2022 · Twitter for iPad

The Thucydides Bot
@Thucydiocy

I'm afraid that this line is not in fact from Thucydides, but nineteenth-century scholar F.B Jevons, writing about prose style. Jevons was quoted, without attribution, by the translator of Thucydides C.F. Smith, in a way that made it seem as if he was quoting Thucydides…

10:43 · 11/03/2022 · Twitter for iPad

Figures 6.1 and 6.2 Tweets from the Thucydides Bot account.

question of whether the account is really a bot, and I have then been happy to explain how it works.[19]

The style and content of the Thucydides Bot's replies have changed over time, through a process of trial and error and further research on how people respond to different sorts of corrections online. In particular, the standard opening has shifted from "This is not in fact Thucydides, but X" to "I'm afraid this is not in fact Thucydides, but X," recognizing that I may be asking people to revise a firm belief, something which could be experienced as a personal attack, and certainly am intruding into their conversations without invitation (Twitter may be a public forum for everyone who does not deliberately lock their account, but users don't necessarily think of this in practice). Further, the response now includes more detail about the identity of X and his text, with the aim of showing that this is a well-founded alternative rather than just a contrary opinion, and where space allows I also add information suggesting why Thucydides is not really a plausible source and/or reassurance that the misattribution is widespread and therefore the error is not a culpable one.

Clearly the Bot is not a known or trusted "person," so it is necessary to emphasise other means of persuasion, anticipating the most likely responses and grounds for resistance. Inevitably, the result is that it sounds very like a formal version of my usual style—but research into the linguistic cues for expertise and authority suggests that this style ought to be reasonably effective: number of words used (uncertainty reduction), avoidance of I-pronouns and anxiety-related words, and use of longer words and more negatives (cognitive complexity) are all taken, according to studies of the users of medical advice websites, as indicators of expertise and trustworthiness.[20] Having 1,700 followers might also be taken as a sign of credibility; research has shown more popular accounts have their tweets shared more, not only in absolute terms but proportionate to their number of followers, but it is unclear what the threshold is for such an authority effect, beyond the vague perception that accounts with only a few followers (fewer than 100?) are unlikely to be trustworthy in the absence of other indicators.[21]

Responses to these corrections are evidence both for the possible impact of this strategy and for the thinking of those tweeting misattributed quotations. The majority of accounts engaged with in this manner do not reply at all, though my impression is that accounts that are run by real humans, as opposed to the social jukebox bots, are then less likely to become repeat offenders, occasionally deleting the tweets in question (and in one instance, modifying subsequent references to the misattributed line to "(not Thucydides)," which is better than nothing). Of the rest, roughly half answer with thanks, occasionally noting that they have looked into the matter and see that the Bot is correct (without indicating where they found this information, but the Wikiquote page seems a reasonable assumption for the majority); one can only guess whether the others have done similar research, or have simply accepted the Bot's correction. Roughly a quarter of the accounts which respond positively in some way to corrections then also follow the Bot, and one or two have taken to correcting the same misattribution themselves, or summoning @Thucydiocy when they encounter it.

From the perspective of understanding both people's image of and feelings towards Thucydides and the dynamics of misinformation and credibility, the most interesting cases are those that push back against the correction, at least initially. There is no single pattern of response, but over the years the same forms of argument have recurred, advanced with varying degrees of conviction and annoyance. (1) Citing the authority of the source of the quotation (most often, collections of military quotations or accounts of contemporary military life, and prominent figures such as the late General Colin Powell or the journalist Chris Hedges), or its prevalence in Google search results: "many attributions to Thucydides online"; "Goodreads says you're wrong"; "it's there on a Greek government website." (2) Questioning the authority of the Bot—"who do we believe? Show us proof!"— and of the Wikiquote page to which I sometimes refer people to find links to supporting material. (3) Claims that the quote clearly reflects Thucydides' character or ideas (this may of course reflect the fact that impressions of key themes in his work are increasingly shaped by such quotations): "Thucydides throughout his work examines history's dependence on human character"; "it doesn't seem to contradict the main themes of Thucydides"; "in multiple places Thucydides tells us about the life of the warrior." (4) Evocation of general principles of critical thought: "the attribution isn't necessarily not authentic if it isn't proved so by later research"; "lack of evidence is not evidence of lacking"; "the sentiment is general enough that both could have independently said the same thing. Both. Do better research." (5) Often in conjunction with the previous, a particular insistence on chronological primacy, often on the reasonable grounds that the modern author could have been quoting Thucydides—"are you sure he didn't just paraphrase Thucydides? He was around thousands of years earlier"; "maybe he was quoting Thucydides and forgot to give proper credit"; "Thucydides came before Butler!"; "Butler ripped off Thucydides!"—but sometimes in the absurd form that, because a version of the quote exists translated into Greek, it must be authentically ancient: "Translated to ancient Greek from English? Greek 1400 BC. English 700 AD. English didn't exist back then. You just proved you have no academic credentials."

Such responses open up the possibility of a continuing conversation, which allows more detailed description of the process by which the quote in question came to be misattributed (at the same time showing how this therefore makes it entirely understandable that people might believe in its authenticity) and further discussion of questions of authority and critical analysis. I can (1) provide detailed information and sources to establish the Bot's knowledge, pointing to the absence of textual references or any other details on quotation webpages); (2) acknowledge issues with Wikiquote (emphasizing that I mention it solely as a place to find links to sources and an academic discussion, namely Morley 2013); (3) acknowledge the real issues involved in proving a negative (not claiming to possess more knowledge than is actually possible, while emphasising that no published translation of Thucydides includes the phrase in question and evoking the principle of the balance of probabilities); and (4) broaden the discussion to consider wider contexts and issues of anachronism (the fact that a distinction between scholars and warriors makes little sense in a classical Greek polis where every citizen was expected to fight for the city, and the fact that Thucydides' account breaks off before the end of the war so he could not have commented on the rule of the Thirty Tyrants).

As far as possible, this effective resort to academic authority (reference to published research, demonstration of detailed knowledge of ancient history) is framed in terms of the exploration of these issues as interesting in themselves, rather than an attack on the person who tweeted the misattribution, to create a safe space for acknowledging error. Perhaps half the time this works, and the conclusion of the conversation is thanks, albeit sometimes rueful: "I stand corrected. Damned interwebs are full of this. I feel like I just learnt that Santa isn't real..." Otherwise, the conversation ends when the original account decides to ignore or block the Bot, most often after I have invited them to prove it wrong by offering a specific reference in Thucydides' text. The positive outcome is that once again these accounts rarely repeat the misattribution (the main exception is an account who insists that their former professor's paraphrase/interpretation should be counted as a valid quotation); perhaps they have accepted the correction but are unwilling to admit this in public, or are simply reluctant to be accosted if they tweet it again.

It is striking how often those who push back against the Bot do so on the basis of claims of knowledge and expertise, of Thucydides' work and/or of principles of critical analysis; their perception of themselves seems to be that they are critical and informed and therefore would not have been taken in by a fake, so the quote they have accepted needs to be defended against criticism. Still more striking is the pattern of which quotes are most likely to be defended in this manner. With many relatively common misattributions, such as "justice will not come to Athens until those who are not injured are as outraged as those who are," the correction is accepted without a qualm, although these are often put forward in the context of emotive political issues (such as Black Lives Matter) and so one might have anticipated greater emotional investment; most likely because it really is the sentiment that matters, and perhaps also because it still has the authority of a classical origin (Solon). "History is philosophy teaching by examples" is much more often defended, with claims about it being a reasonable summary of Thucydides' methodology (despite him not using the term "history"); perhaps because it is an ancient misattribution, long since established in general accounts of historiography and its mission, and perhaps because its real source—"a third-century *Ars Rhetorica* falsely attributed to Dionysius of Halicarnassus"—does indeed lack authority.

The misattribution that is most often defended is, predictably, William F. Butler's "The society that separates its scholars from its warriors ..."; not only, I would suggest, because it is the most common, but also because it appears to be personally meaningful for at least three of the informal communities within which it regularly circulates: military and veteran circles for whom it seems to epitomize a philosophy of military life (the "warrior ethos"—combined on occasion with an explicit disparagement of those who are merely civilians and intellectuals), right-wing groups for whom it expresses the decadence of contemporary "civilized" society, and, in the last two years, weight-lifters ("every intellectual needs to lift; every gym bro needs to read").[22] Questioning the authenticity of the attribution seems at times to be experienced as a questioning of the validity of the whole idea, but in addition the association with Thucydides, as an authoritative soldier-strategist-analyst figure who is seen to embody the philosophy of the statement, is clearly important to many, still more when it is attributed to "a Spartan king" being quoted by Thucydides—William F. Butler is neither familiar, nor ancient, nor authoritative enough. This interpretation is perhaps supported by the fact that the other misattribution most vehemently (if less frequently) defended in recent years has been "who dares wins" or "fortune favors the brave," as a sentiment prized by admirers of specific military units and their ethos; the conviction that this *must* be Thucydides, on the basis both of prior conceptions of his views and of sense of the importance of this identification, is striking.

Conclusion

The Thucydides encountered on Twitter is in most respects a familiar figure—even if he is associated with a range of ideas that are not actually found in his text, they reinforce rather than contradict his established image as an authority on war, politics, and power, who offers a clear and illusionless view of the world as it really is. It is a received perspective that has been shaped by scholarly receptions, above all the traditions of international relations theory, but it does not habitually appeal to academic authority. It is not that academic authority is rejected, for the most part—it can be the successful final gambit in debates about the authenticity of "Thucydides" quotations—but for the most part the quotes and ideas are assumed to speak for themselves, even to the point of powerful emotional identification with them, and Thucydides' authority is taken as read.

Appendix: On Social Media Research

A critical issue for the quality and integrity of this project is the fact that the study of social media is a relatively young field, and there are not yet agreed protocols for many aspects; for example, debate continues as to whether posts on social media can be assumed to have been consciously "published" in a public forum, hence free for researchers to use without any further concerns—the prevalent assumption in the early years—or whether there are continuing ethical obligations to the users. This is clearly a significant point when it comes to detailed qualitative analysis of the contents of tweets, with the aim of drawing inferences about the authors and their beliefs or commenting on their styles of argument and (self-) representation. Even attributing the tweet to the author's online identity creates the possibility that they might be identifiable, and hence the view among researchers is increasingly that social media posts should be treated as personal data, and hence research in this field requires ethical oversight.[23]

The approach adopted in this project has been shaped above all by the ideas of best practice set out in Williams et al.,[24] and through ongoing discussion with the College of Humanities Ethics Committee. All social media posts are treated as personal data rather than regarded as effectively public domain; the authors are not identified (the discussion of accounts that adopt Thucydides as part of their online persona enumerates types of user IDs rather than actual examples), and as far as possible material which would be identified easily through a search engine is paraphrased rather than directly quoted, except where this would significantly undermine the analysis.

Notes

1 Morley (2014).
2 Keene (2015); Ruback (2015).
3 Allison (2017); Jaffe (2017).
4 Morley (2018, 2021).
5 See for example https://www.belfercenter.org/project/applied-history-project, and especially https://www.belfercenter.org/thucydides-trap/book/wonder-woman, together with https://thesphinxblog.com/2017/06/04/talk-thucydides-to-me/, accessed March 13, 2022.
6 On anxieties about the ever-reducing amount of text and obsession with "likes," see Derakhshan (2015).

7 See e.g. Bateman (2017).
8 Appleby (2021).
9 This section is based on the analysis of relevant tweets from the same periods each year (January 16–22, April, July, and October, from 2010 to 2021), identified through the Twitter search engine and organized into a series of categories: genuine quote, fake quote, retweet of article, study discussion, topic discussion etc., as well as identifying the specific quotes and references deployed.
10 On this and other fake Thucydides quotations, see Morley (2013).
11 Geva, Oestreicher-Singer, and Saar-Tsechansky (2019).
12 Correspondence on the Goodreads' chat, June 25, 18. This attitude—the idea that the authenticity of quotations may be established by the number of upvotes—can be compared plausibly with the "market epistemology" discussed by Mirowski (2019).
13 In contrast, the vast majority of tweets citing the Thucydides Trap in this context, mostly treated as a neutral description of the world rather than an idea associated with Thucydides, used it to blame the United States and NATO for the outbreak of hostilities.
14 Please see the appendix on the way this research was conducted, especially in relation to the use of personal data and the identification of individuals. A project to collect and analyse the data more systematically, to be combined with issuing an invitation to all identified accounts to complete a questionnaire on their knowledge of and attitudes towards Thucydides, is currently under review by a research ethics committee.
15 This relentless seriousness of purpose is relieved only on rare occasions, most obviously at Christmas, when for the last few years the account has tweeted out The Twelve Days of Thucydides as a commentary on patterns of Thucydides references over the previous twelve months.
16 See Wu et al. (2019); Ecker et al. (2022).
17 Excellent summary of the literature in Metzger and Flanagin (2013).
18 On "epistemic vigilance," see Sperber et al. (2010).
19 One of the most entertaining comments, from a Turkish account, was: "Like Voldemort, the man has set up a trap in Thucydides' name, catching up when his name is mentioned. Even tweets in Turkish do not escape his eyes."
20 Sparks and Areni (2008); Toma and D'Angelo (2015).
21 Weismueller et al. (2021).
22 On the "warrior ethos," Noordally (2020), and more generally (with reference to the role of the classical tradition) Kaurin (2014). On the construction of community through the retweeting of appropriate memes, as an assertion of common knowledge and values, see Peck (2017).
23 See Golder et al. (2017), Townsend and Wallace (2018), and the guidance developed at the University of St. Andrews (https://www.st-andrews.ac.uk/research/integrity-ethics/humans/ethical-guidance/social-media-research/, accessed March 14, 2022.).
24 Williams et al. (2017).

Is Livy a Good Wikipedian? Authority and Audience in Ancient Historiography and Contemporary Anonymous Writing[1]

Juliana Bastos Marques

Current scholarship has been shifting away from the pervasive need to evaluate Livy's merits as a historian. Still, while numerous new topics have been discussed, traditional themes in Livian scholarship are far from exhausted, such as, for instance, the apparent dissonance between his pessimism in the preface and support for Augustus' policies,[2] or the way he uses and transforms his sources. We still try to understand the uncertain but crucial relation between Livy's discourse and his *persona*, struggling to elucidate the details of his career and to make sense of his role in the elite circle close to Augustus, in relation to his *Patavinitas*.[3] Precisely because of these questions, reading him as a mere compiler, or as a distinct authorial voice, as we do, means that it is not possible to read his text *per se*, as if authorship could be dismissed. We should assume that questions such as who Livy was, how he was seen in his social environment, and how he chose to present himself in his work, are deeply connected to the acceptance of his text by his readers and peers, and not just through an acknowledgement of his textual abilities. In other words, his authority as a historian cannot be detached from either his individual authorship or his audience.

I want to introduce this question because there seems to be a specific relationship between authority and authorship in Western historiography.[4] In that sense, Livy presents an interesting case study, because many of the issues concerning his work are related to these broader questions: how much does he choose to present himself in the preface, and how much of it is just a *topos*? How much does his choice and arrangement of sources reveal about his method and knowledge? How highly was he esteemed among the Roman elites? Let's assume for a start these were his audience, since he was not a senator himself. In other words, how does Livy build his authority as a historian, in terms both of his mastery of historiographical rules and the presentation of his *persona*?

The nature of these questions is the background to an experiment in which I selected three texts from Livy and presented them to Wikipedia editors for review, removing the original attribution of authorship. The editors were asked to review these texts and evaluate whether they would comply to current Wikipedia standards for "appropriate" writing. Within this context, we tried to ask some interrelated questions: how much is the knowledge of the author, or of their *persona*, a prerequisite for the audience to validate the authority of a text? How much can we assess of the role the audience plays in this exchange of legitimacy? What do we make of historical differences between audiences and their power to confer authority to a text?

Pillars of Historiography, Pillars of Wikipedia

Authors on Wikipedia, referred to as "editors" or "Wikipedians," are by definition anonymous—like anyone else using the internet, because what the network actually recognizes are connections between remote machines, called IPs.[5] For the authorship of every contribution to the encyclopaedia, what is effectively recorded is either the IP of a certain computer used to connect to the remote wiki server, or a pseudonym by which that editors choose to identify themselves when they register at the website, although this is not mandatory. Online pseudonyms, even because of these technical reasons, have a life of their own. Therefore, an article about, for instance, the history of the Roman Republic, could theoretically be written either by a distinguished scholar, by a talented fifteen-year-old student, or by a retired engineer who happens to like ancient history. How then do we assess the quality of writing in these articles, if authority cannot be ascertained by knowing authorship?[6]

The question also calls for a better definition of "quality." It will come as no surprise that there are points of contact between Livy's assessment of quality, as we understand from the distinctive characteristics of his text and his adherence to a set of traditional rules in ancient historical writing, and what Wikipedia uses as core policies, or "pillars," in order to validate information. Wikipedia has three core policies: neutrality, verifiability, and an absence of original research.[7] In another compilation of "non-negotiable" guidelines, called the "Five pillars," these three main policies are condensed into the first two pillars: 1. "Wikipedia is an encyclopaedia," encompassing "notability" and "no original research"; and 2. "Wikipedia is written from a neutral point of view."[8]

Although there are fundamental differences between ancient and modern historiography,[9] I would like to argue that it is possible to draw a parallel between the rules established by Livy and these Wikipedia guidelines. Notability has been a fundamental definition of historiography ever since Herodotus framed his subject in and around a particular topic, "the great and marvelous deeds" concerning the war between Greeks and barbarians. Successive historians may have differed as to what a notable subject meant, but even "universal" historians such as Polybius defined a certain theme that guided their criteria of notability. In the case of Roman historians, the city of Rome is from the time of Fabius Pictor the unifying core of their narrative, a focus that also appears in Livy's textual arrangement.[10]

Notability is also connected to the historians' use of sources, meaning how they chose to use or to leave out previous works. This has been a favourite topic of Livian *Quellenforschung*, in particular because he cites and criticizes some of them, such as in the case of the constantly attacked Valerius Antias,[11] and because we can compare a considerable amount of his text with the earlier account of Polybius, which is sometimes quoted almost *verbatim*.[12] The concept of "no original research" is somehow equivalent to the ancients' use of sources, considering that originality was not a primary goal (for the Romans, in particular); a historian's work would be assessed instead through their mastery of truth, impartiality, erudition, and style in reference to their predecessors.[13]

However, it is true that we cannot say that Livy's writing was encyclopaedic, in the manner of Wikipedia. Narrative history has its own structure, content, and purposes, while the ancient genre closest to an encyclopaedia was the antiquarianism of Varro or the Elder Pliny.[14] Most of Livy's text, as "standard" factual narrative, is often full of what Wikipedia editors would call POV—point of view—such as the use of adjectives and adverbs; however, as we know, this does not detract from Livy's impartiality within his own set of values. These more subjective characteristics were indeed expected from Livy by his audience, as ancient historians were supposed to display mastery of the craft also by embellishing facts.[15] Therefore, only a few passages of Livy's text would be adequate for this experiment, whether being in the style of antiquarian digressions or unadorned descriptions.[16]

The other Wikipedia pillar that may be likened to Livy's concerns is related to impartiality—a *topos* full of contradictions in the writing of history in our deconstructed world, as much as a well-meant, but rather utopian intention in Wikipedia. The claim is a cornerstone of Greek and Roman historiography, but is also filled with apparent contradictions, such as the presence of what seem to our standards flagrant biases against barbarians, forthright praise of current emperors, or frank group partisanship.[17] Impartiality is related to the ancients' method of ascertaining truth, in the sense that the opposite of truth would not be falsehood, but bias.[18] For Roman historians such as Livy, there would be no sense of bias in writing their very own "patriotic" history, only a potential risk in the passionate moral judgement of individuals[19] or, of course, the "political bias" of one's enemy. Coincidentally, it is very easy to find the same problem of "passionate judgment" or accusations of political bias in the discussion sections of Wikipedia articles, in what are called "editing wars."[20]

Setting the Experiment

According to our departure assumptions, knowledge of real authorship could prevent editors from objectively evaluating Livy's own claims to notability and impartiality, and therefore to being an intrinsic literary authority. Since the rules of Wikipedia writing do not rely on content expertise *per se*, but rather on a set of writing principles, it was not expected that reviewers would have any familiarity with Livy or Roman history, and indeed some of them expressed concerns about not being particularly knowledgeable on the subject of the selected texts—although this did not prevent them from reviewing.

Potential reviewers had to meet specific criteria. It is assumed that editors with a high number of consistent edits, and who regularly participate in discussions about the project and act as administrators or in other maintenance roles,[21] are most likely to be fully proficient around Wikipedia rules and policies, so the sample selected and invited for participation in the survey were the 200 users with more edits in September 2017 on Portuguese Wikipedia.[22] The decision to work with this particular language community rests on the fact that it is the environment most familiar with my own Wikipedia edits[23] and my previous work on the use of Wikipedia in Higher Education.[24] Moreover, as the Portuguese-speaking Wikipedia community is considerably smaller than the English-speaking community,[25] it was considerably easier for me to contact and manage a smaller sample of editors.

However, in order to control the access of the selected texts for review, while also avoiding disruption of regular work on Wikipedia, I chose to conduct the experiment on another website, identical to Wikipedia in code, navigation, and layout, but not subject to the same content rules, called Miraheze.[26] All selected editors were contacted through their Wikipedia user discussion pages with the following message:

Hello, (username)! I have been working with Wikipedia in higher education for 8 years, and my interest is to understand the need for information literacy of students, validating knowledge through the principles of Wikipedia. I am doing research on encyclopaedic writing and making a few small online article drafts for evaluation. Could you help me with comments on the quality and adequacy of these texts? To help validate the results, I'm doing the search on another site, which uses Mediawiki and the same Wikipedia layout. It is not necessary to register for Miraheze, just cite your username from here or create another one. Thank you very much, Domusaurea.

Prof. Dr. Juliana Bastos Marques—UNIRIO

After following the provided link, instructions were as follows:

Participants are asked to provide feedback on the following texts, on their respective discussion pages: Text 1—by Prof. Dr. Juliana Bastos Marques; Text 2—by an undergraduate History student at UNIRIO; Text 3—authorship will not be stated. GOAL: This research aims to verify the adequacy of encyclopaedic writing by different users to Wikipedia standards required for good writing. IMPORTANT INSTRUCTIONS: For each text, create a sub-page of the discussion page to write your comments.[27] Discussions between participants is welcome in the sub-pages, and the discussion dynamics will be observed. To validate research findings, it is requested that no query of any kind beyond the text provided be used (*i.e.* through online searches or printed publications). Your feedback should be based only on your knowledge of Wikipedia rules, such as the Five Pillars and the protocols agreed through consensus by the Portuguese-speaking community; because these are simple, unformatted paragraphs, no references were included. Please write where on the text you consider that references are needed and why (there is no need to make searches to refer to external material); it is interesting, but not required, that you identify yourself in the discussion by signing your username on Wikipedia. Participants will not have their real names requested or disclosed. CONSENT: By participating in this survey, you agree to its terms and grant your participation under the terms of the CC BY-NC-SA 3.0 license.

Three texts were selected at random and presented to the editors, with different attributions of authorship, as stated in the instructions:

- Text 1: Livy, 7.2.4–12 (the birth of theater in Rome);
- Text 2: Livy, 39.14.5–10 (Senatorial repression of the *Bacchanalia*);
- Text 3: Livy, 1.43.1–11 (reforms of Servius Tullius).

I translated these texts into Portuguese so that editors would not be able to find another translation on Google. My translations tried to preserve the original wording and phrase structure as much as possible; authorship attributions and order of the texts were chosen randomly.

The first fragment, on the origin of drama, has been studied extensively by scholars and its interpretation is notoriously difficult. The question of the sources used by Livy is very disputed, with some arguing in favor of (and others against) an extensive use of Varro.[28] As Feldherr summarizes:

> As even a cursory reading will show, Livy's excursus is anything but straightforward. Over two centuries of literary history are packed into slightly over a page of the author's most obscure prose. The general tendency of his account emerges clearly enough: the drama grew from small but respectable beginnings to a form of madness. But almost every detail of the process has raised a host of questions.[29]

For the second text, the senatorial measures against the Bacchanalia, there is also a wide range of interpretations concerning Livy's use of sources and his level of rhetorical invention. Did he use the official senatorial decree as a primary source, or did he fabricate a narrative with the purpose of praising the senate's appeal to restore tradition?[30] In fact, as Paillier reminds us, concerning Livy's treatment of the issue:

> (…) il est vain de prétendre distinguer avec certitude l'aspect "subjectif" de l'aspect "objectif" du récit. Non seulement parce que l'art de Tite-Live, dans un morceau aussi travaillé que celui-là, tend à rendre indissociables le fond et la forme. Mais de plus il se peut fort bien que le matériau historique dont il disposait ait, sur certains points, si parfaitement convenu à ses intentions qu'il n'a guère eu à le modifier ou à le commenter.[31]

Livy had access to a number of sources, which could well have included the Tiriolo decree,[32] and was certainly familiar with the works of the annalists who treated the subject before him. Either way, his approach would ultimately be affected by bias from the senatorial investigation coming from Postumius' report, the only available primary source for the event. Since the whole affair is reconstructed from a set of private events, the tone of this paragraph bears a difference in style to the "dramatic and entertaining soap-opera"[33] of the preceding text, as an adaptation of a series of objective measures derived from the official document. The context of the sources is therefore fundamental to the understanding of this episode.

The probable source for the third text, on the reforms of Servius Tullius, seems to coincide with the one used by Dionysius of Halicarnassus (4.16–18), except for some details on the last two classes. Both accounts are considered by scholars as anachronistic, probably revealing instead the structure of the army in the fourth or third century BC,[34] and have been interpreted as a rhetorical counterpart of the Cleisthenic reforms in Athens, forcing the construction of a parallel connection between the developments of the Roman and Athenian polities.[35] Mommsen has first shown that they may ultimately come from an official inscription mentioned by Festus,[36] and Cornell describes Livy's treatment as "artificial and contrived."[37] Therefore, the dry, descriptive tone of the text possibly reflects the indirect use of an official epigraphic source.

This small treatment of the selected texts aims to contextualize some of the difficulties that the Wikipedia editors would face when reading and reviewing them. Since they were not specialists in Roman historiography, it was expected that some of their difficulties in interpreting information and style would be unconsciously related to informed interpretations of "obscure" or "contrived" tones that we find in scholarly readings of Livy. It was also expected that their evaluations would take the different authorial attributions into account: would the article written by the "scholar" be better rated than the one produced by the "student"? In that arrangement, the third selection, with an unnamed attribution, acted as control group.

Analysis of Answers

Of the 200 most frequent editors, eleven participated in the experiment, equating to a response rate of 5.5 percent. Although this may seem low, it is consistent with a generally low level of involvement in Wikipedia-related activities, where a small number of frequent editors contributes a high percentage of edits.[38]

All nicknames used were apparently the same as their Wikipedia usernames, meaning none of the participants decided to create new usernames. This angle of editorial scrutiny, however, is subject to the potential problem of multiple usernames created by the same person, a change in some cases revealed openly to the Wikipedia community (as was the case with one participant). Sometimes, this is made in secret—known as "sock puppetry"—and is regarded very poorly in the community.[39] Sock puppets have the potential to create different personae from one single original author, disrupting the essential admission of good faith that allows the anonymous collaborative writing effort.[40] This practice has created many conflicts in Portuguese Wikipedia, and was surprisingly replicated even in this small-scale environment on Miraheze: one editor contacted me in private complaining that someone else had written a comment on one of the texts and signed with his username. Sock puppetry has also been one way to override blocks or to rig votes, as well as to reinforce arguments in editing wars over contentious issues, but it is of particular note that such practice ended up replicated in our topic. Another editor, who contributed via a comment on the second text only, also helped to edit the Miraheze website as they did Wikipedia, which shows that the similar layout may have contributed to a perception of a similar usage and exchange between editors.

Ultimately, Wikipedia editors encountered a situation all too familiar to classicists: small chunks of unidentified fragments. Only one editor, a long-time contributor to Wikipedia, made it clear in their comments that the passages did not seem to have been written by the authors to which they were attributed (this person's review was the same for the three texts):

> I have read the narrative and it seemed to me an unidentified book excerpt, unknown to me. In order to be part of Wikipedia it would logically be necessary to assert the text origins through references. On a second reading, I found the text to be more appropriate for Wikibooks (because it is very descriptive) than for Wikipedia.

Wikibooks is another project by Wikimedia Foundation, containing "... textbooks, annotated texts, instructional guides, and manuals. (...) As a general rule, only instructional books are suitable for inclusion."[41] It is interesting to note that this editor thinks about different levels of description, since the encyclopaedia itself also requires a descriptive tone. This comment implies an association between descriptiveness and instruction, such as in a factual textbook about Roman history. My hypothesis is that this perception sums up the other comments in the sense that, since the editor does not have any background on the authorship of the text, it is impossible for them to consider it appropriate or not to the intended medium.

The narrative style of the texts was repeatedly observed through the comments, but with mixed appreciation. The text on the origins of theater, characterized above by Feldherr as Livy's "most obscure prose," is similarly confusing to Wikipedians. It is described as either "too academic" or "too informal," filled with "technical jargon" or "a bit childish," containing unexplained concepts such as a particular meaning of "art," having "unnecessary mannered language" and a general perception of lack of structure and coherence. For instance:

> There are many expressions of doubtful or unclear character. For example: "The games started small." What does this mean exactly? "They came from a foreign source..." In addition to "coming" not being suitable, what exactly is this foreign

origin? Which "young people" began to imitate what? What continued, until when? "In the past" in which century? The whole paragraph lacks description, objectivity and geographical and chronological contextualization.

Almost all participants presented clear reasons for their negative assessment of the language and structure used in the text: there are no dates, no "introductory contextualization," or "it seems the editor was trying to insert the maximum amount of information without any concern for legibility." This lack of temporal and descriptive contexts is at odds with the readership focus, according to this editor: "When writing or reviewing an article, I will always keep in mind that the main audience of an article is a 15-year-old student in Angola."

This also means that the characteristics of the target readership are essential to evaluating success in transmitting information, since it is expected that the audience would have a similar cultural background as the author.[42] Ancient readers of Livy were naturally supposed to have had previous knowledge of the meaning of "scenic games," "Fescennine verses," or even "the young," or why games "always" start as small venues, *mutatis mutandis* like classicists who read Livy. Wikipedia readers, however, would expect to receive further background help, through links to related Wikipedia articles on names, places, and concepts. All editors have strongly emphasized the need for internal links, "wikification" (using wiki markup and layout) and, most notably, external references, although it was clearly stated in the instructions that all texts lacked these features on purpose, and comments should indicate where and why they were needed. Therefore, as participants consistently disregarded the disclaimers for these omissions, the recurring criticism of lack of references and Wikification revealed a standard reading behavior in this audience, since these admonitions and corrections are a common task for all experienced editors. Not only did these editors need some external background, as readers without previous knowledge of context, but they also discredited the "author" because they did not recognize their authority, both internal and external to the text—hence their claim on the need of external references.

The second text was presented as a proposed new section for the existing article on the Bacchanalia, which was still a small entry in Portuguese Wikipedia.[43] Perhaps not aware of this, two commentators complained that the text did not offer an introductory piece on the subject, and again six of the eight commentators criticized the lack of references and Wikification; once again this reveals a constant need for reaffirming the core concepts of Wikipedia, and shows that the assigned authors for these texts were perceived as lacking enough authority according to these quality parameters.

The perception of clarity on the second text was also mixed: two editors stated that this text was clearer and more objective than the first—or more "encyclopaedic," as one of them put it. One stated explicitly that the text was better than the first one, thus contradicting my initial hypothesis that the text written by the "student" would be considered *a priori* of lower quality. Others noted the opposite: "the wording of this text is a little poorer and harsher than the first, and information does not seem well ordered," or, "the text lacks cohesiveness—it seems more like a collection of excerpts than a structured exposition." This actually does not come as a surprise: as Paillier and other scholars noticed, it may well be that Livy's text could have been based on a collection of excerpts after all, coming both from the official senatorial decree and private reports turned to historical narrative by Livy's predecessors, whom he used as sources. The questions raised by editors end up being similar to the textual criticism applied by scholars:

> There are vague and not very strict terms, such as "being at the disposal of the consuls." What is this exactly? Another example of a vague term is the use of "should" in the expression "should be proclaimed." The reader is not certain whether the edicts were actually proclaimed or should, but were not. Another example of vague and not strict terms: who are the "all" in "decreed before all"?

All but one of the editors explicitly stated that the third text was the best of the three. Is this somehow related to the lack of "known" authorship, or does the way the content itself is presented provide more authority to the intended information? The list of reforms by Servius Tullius was considered by one editor:

> ... clearly the best quality text among the three, and the one using encyclopaedic language: the clearest, most rigorous, factual, descriptive and structured [of them]. It is clear that small observations could be made on minor issues, but we are already talking about final FA/GA[44] adjustments that I believe are beyond the scope of this study.

Other praise included: "In essence it's good"; "Best of the three texts, written clearly, coherently, almost always self-explanatory. No mistakes, simple Portuguese"; and "Except for the absence of references, the text seems to me of excellent quality, I do not have any other repairs to make." The relationship between perception of good quality and the need for internal links and references is especially noteworthy in this comment: "Text three is (by far) the most developed, compared to the previous ones. *Because of this* [my stress], it is also the one that most lacks wikification and references to its claims." In other words, this editor may be indirectly stating that this is the only text worthy of future use in an article.

Why does this text seem to the editors to be the best of them all? Indeed, the description of measures taken by Servius Tullius to divide Roman citizens and army is factual, descriptive, schematic and full of numbers, (thus "artificial" and "contrived," as Cornell states). Lacking a broader historical context, it does not matter for the editors whether this information is anachronistic or not, and even Livy's interpretation that the distribution of votes favoured oligarchs is not considered as lacking neutral point of view.

Therefore, when we consider that authorship for this text was purposefully informed as undisclosed, what does this mean for the initial hypothesis of establishing authority through authorship? One possible interpretation is that a combination of a particular objective style (e.g. many numbers, a schematic structure) and factual descriptions were factors revealing mastery of the Wikipedia writing rules, notability, and impartiality. The anonymous author could be anyone: a scholar, an Angolan high-school student, a retired engineer, an experienced Wikipedian, or even Livy himself.

Conclusion

The small sample of reviews in the experiment prevents us from reaching a more solid conclusion about the mixed perception of authority for the first and the second texts (i.e the one on the origins of drama and the one on the Bacchanalia). The last text, however, lacking attribution of authorship, benefitted from its particular "objectiveness" because of its more unadorned style and the presence of information that could be regarded as straightforward "facts." However, the most remarkable finding of the study was the overlap of the editors' analyses with the scholarly readings—both groups are essentially raising the same issues, although with different wordings and coming from different contexts. In that sense, these findings validate some level of equivalence in the sophisticated informational literacy skills of the experienced wikipedians and the trained skills of the scholars. Wikipedia editors noted, albeit unknowingly, that since we are not the audience that Livy intended, we lack the common background that would explain facts and concepts that to us seem "obscure" and "lacking" in his text. Indeed, Livy's readers, first of all the elite circles to which he was connected,[45] would supposedly not have missed his "omissions" and indeed enjoyed—and expected—what to us seems an "excessively adorned" style.

Since the methodology for this study has been hardly adopted in the Humanities, let alone in Classics, its novelty inevitably produced some shortcomings. Choosing the English-speaking Wikipedia community would have provided a much more statistically significant number of responses, even with the same rate of around 5 percent. However, this would probably require a bigger research team and structure, and English Wikipedia is particularly resistant to being the subject to academic research.[46] Moreover, a more accurate measurement of the weight of authority in different *personae* would have been achieved if only one text was used (maybe the third one, on the Servian reform), thus reducing variables, but that would have also required a more complex operation for dividing respondent groups, who would need to have no contact with each other. In this sense, the current results are an invitation for further work using online wiki environments in order to assess the relationship between a created *persona* and their authority, which is a pressing and problematic issue, notably in social media, in the early decades of the twenty-first century.

However, I hope that this experiment was able to show a complex and compelling correlation between literary and socio-political authorities. Livy's literary authority, which is predicated on the mastery of the rhetorical rules of historical narrative, internal to the text, could be equivalent to knowledge of "Wikipedia's core content policy": notability and impartiality. The social and political authority coming from Livy's self-presentation to his intended audience allowed him to expect a priori recognition from his readership, and added to his *auctoritas*. This same authority is achieved in Wikipedia through the building of a completely made-up persona, which is also recognized by peers through the mastery and display of the same set of rules. In both cases, the essence of the "author," whoever they may be, plays a lesser role than their self-presentation to a group that has the ultimate authority of conveying or withholding their intended legitimacy. A "good Wikipedian" could never be the real person Titus Livius, but only a fantasy pseudonym "Livy" created and maintained by anyone: either me, a student or, well, Livy. In the end, of course, the question whether Livy would be a good Wikipedian was always a *non sequitur*. This experiment was not about Livy, but about the power of contemporary audiences in yielding authority, to anyone as well as to ancient historians. Quite a distinctive case can be made with qualified audiences in Wikipedia, since editors not only create content, but also have means to decide whether to erase or not previous contributions, and establish a stable text.

Notes

1. This chapter took many more years to be completed than I intended, and not only because of the great Covid pandemic that befell us all. Since its outline is fairly unusual for the field, the methodology used was subjected to constant discussion and realignment. Ancient historians and classicists, public historians and theorists, scholars of information science and Wikipedians all contributed in their own fields of expertise through debates in conferences, peer reviews, and passionate conversations—I am grateful to them all.
2. Walsh's claim, made more than forty years ago, still stands: "The dominant preoccupation of scholars writing on Livy has been the relationship between the historian and the emperor Augustus" (1974) 5.
3. The bibliography on these questions is gigantic. Syme (1959), Peterson (1961), Walsh (1961), Badian (1993), and, more recently, Sailor (2006), Muñiz Coello (2009), and Moreno (2021) are especially relevant contributions.
4. As in other non-fiction genres. We should not assume, however, that this ingrained relationship is unique to Western historiography: it is, for instance, characteristic of Chinese historiography from its early beginnings. Indeed, the contrast would be closer to Near Eastern and Egyptian forms of historiography, together with the singular role of Homer in the establishment of a proto-historical narrative in archaic Greece. For an introduction to non-Western historiography, see Glassner (2004), van Seters (1997), and Raaflaub (2013). For Homer, see West (1999).
5. Literature on internet anonymity is vast and growing. See Nissenbaum (1999), Froomkin (1999), and, for Wikipedia, Tsikerdekis (2013).
6. Criticism of Wikipedia abounds, in popular titles such as Keen (2011) or by former members of the project, such as Sanger (2009). Giles (2005) is a famous opposite view. See http://en.wikipedia.org/wiki/Reliability_of_Wikipedia (accessed January 14, 2022).
7. https://en.wikipedia.org/wiki/Wikipedia:Core_content_policies (accessed January 14, 2022); also Reagle (2010).
8. The other pillars are related to free copyright, community etiquette, and proactivity in the project ("be bold"), https://en.wikipedia.org/wiki/Wikipedia:Five_pillars (accessed January 14, 2022).
9. Though, away from academia, this is not so simple: see Marques (2013).
10. Edwards (1996); for Livy, see Miles (1995).
11. Livy continuously disproves, but largely uses Antias. See Howard (1906), Laroche (1977), Rich (2013), and Richardson (2018).
12. See Luce (1977) and Tränkle (1977); also Levene (2010).
13. J. Marincola (1997). It is surely fitting to remember Livy's literary ambitions and agenda, however we might manage to establish them, but Wikipedians also seem to have them—see Marques (2019).

14 Although, as is well known, Pliny's encyclopaedia is not equivalent to our own concept of the genre, see Doody (2009).
15 This is the *exaedificatio* that Cicero advocates through Antonius in *De Oratore*; see Woodman (2011).
16 Livy is known for not using many of these, such as in 9.17.1, excusing himself for introducing the Alexander digression. See Forsythe (1999), esp. chapter 7; for Livian digressions, Oakley (1997: 184–6).
17 As in the Roman justification of war *contra* Carthaginian historians, the apparently perfect relationship of Nerva and Trajan with senatorial *libertas* (Tacitus, *Agr.* 3), or the political stance of Sallust.
18 Woodman (2011).
19 Luce (1989 [reprinted in Marincola, 2011]).
20 Gustafsson (2020). Most studies about editing wars on Wikipedia are based on computational models and algorithms to predict these dynamics, such as Borra (2015) and Yasseri (2012).
21 Panciera et al. (2009) discuss previous findings on this subject.
22 These users were selected with the aid of the Quarry tool, from Wikimedia Foundation labs, by editor OTAVIO1981 (https://quarry.wmflabs.org/query/21953, accessed January 14, 2022) and sent to users by administrator Leon saudanha, whom I would like to thank for their kind help.
23 I am user Domusaurea, registered on July 31, 2006, with more than 2,000 edits on Portuguese Wikipedia in October 2017: https://xtools.wmflabs.org/ec/pt.wikipedia.org/Domusaurea (accessed January 14, 2022).
24 See Marques (2012) and Marques and Louvem (2013). For a full list of my educational activities with Wikipedia, see https://pt.wikipedia.org/wiki/Usuária:Domusaurea (accessed January 14, 2022). In English, an introduction to my teaching experience can be found at https://diff.wikimedia.org/2012/01/06/things-i-learned-through-teaching-with-wikipedia/ (accessed May 10, 2022).
25 Portuguese Wikipedia ranks currently as eighteenth among all languages (higher article counts in less commonly spoken languages, such as Cebuano and Waray-Waray, were translated automatically by bots), with sixyt-six administrators, against 1061 on English Wikipedia. https://meta.wikimedia.org/wiki/List_of_Wikipedias (accessed January 14, 2022).
26 The purpose and functioning of the website can be viewed in https://meta.miraheze.org/wiki/FAQ (accessed January 14, 2022).
27 Previous knowledge of this procedure was expected from the participating experienced editors.
28 Livy used Varro: Jahn (1867), Waszink (1948); *contra* Leo (1904).
29 Feldherr (1998: 180).
30 Paillier (1988: chap. 7).

31 Ibid., 334.
32 *CIL* I² 581 = *ILS* 18.
33 Walsh (1996: 202) and Briscoe (2008: 230–50).
34 Cornell (1995: chap. 7). For a military focus, see Last (1945) and Forsythe (2007).
35 Ogilvie (1965), Smith (1997), and Pelling (2018).
36 Mommsen (1887: 245, n. 1).
37 Cornell (2012: 180).
38 Priedhorsky et al. (2007). A series of detailed statistics can be viewed at https://stats.wikimedia.org/#/all- projects (accessed January 14, 2022).
39 https://en.wikipedia.org/wiki/Wikipedia:Sockpuppetry lists both potentially harmful and legitimate uses of *sock puppets* (accessed January 14, 2022).
40 https://en.wikipedia.org/wiki/Wikipedia:Assume_good_faith (accessed January 14, 2022).
41 https://en.wikibooks.org/wiki/Wikibooks:What_is_Wikibooks (accessed January 14, 2022).
42 Marincola (2009: 11–23).
43 https://pt.wikipedia.org/wiki/Bacanal (accessed January 14, 2022). Page versions through time can be viewed in the "Ver Histórico" section.
44 "Featured article" and "good article."
45 Marincola (2009: 12). Roller (2004) speaks of "primary" and "secondary" audiences based on the criteria of closeness in experiencing actions, either as themselves (as eyewitnesses), or as commemoration through *monumenta* of actions past. Alternatively, I would suggest a definition of primary audiences as the holders of the political and economic structure—i.e. the elites in the broader sense (not only senators)—and secondary audiences as the common people, mostly even illiterate, who would presumably attend readings in public venues. Spreading the elite discourse to this secondary audience would serve as either a model set of values for social climbing or at least reinforcing social structures—a dynamic not very much unlike the one we witness today.
46 The current official policy of the community is "Wikipedia is not a laboratory" (https://en.wikipedia.org/wiki/Wikipedia:What_Wikipedia_is_not#Wikipedia_is_not_a_laboratory (accessed January 14, 2022). A very thorough introduction to academic research on Wikipedia is Nielsen (2019).

The New *Agora*? Online Communities and a New Rhetoric

Catalina Popescu

Online life has expanded significantly. The virtual world is now comparable in many ways to any other physical space of action. It is a place for selling, for buying, for reading, for meeting friends, for taking a serene "walk" among virtual cities, and even a place for debate and discovery. It fulfills the functions of an inhabited land, works as an organism, and displays the needs of an actual *polis* and the polyvalences of a real marketplace. Extreme selfies, photoshopped pictures, and even the "creative" world of fake news produce at times (besides amazement or annoyance) unusual hybrids between the "outside" world and the fantasies of the virtual space, by combining the two in a new hyper-reality. It is an *agora*, or if we prefer the more commonly used Roman term, a *forum*. The world of megabytes and pixels is just as real as any place one can measure in feet and miles. It is in actuality a mixture between our world and a fantasy land where everyone can be whatever they choose to be: in this case, the nicknames and the avatars of Internet users display a great deal of creativity and also testify to their interest in a world alternative to that of daily reality. The Internet harbors blogs by 'Diogenes', 'Aristophanes', and 'Socrates', where ancient modes of persuasion come to life to argue and mingle.

It was the fact that online *personae* take at time the names of ancient philosophers, orators, and rhetoricians, that persuaded me to design a survey for young students regarding online debating. It took me two years of teaching Latin to middle- and high-school students to finally realize that there is a spectacular parallel world of classical debating tools which extends in our education system beyond school debates and other "serious," organized events.

When checking the validity of Greek arguments, one can always find manuals about the proper way to use the old logic in modern debates in scholarly environments. Nevertheless, I was lucky enough to discover another side of modern rhetoric: the online world inhabited by young people is keeping the Greek debating tools more alive than the efforts of law school professors and rhetoricians.

When I was working with high-school students, I used Survey Monkey to create a poll for students from eighth to twelfth grade: 104 participants replied with useful information. The survey allowed for anonymity and contained questions with suggested answers to choose from, as well as space for write-in answers. The results are described in this chapter and represent the view of my survey-takers regarding their experience and their view of *ad hominem* arguments in the virtual debate space. Thus, this chapter discusses the results of the poll regarding old rhetorical tools and online identity, and deals with the modern use of ancient diatribe in youths' debate practices.[1]

Debaters themselves recognize the use of *ad hominem* argument in their interactions, particularly when the topics are sensitive and the atmosphere is tense. According to Douglas Walton, various scholars of *logos* used the term *ad hominem* to denote either a rhetorical fallacy, when someone attacks the person making an argument rather than the argument itself, or an argument *ex concessis*, when someone attacks a core belief of the interlocutor to later invalidate his/her whole argument:[2]

> Not all arguments from commitment (*ex concessis* arguments) are personal-attack arguments. And not all *ad hominem* arguments in the personal-attack sense are arguments from commitment (although many of them are, as will be shown below). [...] This meaning also stems from ancient teachers of rhetoric, who distinguished between the substantive issues in a debate and the personal aspect that can also be involved.[3]

In the situation when the *ad hominem* argument constitutes an attack directed towards a rival's personality, Walton identifies three possible forms: it is either circumstantial (based on the adversary's acts); biased (based on intentions); or of the "poison the well"-type, the latter invalidating everything the interlocutor might say, due to one major flaw that permanently annuls his/her opinions.[4] According to his view on the reception of such an argument, the philosophical and rhetorical tradition post-Aristotle, moving from Boethius and Thomas Aquinas to Locke in 1690 and Charles L. Hamblin in 1970, perceived this form of argumentation as a logical fallacy or, at best, as an inferior form of argumentation which depends significantly on outside evidence. As Walton concludes, the *ad* type rhetorical tools include problematic approaches to a debated issue (*ad verecundiam*, *ad ignorantiam*, *ad populum*, and even *ad* baculum).[5] According to Franz E. van Eemeran, after Aristotle these were generally regarded as tricks, as were the more common fallacies *e dictione* or *extra dictionem*, namely the circular argument and the divagation.[6] Van Eemeran explained that if earlier logical treaties considered these to simply fall into the categories of arguments "which seemed to be valid, but are not so", this idea is currently under metamorphosis by scholars.[7] In other words, while circular argument and divagation remain rhetorical flaws today, the *ad hominem* argument appears to have been upgraded from the list of perceived mistakes to that of acceptable practices in certain circumstances. The *agora* realities of the ancient Greeks played a role in this re-evaluation of the importance of *ad hominem* arguments in modern rhetorical analysis:

> The legitimacy of the character attack, the main meaning of *ad hominem*, has also been widely recognized in rhetoric, where *ethos*[8] or persuading an audience using argumentation based on the perceived character (good or bad) of a speaker, can be an acceptable form of argument. In political debate, for example, character is a relevant issue in a democratic system, where voters cannot reasonably be expected to know all the facts on all issues and will often vote on the basis of the perception of a candidate's character.[9]

While the *ad hominem* argument is the same in ancient and modern times, namely attempting to eliminate the adversary's credibility by revealing a deep contradiction within his core beliefs or practices outside speech, those involved in the modern online *agora* feel apprehensive to admit the rhetorical or moral values of such practice. From those who took my survey, 28 percent strongly believe that they do not use *ad hominem* responses and moreover, that such practice is wrong, while about half of the interviewed admitted discomfort regarding the usage of such rhetorical tool (even when 32.1 percent of survey respondents declared that they used it before). Surprisingly, the majority (about 63.5 percent of those interviewed) admitted the usage of *ad hominem* arguments. For those interviewed, the *ad hominem* argument meant only one type: the abusive kind, where the adversary is tormented with insults that have no relevance to the substance of their argument but are meant to deter them from the debate. In such context, in an age where the most common accusation online is being a cyber-bully, *ad hominem* arguments appear specious not only for clouding the core of the arguments itself, but also for degenerating into the oldest form of bullying, where name-calling, threats, and curses coalesce. Paul Graham, speaking about the extra-academic culture, and also including the corporate world, lists the *ad hominem* argument as the second lowest type of debating strategy, after the name calling, in his "Pyramid of Disagreement" part of "How I disagree."[10]

A clearer picture unraveled when those survey respondents who admitted having used *ad hominem* arguments explained why they had used such rhetoric. The majority appeared troubled by the question and embarrassed at their behavior: about half of them (32.1 percent of the total) believed that they used it "sometimes" and only because it is hard to distinguish between the individual and their ideas. From the remaining half of my responders who affirmed that such argumentation is acceptable, about 50 percent relied on Greek tradition (15.1 percent of the total), when given the opportunity to defend the practice (with a sentence such as "Yes, I do, but so did the Greeks"), using an *ipse dixit*,[11] or *ad verecundiam* type of argument. The remaining fraction (17.2 percent of the total) believes that it is acceptable in its own merit. Therefore, when asked "Do you feel like you attack the argument, or the person?," this group chose the response: "It's all the same to me: stupid people make stupid arguments." In such assumption, survey respondents combine the "flesh and blood" arguer and their argument into one identity and in doing so, they unknowingly use an ancient assumption. According to the scholarship listed by S. Johnstone, it was normal for an Athenian orator to believe that someone's character was a constant and that actions spoke daily on behalf of that character:[12] "A person who habitually behaved one way was unlikely to act to the contrary."

Those who disagree with *ad hominem* arguments believe that the individual has to be carefully separated from the principles he or she supports ("No, this would be a mistake. I am rejecting my opponent's arguments only. His/her person is not relevant to our duel."). In other words, the *ad hominem* argument brings the debater into an area where the dominant instances are *logos* and the Aristotelian "reason free from passion." For these who resent the intrusion of the "outside" reality in the world of rhetoric, the concept of "reality" itself switches from the pedestrian *res* to the purity of *logos*, in a Platonic way. Thus, the real argument, the one with "substance," scrutinizes only the universe of ideas, while their author and his *ethos* detach completely as separate entities. As mentioned above, this opinion appears in Graham's "How I Disagree. Pyramid of Disagreement": "ad Hominem: attacks the characteristics or authority of the writer without addressing the substance of the argument."[13] Similarly, on *pathosethoslogos.com*, the concept of *logos* is emphasized over all the other rhetorical tools, as the very seat of pure ideas: "*Logos* is the Greek word for 'word,' however the true definition goes beyond that, and can be most closely described as 'the word' or 'that by which the inward thought is expressed' and, 'the inward thought itself." In addition to this extolling of *logos*, Martha Henning's *Classical Rhetoric Now* stated the ancillary status of *ethos* in a written or oral argument, thus arguing that it is best for any modern debater to just stick to the issue of the debate.

The taboo of conflating an individual's personality and his/her ideas is so prevalent among debaters that websites against cyber-bullying, like SketWeb, post the following equation between *ad hominem* arguments and unethical harassment:

> Stay focused on topic. If someone calls you names, attacks your personality, your credibility, your knowledge, do NOT reply to such remarks. This type of harassment is called *Ad Hominem* attacks. Instead prefer to stay on topic and ask his/her arguments regarding the topic at hand, and his arguments/rebuttal against your argument. If they insist, tell them that personal attacks do not make an argument. If they do not start talking rationally, tell them that such discussion with personal attacks instead of arguments is unproductive, and you are bailing out of discussing with them.

Nevertheless, the *ad hominem* argument is common in rhetoric, and it is even more common in trials where character revelation can raise questions regarding the witness' credibility. This tool was frequent in Greek *agora* and writers like Lysias (*On the Murder of Eratoshtenes*) or Antiphon (*Against the Stepmother*) used it successfully in their published speeches against characters deemed unworthy of Athenian citizenship or of their social status. In a certain form, these elements were not deemed fallacious, but the *ethos* of an adversary was an important piece of the forensic puzzle where the trials involved flesh-and-blood individuals and a network of interests and values. Thus, appealing to the audience's knowledge of past goods, to their sense of citizenship and public worth, was just as crucial as proving that a certain fact happened due to irrefutable logical proof. *Logos* (the logical substance of the argument), *ethos* (the use of one's character), and *pathos* (the use of emotions) were immersed masterfully and recognized as valued rhetoric techniques.[14] In such a context, as Walton[15] and H. W. Johnstone before him suggested, *ad hominem* arguments are not entering the areas of fallacies, unless they are abusing their role in argumentation.[16] When used correctly, they shine a light on the character of the opponent in contexts where certain flaws constitute impediments to the speaker's commitment to a particular argument. The intrinsic tie between the individual and his or her cause was the reason why the Greeks used the "character" argument to begin with, namely the chance to be free from the structures of abstract logic: "They were part of the complex competition of litigants to represent their own speech as more authoritative: Defendants recalled such 'actions' both to erode the authority of the prosecutor's story and to construct a relationship between themselves and the jurors that did not depend on the vagaries of rhetorical language."[17]

The world of online diatribe follows the same subconscious path and is deemed fiercely addictive. This world reminded me of what Petronius' Encolpius (*Satyrica*, 1–3) craved when he complained about the tediousness of *suasoria* (school practice speeches on a given topic): unlike schools' debating societies, which operate in a controlled, scholastic, and as a result, unsatisfying environment, the virtual arena is at the same time less and more real than the outside world. It is also less sanitized or gentlemanly: it operates under false names and uses the protective screen of a computer, but it has the spontaneity and zest of a street fight.

The transition I used in my survey between the use of Internet and online debating was a question about gaming. "Do you use the Internet for games?" The question was meant to bridge the virtual and non-virtual reality through the lenses of play culture, since the nature of games implies competition and resolution of conflicts through rhetoric and negotiation. According to Johan Huizinga's *Homo Ludens, A Study of the Play-Element in Culture*, playfulness has *in nuce* the principles of realities[18]: it is a facsimile which at times prepares the individuals for the real-life performance. It is through this gate of fantasy that debaters discovered their appetite for diatribe. There is an additional connection between the world of theatrical pretense and the *persona* of an orator. In ancient Athenian times, the *agora* was the ultimate *theatron* where orators put on masks and, by playing their intricate roles with conviction, they ended up affecting the lives of the flesh-and-blood citizens they represented.[19] In his article "Thespians in the Law Court," Andreas Serafim discusses this paradoxical use of theatrics and drama in an environment where real lives were at stake and the purpose of the speeches in the agora was to convey sincerity.[20] Similarly, in modern times, the virtual world's "appearance of life" eased the debaters' intrusions into the real life. For those who assume online identity, sometimes the borders between reality and fiction blur. Some survey takers acknowledged the difficulty of detaching the "mask" (*persona*) of the opponent from the reality of the speaker behind it.

The online world uses its virtual tendrils to probe the private world of its users, breaking the wall of anonymity which separates the online identities from the realities behind. Bridging reality is the ultimate taboo and temptation. For many so-called "trolls," peeking into the forbidden private realm is the ultimate

El Dorado while at the same time they construct solid boundaries between themselves and the world. *Ad hominem* arguments allow their users the first step outside the virtual world and the penetration of the opponent's reality. At times, that subtle probing could turn brutal. We now leave behind the world of my survey, for a more aggressive reality of insults. Much like the Greeks entered the private sanctum when debaters looked for disreputable details in each other's life or imagined unsavory intimate commerce (see Aeschines' depiction of Neaira's past as a courtesan or Lysias' details about Timarchos' alleged prostitution), the online debaters compete in offensive name-calling and quest for lurid details. E. Cohen specifies that the agora was probably the most sensitive environment to such accusations and constituted sometimes "the only disincentive to sale by *politai* of their own sexual services," since the consequence was "enforced exclusion from leadership rules in political activities."[21] Thomas A. J. McGinn establishes that Greeks saw in individual deviancy an attack against the well-being of the *polis*. Just like the ancient Greeks, the private realm is claimed as public domain by the aggressive debaters today.[22]

Some modern debaters updated their accusation to fit our current sexual taboos, but they use this with the same purpose of silencing the accused, prevented them from voicing opinions in the forum.[23] Rumors of "deviancy" are peddled with the intent of ruining reputations.[24] Like the Greeks, they use *logos*, *ethos*, and *pathos*, but claim to function only according to the laws of "pure" *logos*. What ancient Greeks, online gamers, and YouTubers have in common is the weaponizing of such *logos* and the equation between words, proofs, and deeds. In other words, it is a fight between *logoi* (statements) and *erga* (deeds or facts) for the title of *tekmeria* (proofs). The Greeks were much the same when claiming to have facts speak for themselves, since their statements too "were not objectively more factual or known in a different way than other kinds of claim a litigant might make. [...] If defendants were to contend that liturgies were *erga* that overthrew the *logoi* of the prosecutor, it was only because as *logoi* themselves the defendants' claims had successfully masked their own character."[25] Cohen even specifies that certain liturgies or *erga* were not even real, but were attempts *ad ignorantiam*.[26]

If modern Internet personalities wear a virtual mask to detach themselves from others or to prevent emotional connection to others, lawyers in the Greek *agora* were doing just the opposite: their speech was in first person when talking about their clients, as if they were about to inhabit the physical body of their client, as Serafim discusses. When a lawyer was speaking, he was becoming an amplifier of the defendant's voice, wearing throughout the trial his *persona* like a suit. Like Internet trolls, they were also parading "slices" of someone's life, but with the distinct purpose of eliciting sympathy. Both the modern and the ancient had a flare for live drama, for a voyeuristic "reality show"; of course, the real life was a pretense, sometimes excessively idealized, up to the point of being unrealistic.[27] For example, Lysias, in his speech *Against Simon*, defends a man accused of killing an opponent, by revealing that this rival has committed a home invasion, where several female inhabitants were traumatized: "Hearing that the boy was at my house, he came there at night in a drunken state, broke down the doors, and entered the women's rooms: within were my sister and my nieces, whose lives have been so well-ordered that they are ashamed to be seen even by their kinsmen" (3.6) For the translated Greek texts quoted here, I use the editions mentioned in the References. To contrast their unbelievable *aidos* (pudor) with the shamelessness of the intruder, Lysias puts on a dramatic scene: "This man, then, carried insolence to such a pitch that he refused to go away until the people who appeared on the spot, and those who had accompanied him, feeling it a monstrous thing that he should intrude on young girls and orphans, drove him out by force" (3.7). In a world which lacks YouTubers' HD cameras, the home invasion depicted barely has the quality of radiophonic theater, but still delivers.

In his speech *On the Murder of Eratosthenes*, Lysias has another brilliant depiction of a family life that he had never witnessed: and yet, he tries to feel what his client Euphiletos might have felt, in a way which reminds us of method acting and the dramatic technique of Stanislavski. The result is a heartbreaking depiction of the damaging onset of paranoia:

> With these words, sirs, she took herself off; I was at once perturbed; all that had happened came into my mind, and I was filled with suspicion,—reflecting first how I was shut up in my chamber, and then remembering how on that night the inner and outer doors made a noise, which had never occurred before, and how it struck me that my wife had put on powder. All these things came into my mind, and I was filled with suspicion.
>
> 1.17

At times, even for the Greeks, *ethos* and *pathos* indeed fused. Emotions are always stirred by powerful character attacks and when they do, both *ethos* and *pathos* appear as the enemies of *logos* rather than its natural allies. While *logos*, *ethos*, and *pathos* were meant to be intertwined means of persuasion,[28] Aristotle himself felt that *ethos* and *pathos* occupy in fact the most influential in terms of convincing an emotional audience.[29] The ancient debaters felt the connection:

both Demosthenes (19, 227–40) and Lysias (6.53) knew the destabilizing power of *charis* (grace, charisma), a weapon of *ethos*, when a lawyer uses his client's past munificence to emotionally blackmail his audience. As Aristotle puts it in *Rhetoric* 1.2.4: "we feel confidence in a greater degree and more readily in persons of worth in regard to everything in general." S. Johnstone believes that as a tool of *ethos*, *charis* was more meaningful than a simple appeal to *pathos* and worked as an excellent tool to fuse the jurors with the interests of the *polis* "by reproducing its group consciousness." Lysias (6.53), as a rival of Andocides' client, had to "disintegrate a collective identity by positioning each juror as an individual."[30] "What kind of friend, what kind of relative, what kind of demesman finds it necessary to be openly hated by the gods by secretly giving *charis* to this man?" Much like the modern debaters, revealing the opponent's human nature was a mean of winning, according to S. Johnstone "by asserting juror's identity as mere individuals."[31]

Additionally, through the power of *pathos* and fellow-feeling, Lysias taps into the jurors' sense of gratitude and pity, thus making them not only witnesses, but also emotional characters in his client's personal drama, even from *captatio benevolentiae*:

> I should be only too pleased, sirs, to have you so disposed towards me in judging this case as you would be to yourselves, if you found yourselves in my plight. For I am sure that, if you had the same feelings about others as about yourselves, not one of you but would be indignant at what has been done; you would all regard the penalties appointed for those who resort to such practices as too mild. And these feelings would be found, not only among you, but in the whole of Greece: for in the case of this crime alone, under both democracy and oligarchy, the same requital is accorded to the weakest against the strongest, so that the lowest gets the same treatment as the highest. Thus, you see, sirs, how all men abominate this outrage.
>
> 1.1–2

According to Serafim's view, orators who embodied their clients were also operating in an environment that was fully aware of their ability to lie, impersonate, and mimic sincerity, and was, as a result, equipped to resist such emotional assaults.[32] This apprehension translates well even today and is partly responsible for the response my students had when confronted with my questions regarding the legitimacy of arguments of *ethos* and *pathos* in their debates. Since emotional response brings with it a feeling of impotence and subservience to the illusionist tricks of a conman, the validity of *pathos* and *ethos* appear questionable.

As M. Gleason argues in her book *Making Men: Sophists and Self-Presentation in Ancient Rome*, the ancients went even a step further in comparing the one "displaying signs of emotional passivity to the sexually submissive, namely the effeminate and the *pathicus* (term designating the passive adult homosexual and meant as an offense in those times).[33] They were looking for such signs in an orator's voice, posture, and (of course) behavior. Being the passive "recipient" of emotions meant defeat.

In opposition, the claim at pure logic and *logos* creates a cocoon around a debater's *persona*, by which he/she becomes impervious to the attacks on their emotions. Also, reliance on "pure" *logos* creates the image of a superior intellect. Response to *pathos* is marginalized as failure, inability to control oneself, or a detachment of the mask meant to be worn during the debate. The modern winning game is described as making the opponent feel ashamed, embarrassed, even sad. Thus, the weapon of *pathos*, which was usually directed towards a tertiary in the ancient days (the audience), is now actually a tool targeted at the debasing one's opponent. According to K. Leigh, in her essay on modern cyber-trolling, the key to defeat even in modern times implies an emotional surrender, since the debates most of the time imply a psychological war between arguers.[34] Thus, to be subjected to *pathos* when all one wants is to validate his/her world view and strengthen a projected image, means to be on the losing team: "Their [bullies] weakness is that they *feel* like they have something to prove intellectually, so the most effective way to deal with them is with condescension."[35]

Thus, according to such view, the *ad hominem* arguments do not enter the area of legitimate *ethos* but feed the basest form of *pathos*: an individual dealing in such terms is at loss of "real" arguments which rely strictly on logic and collection of data. When a perceived "troll" tries to discuss *ethos*, his/her detractors claim that he/she is trying to set an emotional trap to someone painfully susceptible to the devious weapons of *pathos*. *Pathos* is thus equated to illegitimacy and swindling. Due to its perceived deviancy, it loses its status, because of its tendency to prey on emotions, to penetrate the most intimate sanctum of *psyche* and castrate the intellect of its cognitive powers. Even worse, a quest for *proof* raises the suspicions of fictitious statements or *muthos*: "If your troll is asking for 'evidence,' or 'proof' of your claims, it's a trap. Anything you post will be dismissed *ad hominem* or written off as fake news, and meanwhile they wasted your time and got you to perform a task for them."[36] Due to this bizarre online commerce in emotionality, some interviewers felt the need to claim immunity to the touch of *pathos*: many of those (44 percent) who responded to my survey either deny any change in their rhetorical abilities and emotionality or believe that they have improved (with 39 percent of the rest replying that this was not applicable to them in the first place).

The need to self-censure and to project a controlled, mature, and intellectual *persona* to one's audience is not a modern invention. It should not be underestimated as vapid or useless. The ancient orators were working as hard at their appearance of self-control, as they did at articulating valid arguments. As Gleason asserts, the *agora* was one of the most enduring arenas for manly pageantry and rivalry. Showing oneself as controlled and impervious to emotions was key:

> Rhetoric was a calisthenics of manhood. This is easier for us to grasp for we remember that the art of self-presentation through rhetoric entailed much more than mastery of words: physical control of one's voice, carriage, facial expression, and gesture, control of one's emotions under conditions of competitive stress— in a word, all the arts of deportment necessary in a face-to-face society where one's adequacy as a man was always under suspicion and one's performance was constantly being judged.[37]

The modern online debater is also prone to such exaggerations of his emotional autonomy. A feeling of alienation issues sometimes, as a result. Whitney Phillips, lecturer at Humboldt State University and author of *This is Why We Cannot Have Nice Things*, declared in an interview that trolls appear sociopathic because they emotionally disconnect themselves from the realities of the events that they mock inappropriately:

> That sidesteps the ways in which trolling necessitates the trolling mask. Instead of thinking about [a tragedy] as a totality, they think about individual, tiny, fetishized details. If a young person was killed in a particular way and there was an "amusing" detail about the death, they would focus on that. They're not thinking about the person who died, and the people affected by that death. It's not that they're laughing necessarily at other people's pain. They're in a privileged position where they don't need to think about it.[38]

The author claims that the cyber-bully mask is nothing more than a façade, ready to crack under the pressure of an emotional attack. The idea of reverse manipulation of emotions to fight bullies fits particularly into the arsenal of those who envision a war against trolling.[39] At advice point 8, the troll's potential emotional vulnerability is exposed: "Take pity on cyberbullies: Bullies, both in real and online worlds, are usually people with unfulfilled lives. They divert frustration by unleashing uncivil comments on anonymous people online." This is quite intriguing, given that many "bullies" claim to be impervious to emotional attacks and fully prepared against the arsenal of *pathos*. The whole purpose of the duel with *ad hominem* attacks is to render your adversaries penetrable to insults, while claiming immune status.

Nevertheless, Internet interactions can go beyond affecting emotions. Through the online world, *ad hominem* graduates from a tool of *ethos* to an attack on emotions and an argument *ad baculum*. For example, online debaters send each other threats of doxing, which implies finding and posting online everything about someone's identity, from real name and address to other more intimate life details, and exposing them to an army of bullies. The paradox lies in the fact that, while the online realities are meant to mimic the extra-network world, these two worlds are no longer the "original" and the "copy," but rather two competing realities in danger of colliding and even fusing. The troll's success in controlling his adversary also implies his ability to bridge the other individual's private space. Empty threats about document revelations take at times the more serious attempts of privacy invasion, such as "swatting." According to B. Koerner's article, "It Started as An Online Prank. Then It Turned Deadly," some online trolls turned into real-life invaders, enjoying the ultimate power game of controlling fictitious infantry troops by sending SWAT teams into the adversary's home. Once more, reality and game negotiated poorly their places and boundaries:[40]

> When you're on the internet and your actions have little weight in real life, and then suddenly that translates into something as physically heavy as a swatting, it makes you realize the weight of your actions on a computer a lot more than you normally would,' says one former Call of Duty fanatic who has taken part in swattings. He maintains that his adversaries usually tempered their behavior after getting startled by a horde of cops: 'It did reestablish boundaries on the internet for them and remind them that just because they were behind a computer talking sh*t, it didn't mean they were untouchable.

As a paradox, the "unreal" world of online debate moves this way from the fringes of reality right into its visceral middle, filled up with dangers like a dark ally in an unfamiliar neighborhood. As Koerner specifies, the troll in such case "became addicted to the thrill of swatting. He loved having the power to transform police into playthings as if they were videogame characters."[41] They might be labeled with terms coined from the realm of fantasy, but online "trolling" appears able to wage wars outside their virtual world. "Trolls" or "cyber-bullies," these illusory *Polyphemoi* appear adequately equipped to bring enduring harm. Even the tongue-in-cheek phrase used in the meme "Do not feed the trolls!" to mockingly dismiss them, raises images of voracity and potential bodily harm.

At the opposite end, when faced with accusations of affecting people's emotionality, some Internet personalities take a step back into the realm of fantasy from which they originally emerged, admitting their work to be nothing more than a game, a form of entertainment that was never meant to affect one's real world.[42] The testimony of journalists interested in the topic shows that for most part, during early 2000s, the public perceived online "trolling" interactions as merely entertaining or only vaguely annoying.[43] Thus, these personalities do not only fall outside the reality of the perceived "serious" debate, but are also alien to reality itself. Like cyclopes or ogres, their name ("trolls") relegates them to the realm of fantasy and *muthos* (the Aristotelian adversary of *logos*).

In conclusion, my initial intention was to see how far the world of Greek debate stretches into the modern time, beyond the environment of debating societies or televized political debates. I found a lively world of debate that has all the elements of the Greek *agora* and affects our world in ways which I could have only imagined. Before launching my survey, I was teaching a dead language in the hope that if I argue well enough in favor of Classics, someone might be open to an artificial encounter with the ancient roots in modern medical terminology or agree to learn about debate points and logical fallacies when applying to law school. Instead, I discovered that the ancient world of arguments is alive and well in daily interactions among young people and has never lost its biting vitality, for better or for worse.

Notes

1 I want to take this opportunity to thank all my anonymous participants. This chapter goes beyond their responses, discussing the topics of "trolling" and "cyber-bullying," which were not part of the survey. The translated Greek texts quoted in here are those from the editions mentioned in the References.
2 Walton (1998: 248–83).
3 Walton (2001: 1).
4 Walton (2001: 1–2).
5 The *ad verecundiam* argument implies that the audience should accept an argument based on their reverence for the authority of a certain individual supporting it. The theory postulates that an argument is valid because there is no evidence that it is false or that the contrary is true. The *ad populum* fallacy relies on unproven views that are accepted by the wider public to validate an opinion, while the *ad baculum* error is based on threats and promise of negative consequence if one does not agree with an argument.

6 Van Emeran (2001: 298–9).
7 See also Woods and Walton (1982: 298).
8 Aristotle himself agreed that it was important to discuss the character of the opponent and use it within the argument: "Evidence partly concerns ourselves, partly our adversary, as to the fact itself or moral character; so that it is evident that one never need lack useful evidence. For, if we have no evidence as to the fact itself, neither in confirmation of our own case nor against our opponent, it will always be possible to obtain some evidence as to character that will establish either our own respectability or the worthlessness of our opponent" (Aristot. *Rhet.* 1376a, 18).
9 Walton (2001: 2).
10 Graham (2008), listed also on Wikipedia.
11 It literally means "he himself said it," representing a type of argument where the audience is expected to accept the validity of an opinion because a respected individual or a figure of authority sustained it.
12 Johnstone (1999: 97).
13 Graham (2018).
14 Aristotle, once again, enlightens the student of rhetoric: "Of the modes of persuasion furnished by the spoken word there are three kinds. The first kind depends on the personal character of the speaker; the second on putting the audience into a certain frame of mind; the third on the proof, or apparent proof, provided by the words of the speech itself" (Aristot. *Rh.* 1.5–6). Aristotle elaborates further in respect to the value of *logos*, the argument provided by the subject under discussion: "we must look, not at what is indefinite but at what is inherent in the subject treated of in the speech, marking off as many facts as possible, particularly those intimately connected with the subject; for the more facts one has, the easier it is to demonstrate, and the more closely connected they are with the subject, the more suitable are they and less common" (Aristot. *Rh.* 1. 11).
15 Walton (1998: 248–63).
16 Johnstone (1978: 9).
17 Johnstone (1999: 94).
18 Huizinga (1980: 1–27).
19 Worthen (2015); Serafim (2019).
20 Serafim (2019).
21 Cohen (2000: 158).
22 McGinn (2014: 90–1).
23 See Ortiz (2020) for an in-depth view on harassment based on social status, race, gender, and sexual orientation.
24 The most common insult nowadays in a gaming environment is calling someone a "pedophile," which replaces the slurs used in the past decades to denote homosexuality or non-binary identities. Gamers' insults cover many areas of

harassment, ranging from gender and race to sexual orientation. For more in-depth analysis, see Gray (2012) and (2014).
25 Johnstone (1999: 96–7).
26 Cohen (1995: 107–12).
27 Just (1991: 96).
28 "Now, since proofs are effected by these means, it is evident that, to be able to grasp them, a man must be capable of logical reasoning, of studying characters and the virtues, and thirdly the emotions—the nature and character of each, its origin, and the manner in which it is produced" (Arist. *Rhet.* 1.7).
29 Arist. *Rhet.* 1.2.4-6: "for it is not the case, as some writers of rhetorical treatises lay down in their 'Art', that the worth of the orator in no way contributes to his powers of persuasion; on the contrary, moral character [*ethos*], so to say, constitutes the most effective means of proof. The orator persuades by means of his hearers, when they are roused to emotion by his speech [*pathos*]; for the judgements we deliver are not the same when we are influenced by joy or sorrow, love or hate; and it is to this alone that, as we have said, the present-day writers of treatises endeavor to devote their attention. [...] Lastly, persuasion is produced by the speech itself [*logos*], when we establish the true or apparently true from the means of persuasion applicable to each individual subject."
30 Johnstone (1999: 105).
31 Ibid.
32 Serafim (2019: 1).
33 Gleason (1995, 3–9, 36, 38, 68).
34 Leigh (2016).
35 Pothast (2017).
36 Pothast (2017).
37 Gleason (1995: XXII).
38 Morrison (2015).
39 See also Pothast (2017).
40 Koerner (2018).
41 Ibid.
42 Dynel (2016).
43 Daley (2019): "In 2002, one of the earliest definitions of internet 'trolling' described the behavior as: 'luring others online (commonly on discussion forums) into pointless and time-consuming activities.' Trolling often started with a message that was intentionally incorrect, but not overly controversial. By contrast, internet 'flaming' described online behavior with hostile intentions, characterized by profanity, obscenity, and insults that inflict harm to a person or an organization."

Classical Literature and Contemporary Classics

Ayelet Haimson Lushkov

The Problem with Literature

Classical literature lays claim to a lofty authority: both the literature of the ancient Greeks and Romans and the idiom of the cultured elites of Europe still occupy a powerful place in the literary and therapeutic imaginations of many.[1] But as the canon becomes more globalized and de-colonized, classical literature must also come to terms with the consequences of that lofty status: being the purview of the few and not the many, and especially not of the current generation of students, young people emerging into adulthood in an age of political, financial, moral, and environmental turbulence. With the future of the planet urgently on the line, classical literature is a much harder "sell" than history or archaeology, with their visual aids and concrete relationships to the problems of the moment. Whatever stamp of authority classical literature used to confer, the ground has shifted sufficiently that we must urgently ask how to convince students and members of the public to pay attention to (not to mention pay *for*) the study of old stories and the skills required to analyze and understand them.

There are, of course, utilitarian answers to this question: that the study of literature increases empathy and moral reasoning, that the study of foreign languages makes the mind more supple, and that close critical engagement with any text produces the questioning mind demanded by a well-functioning society, not to mention democracy.[2] Still, these are not easy skills to promote, especially as they are known as "soft" skills, skills that require transferring and modifying, rather than resulting in a clear career path with a paycheck, benefits, and the prospect of home-ownership. For a generation called to do something "use-ful," how do we teach something that for generations, including the very people who wrote the texts we today study, prided itself on being *otiose*, "use-less," from the Latin *otium*, a pleasant break from the demands of running the state or making money, even when the topics they treated were very much political in nature.[3]

Literature, and indeed the Humanities in general, has always had the fear of irrelevance built in to its very core, in what Richard Lanham has called "the Q Question," after the Roman rhetorician Quintilian who first formulated it: "is there a connection between literature and living well?"[4] Various answers to this problem have been floated, for example by classicist Joy Connolly, who sees in the close reading of Latin literature and its reception an important avenue to a fuller and more informed citizenship.[5] The question, however, is of particular urgency for our present moment more generally, not least because the project of living well, or well-being, is perhaps the quintessential contemporary project, whether manifested in a cult of fitness and self-care or in political, social or environmental activism, within academia or on a national level.

Living, and especially living well, has long been a concern of classical literature. Philosophers, educators, and the writers of and commentators on epic and history all strove to produce men who would live well in society, though the exact product could vary dramatically.[6] The reception of such classical education has also varied. Donna Zuckerberg, in her excellent *Not All Dead White Men* (2018), has discussed how the literature of explicit well-living, especially Stoic philosophy, has been appropriated by the Alt-Right, for whom such philosophies help produce an especially toxic brand of exclusionary masculinity. The problem, as Dr. Zuckerberg amply demonstrates, is that this brand of masculinity is all too easily found in our literary texts, bolstered not only by ancient sensibilities, but also by some of the ways in which we still teach these texts, ways that flow from and still replicate the teachings that gave us, for example, the classicism of the British Empire or American slave-owning.[7] To be clear, this is not to say that we are all deliberately reinforcing racist or sexist stereotypes when we teach the classics (though some of us inevitably do), but rather that it is ethically difficult, for example, to teach the *Iliad* or the *Aeneid* without acknowledging that these are poems—poems which we say are beautiful and foundational and important— which celebrate mass violence, misogyny, orientalism, imperialism, and a variety of other toxic behaviors. Further, that these are qualities which the ancients, in large or small part, believed were byproducts, if not constituent parts, of living well and actively in the state.[8]

There is a natural reluctance among classicists to admit to the problematic consequences of some types of reception. We much prefer, as a rule, to point to instances of reception where classical literature works therapeutically to help veterans process their trauma (e.g. Louge (1999)), or reflect political realities (e.g. Torrance and O'Rourke (2020)), or interrogate racial divides (e.g. Raji (2005), Alfaro (2020)). But these instances, laudable though they are, still fall short of providing a colloquial idiom for the public to embed classical literature in its mundane every-day conversation. We are quite a way off from the situation in India, for example, where the characters of the great Hindu epics, the Mahabharata and the Ramayana, are households name, their faces part of the industry of cultural phenomena and everyday interaction.[9] The comparison is admittedly imperfect, but it does highlight how we all recognize a dissociation between classical literature and some of its contemporary afterlives. To maintain its lofty status, classical literature, and equally importantly, its study, must remain on a pedestal made of admiration, difficulty, and unattainability—a situation which maintains its prestige, but at the cost of relevance and survival.

As Esch noted on the physical reuses of antiquity, such as architectural spolia, "new uses preserve," and the following sections offer some paths towards those new uses.[10] In the next section, I share some impressions based on my own experiences in the classroom; in the next section, I build on these anecdotes to argue for a brand of reception which I have termed "reception without the classics."[11] By this I mean a kind of reception that looks for classical inheritances in places where they are so deeply embedded in our day-to-day existence that they are no longer visible, worn smooth by use and convention. My specific example is drawn from the study of media, especially television, but its applicability could be extended, especially if it can combine the *kleos aphthiton* of philology and literary criticism with the hard coin of commercial viability. The advantage is two-fold: in the absence of good popular philology, we see not only the extreme phenomena of Alt-Right appropriation of the Classics,[12] but also a growing distance between the best scholarly insights in the field and their everyday application.[13] Classicists have no monopoly on the Classics, but they do have a duty to guide the public in their best and most responsible uses, and to do so, we must be accessible not only to those who wish to pursue the profession at its highest levels, but also to professionals and others who simply wish to be informed by it.

Gen-Z Achilles and the Literary-Critical Gap

The classroom is a primary space in which to practice reception of any kind, and one of the most important venues for engaging with the myths of authority surrounding classical literature, history, and culture.[14] From 2013 to 2019, I taught a first-year seminar on Classics and *Game of Thrones* ("Classics and Modern Fantasy," or "Games of Thrones") in my home institution. The experience was both a pleasant reprieve from my "real" job of reading Livy, and part of a broader attempt to think about how classical literature survives and exists beyond the groves of academe. First-year seminars at my university are a requirement for all entering students, and as a result enrollment is nearly always randomized to some degree: each orientation cycle opens a small number of slots in each seminar, so students are not always able to select among courses based on interest. This administrative reality—which exists in any course but is exaggerated in the first-year seminar context—means that students have a range of backgrounds and expectations, very loosely unified by high-school curricula, and that the instructor can neither assume any familiarity with the material nor reading skills, nor indeed any prior interest.

The seminar, and the book that grew out of it, was based on the premise that *Game of Thrones* is a prose epic of sorts and can profitably be read against a range of classical epics, from the *Iliad* to Statius' *Thebaid*.[15] This premise is rooted partially in the works' scope and thematic interest, but *Game of Thrones* also has various acknowledged classical influences, from Hadrian's Wall to Martin's ideas of moral ambiguity, for which he cites the fight between Achilles and Hector in the *Iliad*.[16] Even without these parallels, however, the combination is actually more intuitive than it seems, since both types of text are world-building within established generic constraints. They are further long and capacious works, both as texts and in any screen adaptation, which is to say that they present various obstacles to access for example: the intimidation factor of a long book, populated by multiple characters with foreign names and complicated relationships. While substantially different in generic form, milieu, and period, both *Game of Thrones* and the classical epic tradition in fact offer the same type of "sand-box": an opportunity to experiment with critical reading skills, at an increasing scale, external demands, and degree of difficulty.

One of the key challenges of this kind of seminar is establishing community and working mastery early on. One of the first assignments, therefore, is "crowd-reading" the *Iliad*: each student reads a single book of the epic, pulling out relevant quotes about a particular topic. We happened to be discussing foodways as a point of entry into the poem and as a basis for comparison with the introduction of the Dothraki in *Game of Thrones*, but what was most striking was that, as I walked in the door, I was shocked—and indeed delighted—to find eighteen almost complete strangers talking about the *Iliad* with verve and vigor. They felt it was incredible, even though when pressed, they admitted to being very confused about specific details: the repetition of name and genealogies, who was on what side, what the gods were doing, and so forth. What they *were* picking up on, of course, was the power of great poetry to capture the imagination and continuously resonate beyond its time and place of production. As discussion unfolded, however, it became clear that, while they remained enthused about the poem, they were markedly less so about any of the people in it.

Achilles makes for a particularly good example: the students found him petulant, petty, childish in his anger, and insensitively focused on his own tragedy in a landscape of tremendous loss and suffering—much of which inflicted by his sulking if not by his fighting skills, which they found almost robotically alienating. This is very far from the standard ancient response to Achilles, which is by and large glorifying, and far, too, from scholarly modern interpretations: for example (and these are in no way a comprehensive view of the scholarly lay of the land), that Achilles refuses to re-enter battle because of a commitment to his public word;[17] that his anger is an index of humanity or lack thereof;[18] that his trauma is a microcosm of the timeless truths about human condition in extreme duress;[19] and that book 24 offers some kind of redemption and recognition of the universalities of human suffering.[20] Strikingly, it was not a response informed by explicit political consideration, especially of our then-specific moment: the students didn't note that Achilles is, for example, a slaver, a trafficker in women, or that there is never any absolution or reparation to be made for what are effectively war crimes against an entire nation.[21]

At the risk of over-simplification, I would like to suggest that this response is characteristic of student experience in general, and specifically of the generation currently inhabiting college classrooms. Whatever label we wish to use for this generation (or more specifically, this cohort of people in the affluent anglophone west, principally the United States), they are broadly characterized by anxiety, an awareness of social, political, or environmental injustice, and a feeling of being locked out of the securities afforded to previous generations: employment, housing, environmental stability, functional government, and so on. Taking my students as a representative sample (with due caveats), we might reasonably wonder why these students articulated their responses to the *Iliad* in terms of character, plot, and personal morality, rather than through the prevalent concerns of their generation. We could explain away this mismatch by appealing to the eternal truths immanent in literature of the best quality, but it would be by far more profitable to point to the literary-critical habits students bring with them into the college classroom, and to acknowledge that these skills, where they exist, do not provide students the language to connect those immediate concerns with the literature they are reading.[22] We might in fact go further and suggest that today's students have a sense of mismatch between the values they hold and the text in front of them, but are unsure how that mismatch can be articulated, or even if it should. In other words, they lack the critical vocabulary to describe their frustration, whether in the lofty speech of academia or in the politicized language of the internet.

Where this language appears is through entertainment media, a world with much constructive similarities to the myth-making we see in antiquity.[23] *Game of Thrones* supplies a wealth of combative young man to compare to Achilles, or indeed any other hero; I have discussed elsewhere the epic resonances in the subplot of Renly Baratheon and Loras Tyrell.[24] But the most interesting parallel I have heard for Achilles out of the *Game of Thrones* universe is Prince Joffrey, a young man who (like Achilles) is capable of great atrocities with few discernible feelings. Indeed, he is instinctively understood by viewers of *Game of Thrones* to be tyrannical in precisely the same ways that tyrants were described by the ancients: cruel, violent, petty, overly attached to his mother, and happy to exercise his vices on those less fortunate.[25]

What does it mean to read Achilles as tyrannical, the possessor of tremendous privilege, and the beneficiary of a quirk of fate and divine machinations? The answer merits its own paper, but what it highlights is the generational mismatch between the way professional classicists read their texts—a way conditioned by what we know of ancient society and its literary culture, scholia, intertexts, reception, and so forth—and the way fresher eyes today see the text: as exciting but nevertheless alienating products of a very different culture, time, and place, that can nevertheless both resonate with contemporary values and hold up a mirror to examine the language we use to talk about them. This mismatch is far from a bad thing, and in fact one that we should lean into and celebrate. We should recognize too the shortcuts that make it possible, in this case the comparison to *Game of Thrones*, but also supportive classroom environments and directed discussions.

However much the ancients venerated him, Achilles was not a "good person" by modern standards, and few of us would want our sons growing into the mold of an epic hero. Achilles does represent, however, the persistence of our fascination with this kind of character: an action hero with a minimal yet compelling interior world, whose personal emotional outburst we can enjoy, and thereby ignore or excuse the background of pain and destruction in which that hero operates. In this, Achilles, and by extension all the other heroes and characters of classical literature, are the stuff of modern media entertainment, and they speak to us, if we can see it, in the same language as the pixelated avatars we consume at the cinema or on our TV screen.

Reception by Analogy

The idea that classical literature has direct inheritors in modern-day Hollywood is not new; in addition to the wealth of movies on Greek and Roman subjects, from *Ben Hur* to *Troy*, classical materials have offered a template for popular entertainment franchises like Star Wars or Harry Potter.[26] But what does it mean, exactly, to think of these products of the entertainment media as a way of teaching not classical reception, but classical literature? There are various methodological commitments entailed here, and I want to draw attention to two in particular: the possibilities in trying to teach the Classics "without the Classics" on the one hand, and the long-standing disciplinary boundary between "literary criticism" as a set of methods and "classical reception" as a specific practice.

Both methodologies ultimately derive from our collective training as philologists or historians, which means that, broadly speaking, we are more attracted to reference than we are to allusion:[27] that is, we privilege texts or phenomena with a demonstrable connection (verbal or visual, but preferably explicit) to the classics than we are to those texts which are just 'like' the classics, however much we enjoy them or use them as paraphernalia to our engagement with the classics. Teaching *Star Wars* or *Game of Thrones* as a method of teaching classical literature therefore involves decentering the canonical and replacing it with something that instinctively feels not-classical, and therefore relevant only in a general way, rather than in the detailed specifics with which we are normally accustomed to work.[28] More worryingly, it might suggest that the study of the classics can easily be replaced with the study of something else—Hollywood media franchising, for example—without any meaningful loss to the public, but only to those of us who love the ancient world.

My answer to this legitimate objection is first, that this dynamic is inherent to literary criticism itself, especially in a field as tradition obsessed as classical literature. It has taken us many years to acknowledge Vergil as a member of the canon on an equal footing to Homer, and decades more to admit Vergil's successors to the same hallowed circle.[29] Second, modern entertainment media offers some very intriguing parallels and challenges to classical literature and its story-telling mechanisms, and more importantly they offer students a vision of myth-making that is immersive and instinctive. It gives them a language in which to speak about culture and literature that cuts through the initial confusion of jargon and foreignness, and allows them to approach the classical material from a position of empowerment rather than as a confused observer.

One of the constant complaints I hear when approaching new material (this holds as true when I teach epic as when I teach Roman history), is that there are too many new names. And so there are. One way to honor this difficulty is to minimize the names (a technique characteristic of some modern art, especially the introspective novel); David Potter's *Ancient Rome: A New History* (2018) has even gone so far as to eliminate those names altogether, speaking instead of a "consul" going to war or a "dictator" issuing a systemic reform. Such an approach can be helpful, but it also has a flattening effect of what was after all a very interpersonal society. But it is also the case that these same students can, for example, have an encyclopedic knowledge of the bannermen of House Stark, as well as of Westeros' geography, climatology, archaeology, religious structures, and political regimes—all of which they might ascribe to the usefulness of various online wikis, but which fundamentally comes from the pleasure and playfulness of repeated exposure to the same literary material. Students have all the cognitive resources required to sort out which heroes are on which side of the Trojan War, or the connection between the various branches of the Julio-Claudian clan, well enough, at least, to enjoy the *Iliad* or Tacitus, and we serve their interests best when we teach them in ways to empower them to practice and transfer these skills from one medium to another. We serve our own interests, as well, when we acknowledge that play is one of the most effective methods of human learning and import that into our classrooms.[30]

Another frequent observation is that those names are often used genealogically, "so and so, the son of such and such," thus burdening them with more information than they need, slowing them down and breaking the fourth wall, thus frustrating pleasure and progress. In fact, this is a standard technique in modern TV and film production, where "beats" or actions, work hard to re-establish relevant knowledge for the audience.[31] This is why, for instance, Giles keeps telling Buffy that he is her Watcher, or why characters explain things to each other that should be obvious to people in such positions (usually to women, as it happens). The fact that students don't recognize this technique when they see it is interesting and invites some conversations about the cultural context that make these triggers invisible. Above all, however, it opens up a conversation about audience and performance that establishes the college student or general reader as an intended member of that audience, removed in time, space and culture, but nevertheless an invited participant rather than an intruder. For constituencies that have historically been excluded as audiences, like women or people of color, such a perspective has especially critical value. In turn, we can then talk about the ways modern media practices its own protocols of exclusion and discrimination and use those conversation to see the ancient disenfranchised as a living presence rather than a forgotten absence.

Teaching by analogy is something we all do instinctively but not consciously, and the practice deserves some theorization, if nothing else because it demands that we reflect upon our own views of the classics, however we define this set of texts, objects, and practices. But perhaps its greatest virtue is that it directly and visibly translates what literary critics do, in the classroom or in the library, into the stuff of contemporary global phenomena. Classical literature is a vast myth-making, world-building enterprise, and it preserves its versions of the ancient world by drawing people into itself, and making them want to know more, to expand the purview of the story and make it their own. This is what all literature does, before and after the Greeks and Romans, only translated to the peculiar language of our specific place and time. Conversely, it allows us to imagine the work of literary criticism, and especially of the fusty classical kind, as relevant to some vast economic interests (just, incidentally, as it was back then) as well as to the private and specific pleasure of the individual consumer, a back and forth acutely relevant for the fate of contemporary classics, and especially for those parts of it which have long segregated themselves from the common crowd.

Notes

1   The scholarship on the afterlives of the classical world is vast and rapidly growing. Besides the traditional focus on (for example) Dante and Milton that characterized the inception of reception studies (Martindale (1993)), the afterlives of classical literature reach firmly to the present and across the globe: Jenkins (2015) offers a compelling survey of classical receptions in the modern American imagination; Johnson (2019) covers classical receptions in Australia and New Zealand; Torlone, Munteanu and Dutsch (2017) do so for Eastern and Balkan Europe; Greenwood (2010) for the Anglophone Caribbean. Examples can be multiplied, but see Greenwood (2013: 359) for the idea of omni-local reception: "omni-localism emphasizes the unpredictable circulation of works of art and ideas, in which any given reception is "local" in relation to every other reception, while together they form part of a larger whole through their connection with a single text or work of art." The therapeutic value of classical literature stretched back to Freud (and to the ancient themselves, who saw poetry as a salve for misery, e.g., Theoc. 11.1) and reaches today to the medical humanities (e.g. McCaffrey (2020)) and projects such as *The Warrior Chorus*, which works with veterans to perform Greek drama.

2 To dip your toes into this debate, see Connolly (2005), Felski (2008), Brooks (2014), Hammond and Kim (2014); *contra*: Fish (1999). Gibson (2014) demonstrates the importance of moral teaching in prose composition exercises in the ancient world.
3 André (1966) remains the standard on *otium*; Hanchey (2013) analyses *otium* as a transcendence of political realities, not a separation from them. Both *otium* and literary production were political in antiquity: drama aimed to educate citizens and interrogate state power, history offered lessons for the budding politician and general. Whatever the genre, however, the Romans imagined the writing itself as part of a world of *otium*.
4 Lanham (1993: 154–94).
5 Connolly (2005: 103–34); (2014).
6 Suffice here to point out Seneca's failure with Nero, Marcus Aurelius' with Commodus, or Aristotle's with Alexander the Great to see how variable educational *exempla* were in antiquity. On education in the Hellenistic and Roman world, see Morgan (1999); on epic as educational vehicle, especially for teaching masculinity, see Keith (2009) 8–35; for modern media doing the same, see Giaccardi (2016).
7 Bradley (2010); Richard (2009). For the challenges of this legacy in the classroom, see Rabinowitz and McHardy (2014).
8 For the *Iliad* specifically as a reflection on "community organization," see Hammer (2002). The military jingoism of the Roman state is nowhere better seen than in the triumphal procession: see Beard (2007), Pittinger (2009), Lange and Vervaet (2014).
9 Dwyer (2006).
10 Esch (2011: 26).
11 Haimson Lushkov (2021: 4–7); (2017b: 310–13).
12 Zuckerberg (2018).
13 E.g. Brown et al. (2018).
14 Forde (2019).
15 Haimson Lushkov (2017a). Earlier iterations included some readings in Tacitus' *Histories* and Shakespeare's War of the Roses plays, with a focus on the theme of civil war, but that proved too unwieldy in the format. Focusing on epic provided both a tighter focus and the opportunity to scaffold the readings.
16 The Wall: "The Wall predates anything else. I can trace back the inspiration for that to 1981. I was in England visiting a friend, and as we approached the border of England and Scotland, we stopped to see Hadrian's Wall. I stood up there and I tried to imagine what it was like to be a Roman legionary, standing on this wall, looking at these distant hills. It was a very profound feeling. For the Romans at that time, this was the end of civilization; it was the end of the world. We know that there were Scots beyond the hills, but they didn't know that. It could have been any kind of monster. It was the sense of this barrier against dark forces – it planted something in

me. But when you write fantasy, everything is bigger and more colorful, so I took the Wall and made it three times as long and 700 feet high, and made it out of ice." (http://www.rollingstone.com/tv/news/george-r-r-martin-the-rolling-stone-interview-20140423)

    Moral ambiguity: "I've been always very impressed by Homer and his *Iliad*, especially the scene of the fight between Achilles and Hektor. Who is the hero and who is the villain? That's the power of the story and I wanted something similar to my books. The hero of one side is the villain of the other side" (as quoted in Kozak (2017: 22); for morally compromised heroism of the classical sort in *Game of Thrones* cf. Haimson Lushkov (2017a: 122–35).

17 Scodel (1989).
18 Muellner (2016).
19 Vandiver (2013: 228–83).
20 Macleod (1983).
21 Such view of the Trojan war tends to find expression in modern retellings of the Trojan War, e.g. Pat Barker's feminist *Silence of the Girls* (2018), which focuses on the story of Briseis, Achilles' concubine. For Achilles' profiteering from slavery: 21.78–80: καί μ' ἐπέρασσας ἄνευθεν ἄγων πατρός τε φίλων τε / Λῆμνον ἐς ἠγαθέην, ἑκατόμβοιον δέ τοι ἦλφον / νῦν δὲ λύμην τρὶς τόσσα πορών ("...and you have led me far from father or friend, and sold me to Lemnos, where I fetched you the price of a hecatomb; but now I have bought my freedom for three time as much...").
22 I should clarify that the issue was not a reluctance to discuss issues that might be perceived as controversial, political, or private—as a group and as individuals, and given a supportive environment, students are generally happy enough to discuss difficult topics. If a gap exists, it is between their lived experience and their reading lives.
23 E.g. Jenkins (2006); Kozak (2017).
24 Haimson Lushkov (2017b).
25 Dunkle (1967); Gwyn (1991).
26 Charles (2015); Olechowka (2016). The tragic elements of Harry Potter are highlighted by J. K. Rowling herself, who uses quotations from Aeschylus' *Libation Bearers* as the epigraph for *Harry Potter and the Deathly Hallows*. Jenkins (2016) notes the prevalence of the *Odyssey* as a story-type, including Star Wars.
27 For the difference, see Hinds (1998: 17–51).
28 See e.g., Charles Martindale's objection that "...many of the films about antiquity that classicists tend to study are neither important works of art nor complexly interesting, and much that is written about them is frankly banal. One suspects that film is often chosen, not without considerable condescension, out of a somewhat desperate desire for 'relevance' or modernity—proof that Classics is somehow still

'alive'" ((2013) 177). One need not disagree with Martindale completely to appreciate that "important" or "complexly interesting" vary, depending on age and experience, and that, at least to begin with, there is value in meeting students where they are, even if that falls short of Milton.
29 An overview of the last century of Vergilian scholarship can be found in Farrell (2001); for the pivot in the study of Vergil's successors, see Hardie (1992).
30 Stegelin (2005).
31 Kozak (2017: 6–9).

Bibliography

Introduction

Alcoff, L. (1991), "The Problem of Speaking for Others," *Cultural Critique* 20: 5–32.
Barthes, R. (1977), "The Death of the Author," in *Image, Music, Text*, 142–8, New York: Fontana.
Bourdieu, P. (1977), "The Economics of Linguistic Exchange," *Information (International Social Science Council)* 16: 650.
Burke, K. ([1950] 1969), *A Rhetoric of Motives*, Berkeley and Los Angeles: University of California Press.
Burke, K. ([1941] 1973), *The Philosophy of Literary Form*, Berkeley and Los Angeles: University of California Press.
Chartier, R. (1994), *The Order of Books: Readers, Authors, and Libraries in Europe between the Fourteenth and Eighteenth Centuries*, trans. L. G. Cochrane, Stanford: Stanford University Press, 1994.
Chartier, R. (2014), *The Author's Hand and the Printer's Mind: Transformations of the Written Word in Early Modern Europe*, trans. L. G. Cochrane, Cambridge: Polity.
Ernout, A., and A. Meillet ([1905] 1951), *Dictionnaire étymologique de la langue latine. Histoire des mots*, Paris: Klincksieck.
Fish, S. (1980), *Is There a Text in This Class? The Authority of Interpretive Communities*, Cambridge, MA: Harvard University Press.
Foucault, M. (1977), "What is an Author?," trans. D. F. Bouchard and S. Simon, in *Language, Counter-Memory, Practice*, ed. D. F. Bouchard, 113–38, Oxford: Blackwell.
Iser, W. (1978), *The Act of Reading: A Theory of Aesthetic Response*, Baltimore: Johns Hopkins University Press.
Jauss, H. R. (1982), *Toward an Aesthetic of Reception*, trans. T. Bahti, Minneapolis: University of Minnesota Press.
Lowenstein, J. (2002), *The Author's Due: Printing and the Prehistory of Copyright*, Chicago: University of Chicago Press.
Minnis, A. (2012), *Medieval Theory of Authorship: Scholastic Literary Attitudes in the Later Middle Ages*, Pennsylvania: University of Pennsylvania Press.
Nettleship, H. (1889), *Contributions to Latin Lexicography*, Oxford: Clarendon Press.
Rose, M. (1993), *Authors and Owners: The Invention of Copyright*, Cambridge, MA: Harvard University Press.
Roth, P. (2012), "An Open Letter to Wikipedia". *The New Yorker*, Sept. 6, 2012. Available online: https://www.newyorker.com/books/page-turner/an-open-letter-to-wikipedia (accessed March 22, 2022).

Scanlon, L. (1994), *Narrative, Authority and Power: The Medieval Exemplum and the Chaucerian Tradition*, Cambridge: Cambridge University Press.

Selle, H. (2008), "Open Content? Ancient Thinking on Copyright," *Revue internationale des droits de l'antiquité*, 55: 469–84.

Chapter 1

Bal, M. (2017), *Narratology: Introduction to the Theory of Narrative*, 4th edn, Toronto: University of Toronto Press.

Berti, E. (2018), *Lo stile e l'uomo: quattro epistole letterarie di Seneca*, Pisa: Scuola Normale Superiore.

Booth, W. C. (1983), *The Rhetoric of Fiction*, 2nd edn, Chicago and London: University of Chicago Press.

Bowen, A. J. (1992), *Plutarch: The Malice of Herodotus*, Warminster: Aris and Phillips.

Bowie, E. L. (2016), "Plutarch's Simonides: A Versatile Gentleman," in J. Opsomer, G. Roskam and F. Titchener (eds), *A Versatile Gentleman: Consistency in Plutarch's Writing*, 71–87, Leuven: Leuven University Press.

Damon, C. (2009), "Déjà vu or déjà lu? History as Intertext," *Papers of the Langford Latin Seminar* 14: 375–88.

de Lacy, P. (1952), "Biography and Tragedy in Plutarch," *American Journal of Philology* 73: 159–71.

Dickie, M. (1981), "The Disavowal of *invidia* in Roman Iamb and Satire," *Papers of the Liverpool Latin Seminar* 3: 183–208.

Duursma, G. (2019), "Fonti sulla vita e fortuna di Sallustio," in R. Funari and G. Duursma (eds), *Lectissimus pensator verborum: tre studi su Sallustio*, 181–326, Bologna: Pàtron.

Goodyear, F. R. D. (1972), *The Annals of Tacitus I: Annals 1.1–54*, Cambridge: Cambridge University Press.

Grossart, P. (1998), *Die Trügreden in der Odyssee und ihr Rezeption in der antiken Literatur*, Bern: P. Lang.

Hogan, B. (2010), "The Presentation of Self in the Age of Social Media: Distinguishing Performances and Exhibitions Online," *Bulletin of Science, Technology, and Society* 30: 377–86.

Ingenkamp, H.-G. (2016), "*De Plutarchi Malignitate*," in J. Opsomer, G. Roskam and F. Titchener (eds), *A Versatile Gentleman: Consistency in Plutarch's Writing*, 229–42, Leuven: Leuven University Press.

Jacoby, F. (1909), "Herodotos (7)," *RE* Suppl. II: 205–520; reprinted in *Griechische Historiker*, 7–164, Stuttgart, 1956.

de Jong, I. J. F. (2014), *Narratology and Classics*, Oxford: Oxford University Press.

Kirkland, N. B. (2019), "The Character of Tradition in Plutarch's *On the Malice of Herodotus*," *American Journal of Philology* 140: 477–511.
Kurfess, A. (1957), *C. Sallusti Crispi Catilina, Iugurtha, Fragmenta Ampliora*, 3rd edn, Leipzig: Teubner.
Luce, T. J. (1989), "Ancient Views on the Causes of Bias in Historical Writing," *Classical Philology* 84: 16–31.
Marincola, J. (1997), *Authority and Tradition in Ancient Historiography*, Cambridge: Cambridge University Press.
Marincola, J. (2009), "Historiography," in A. Erskine (ed.), *A Companion to Ancient History*, 13–22, Malden, MA: Wiley-Blackwell.
Marincola, J. (2015), "Plutarch and the Historian's Character," in R. Ash, J. Mossman and F. B. Titchener (eds), *Fame and Infamy: Essays for Christopher Pelling on Characterization in Greek and Roman Biography and Historiography*, 83–95, Oxford: Oxford University Press.
Marincola, J. (2016), "History without Malice? Plutarch Rewrites the Battle of Plataea," in J. Priestley and V. Zali (eds), *Brill's Companion to the Reception of Herodotus in Antiquity and Beyond*, 101–19, Leiden/Boston: Brill.
Marincola, J. (2017), *On Writing History from Herodotus to Herodian*, Harmondsworth: Penguin.
Nichols, T. (2017), *The Death of Expertise*, New York/Oxford: Oxford University Press.
Opsomer, J., G. Roskam, and F. B. Titchener, eds (2016), *A Versatile Gentleman: Consistency in Plutarch's Writing*, Leuven: Leuven University Press.
Priestley, J. (2014), *Herodotus and Hellenistic Culture*, Oxford: Oxford University Press.
Riemann, K.-A. (1967), *Das herodoteische Geschichtswerk in der Antike*, Diss. Munich.
de Romilly, J. (1975), *Magic and Rhetoric in Ancient Greece*, Cambridge, MA, and London: Harvard University Press.
Romm, J. (1992), *The Edges of the Earth in Ancient Thought*, Princeton: Princeton University Press.
Trilling, L. (1972), *Sincerity and Authenticity*, Cambridge, MA, and London: Harvard University Press.
Van der Stockt, L. (1992), *Twinkling and Twilight: Plutarch's Reflections on Literature*, Brussels: Palais der Academien.
Varga, S. and C. Guignon, (2020), "Authenticity," in *Stanford Encyclopedia of Philosophy*. Available online: https://plato.stanford.edu/entries/authenticity/ (accessed December 1, 2021).
Wiseman, T. P. (1979), *Clio's Cosmetics: Three Studies in Greco-Roman Literature*, Leicester and Totowa, NJ: Rowman and Littlefield.
Woodman, A. J. (1988), *Rhetoric in Classical Historiography: Four Studies*, London, Sydney, and Portland: Croom Helm and Areopagitica Press.

Chapter 2

Ahl, F. (2010), "Quintilian and Lucan," in N. Hömke and C. Reitz (eds), *Lucan's Bellum Civile: Between Epic Tradition and Aesthetic Innovation*, 1–15, Berlin and Boston: de Gruyter.

Arthur, L. (2020), Credita res auctore suo est: *Narrative Authority in the Poetry of Ovid*, DPhil Diss., Oxford.

Asso, P. (2011), "And Then It Rained Shields: Revising Nature and Roman Myth," in P. Asso (ed.), *Brill's Companion to Lucan*, 383–93, Leiden and Boston: Brill.

Bartsch, S. (1997), *Ideology in Cold Blood: A Reading of Lucan's Civil War*, Cambridge, MA: Harvard University Press.

Batstone, W. (2009), "Postmodern Historiographical Theory and the Roman Historians," in A. Feldherr (ed.), *The Cambridge Companion to the Roman Historians*, 24–40, Cambridge: Cambridge University Press.

Bourdieu, P. (1984), *Distinction: A Social Critique of the Judgement of Taste*, London: Routledge.

Charaudeau, P., and D. Maingueneau, eds (2002), *Dictionnaire d'analyse du discours*, Paris: Éditions du Seuil.

Conte, G. B. (1994), *Genres and Readers: Lucretius, Love Elegy, Pliny's Encyclopaedia*, Baltimore: Johns Hopkins University Press.

Davies, J. P. (2004), *Rome's Religious History: Livy, Tacitus, and Ammianus on their Gods*, Cambridge: Cambridge University Press.

Dunkle, J. R. (1967), "The Greek Tyrant and Roman Political Invective of the Late Republic," *Transactions of the American Philological Association* 98: 151–71.

Dunkle, J. R. (1971), "The Rhetorical Tyrant in Roman Historiography: Sallust, Livy and Tacitus," *Classical World* 65: 12–20.

Frazer Jr., R. M. (1966), "Nero the Artist-Criminal," *Classical Journal* 62: 17–20.

Feldherr, A., ed. (2009), *The Cambridge Companion to the Roman Historians*, Cambridge: Cambridge University Press.

Habinek, T. N. (2005), *Ancient Rhetoric and Oratory*, Malden, MA, and Oxford: Blackwell.

Hardie, P. (1997), "Questions of Authority: The Invention of Tradition in Ovid's *Metamorphoses* 15," in T. Habinek and A. Schiesaro (eds), *The Roman Cultural Revolution*, 182–98, Cambridge: Cambridge University Press.

Harries, B. (1989), "Causation and the Authority of the Poet in Ovid's *Fasti*," *Classical Quarterly* 39: 164–85.

Hartog, F. (1999), *L'Histoire d'Homère à Augustin*, Paris: Éditions du Seuil.

Johansson, B. (2013), *Damning Domitian: A Historiographical Study of Three Aspects of His Reign*, PhD Diss., University of Queensland.

Laird, A. (2009), 'The Rhetoric of Roman Historiography," in A. Feldherr (ed.), *The Cambridge Companion to the Roman Historians*, 197–213, Cambridge: Cambridge University Press.

Levene, D. S. (1993), *Religion in Livy*, Leiden: Brill.
Lowrie, M. (2009), *Writing, Performance, and Authority in Augustan Rome*, Cambridge: Cambridge University Press.
Maingueneau, D. (2021), *Discours et analyse du discours. Une introduction*, 2nd edn, Paris: Armand Colin.
Marincola, J. (1997), *Authority and Tradition in Ancient Historiography*, Cambridge: Cambridge University Press.
Rao, V. N. B., D. Shulman, and S. Subrahmanyam (2001), *Textures of Time: Writing History in South India 1600-1800*, Ranikhet: Other Press.
Reed, J. D. (2011), "The *Bellum Civile* as a Roman Epic," in P. Asso (ed.), *Brill's Companion to Lucan*, 21-31, Leiden and Boston: Brill.
Saller. R. (2000), "Domitian and His Successors: Methodological Traps in Assessing Emperors," *American Journal of Ancient History* 15: 4-18.
Southern, P. (1997), *Domitian: Tragic Tyrant*, London and New York: Routledge.
Tabacco, R. (1985), "Il tiranno nelle declamazioni di scuola in lingua latina," *Memorie dell'Accademia delle Scienze di Torino*, 9: 1-141.
Vieira, B. V. G. (2013), "A epopeia histórica em Roma de Névio a Lucano," in Silva, G. V. and Leiter, L. R., *As múltiplas faces do discurso em Roma*, 25-42, Vitória: EDUFES.
Wiseman, T. P. (1979), *Clio's Cosmetics: Three Studies in Greco-Roman Literature*, Leicester and Totowa, NJ: Rowman and Littlefield.
Woodman, A. J. (1988), *Rhetoric in Classical Historiography: Four Studies*, London, Sydney, and Portland: Areopagitica Press.

Chapter 3

Aub, M. (1999), *Jusep Torres Campalans*, Barcelona: Destino.
Balzac, H. de (1971), *Lost Illusions,* trans. H. H. Hunt, London: Penguin.
Barthes, R. (1989), *The Rustle of Language*, Berkeley and Los Angeles: University of California Press.
Bénichou, P. (1996), *Le Sacre de l'écrivain (1750-1830): Essai sur l'avènement d'un pouvoir spirituel laïque dans la France moderne*, Paris: Gallimard.
Bini, E., trans. (2013), *Aristóteles, Retórica*, São Paulo: Edipro.
Borges, J. L. (1985), *Biblioteca personal (prólogos)*, Madrid: Alianza.
Canguilhem, G. (2009), *Idéologie et rationalité dans l'histoire des sciences de la vie*, Paris: J. Vrin.
Caro Baroja, J. (1992), *Las falsificaciones de la historia (en relación con la de España)*, Barcelona: Seix Barral.
de Certeau, M. (1988), *The Writing of History*, New York: Columbia University Press.
Chartier, R. (2006), "Jack Cade, the Skin of a Dead Lamb, and the Hatred for Writing," *Shakespeare Studies* 34: 77-89.

Chartier, R. (2015), *La main de l'auteur et l'esprit de l'imprimeur*, Paris: Gallimard.
Condorcet (2012), *Political Writings*, edited by S. Lukes and N. Urbinati, Cambridge: Cambridge University Press.
Detienne, M. (1996), *The Masters of Truth in Archaic Greece*, New York: Zone Books.
Detienne, M. (2006), *Les Maîtres de vérité dans la Grèce archaïque*, Paris: Librairie générale française.
Farge, A. (2019), *Vies oubliées. Au cœur du XVIIIe siècle*, Paris: La Découverte.
Foucault, M. (1979), "The Life of Infamous Men," in M. Morris and P. Patton (eds), *Michel Foucault. Power, Truth, Strategy*, 76–91, Sydney: Feral Publications.
Foucault, M. (1981), "The Order of Discourse," in R. Young (ed.), *Untying the Text: A Post-Structuralist Reader*, 48–78, Boston and London: Routledge.
Ginzburg, C. (1999), *History, Rhetoric, and Proof*, Hanover and London: University Press of New England.
Ginzburg, C. (2000), *Rapporti di forza. Storia, retorica, prova*, Milan: Feltrinelli.
Ginzburg, C. (2012), *Threads and Traces. True False Fictive*, Berkeley, Los Angeles, and London: University of California Press.
Grafton, A. (1990), *Forgers and Critics: Creativity and Duplicity in Western Scholarship*, Princeton: Princeton University Press.
Greenblatt, S. (1988), *Shakespearean Negotiations: The Circulation of Social Energy in Renaissance England*, Berkeley and Los Angeles: University of California Press.
Hansen, J. A. (2001), "Barroco, Neobarroco e Outras Ruínas," *Teresa. Revista de Literatura Brasileira* 2: 10–66.
Hansen, J. A. (2004), "Notas sobre el 'Barroco'," *Revista de Filología de la Universidad de la Laguna* 22: 111–32.
Hansen, J. A. (2019), *Agudezas Seiscentistas e Outros Ensaios*, São Paulo: EDUSP.
Hartog, F. (2013), *Croire en l'histoire*, Paris: Flammarion.
Kant, I. (1996), *Practical Philosophy*, edited by M. J. Gregor, Cambridge: Cambridge University Press.
Kennedy, G. A., trans. (1991), *Aristotle: On Rhetoric. A Theory of Civic Discourse*, Oxford: Oxford University Press.
Lilti, A. (2014), *Figures publiques: L'invention de la célébrité (1750–1850)*, Paris: Fayard.
Malgat, G. (1999), "*Jusep Torres Campalans* de Max Aub: sur les traces d'un peintre disparu," *Exils et migrations ibériques au XXe siècle* 6: 299–319.
Michon, P. (1984), *Vies minuscules*, Paris: Gallimard.
Quignard, P. (1984), *Les tablettes de bois d'Apronenia Avita*, Paris: Gallimard.
Quignard, P. (2019), *La vie n'est pas une biographie*, Paris: Editions Galilée.
Riccoboni, A. (1588), *Aristotelis Artis Rhetoricae Libri Tres*, Frankfurt: Wechelus.
Ricoeur, P. (2004), *Memory, History, Forgetting*, Chicago: Chicago University Press.
Ricoeur, P. (2015), "Memory, History, Oblivion," in R. Kearney and B. Treanor (eds), *Carnal Hermeneutics*, 148–57, New York: Fordham University Press.
Roberts, W. R. (1924), *Aristotle. Rhetorica*, Oxford: Clarendon Press.

Schwob, M. (2004), *Vies imaginaires*, edited by J.-P. Bertrand and G. Prunelle, Paris: Flammarion.
Spence, J. D. (1978), *The Death of Woman Wang*, London: Penguin.
Thiesse, A.-M. (2019), *La Fabrique de l'écrivain national. Entre littérature et politique*, Paris: Gallimard.
Vernant, J.-P. (1969), "Detienne, 'Les Maîtres de vérité' [compte-rendu]," *Archives de sociologie des religions* 28: 194–6.
Vidal-Naquet, P. (1993), *Assassins of Memory. Essays on the Denial of the Holocaust*, New York: Columbia University Press.
Yerushalmi, Y. (1984), *Zakhor: Histoire juive et mémoire juive*, Paris: La Découverte.

Chapter 4

Bainton, R H. (1953), *Hunted Heretic: The Life and Death of Michael Servetus*, Boston: Bacon Press.
Barral-Baron, Marie (2014), *L'Enfer d'Érasme: L'humanisme chrétien face à l'histoire*, Geneva: Librairie Droz.
Berger, Klaus (2005), *Formen und Gattungen im Neuen Testament*, Tübingen: Francke.
Biagioni, M. and Felici, L. (2012), *La Riforma radicale nell'Europa del Cinquecento*, Rome-Bari: Laterza.
Bietenholz, P.G. (2009), *Encounters with a Radical Erasmus: Erasmus' Work as a Source of Radical Thought in Early Modern Europe*, Toronto: University of Toronto Press.
Chomarat, J. (1981), *Grammaire et rhétorique chez Érasme*, 2 vols, Paris: Les Belles Lettres.
Cohn, N. (1970), *The Pursuit of the Millennium: Revolutionary Millenarians and Mystical Anarchists of the Middle Ages*, Oxford: Oxford University Press.
Calvin, J. (1852), *Commentaries on the Prophet Daniel*, trans. T. Myers, Edinburgh: Calvin Translation Society.
Calvin, J. (1889), *Opera quae supersunt omnia*. vol. 41, edited by E. Cunitz, J. W. Baum, and E. W. E. Reuss, Braunschweig: Schwetschke.
Erasmus, D. (2018), *The Correspondence of Erasmus. Letters 2472–2634. April 1531– March 1532*, translated by C. Fantazzi, edited by J. M. Estes, Toronto, Buffalo, and London: University of Toronto Press.
Erasmus, D. (1938), *The Complete Letters of Erasmus. Letters 2357–2634*, vol. 9, edited by P. S. Allen, Oxford: Oxford University Press.
Foucault, M. (1995), *Discipline and Punish: The Birth of the Prison*, translated by A. Sheridan, 2nd edn, New York: Vintage Books.
Friedman, J. (1975), "Archangel Michael vs. the Antichrist: the Servetan Drama of the Apocalypse," *Renaissance and Reformation* 11: 45–51.

Friedman, J. (1974), "Michael Servetus: Exegete of Divine History," *Church History* 43: 460–9.

Friedman, J. (1978), *Michael Servetus: A Case Study in Total Heresy*, Geneva: Droz.

Friesen, A. (1998), *Erasmus, the Anabaptists, and the Great Commission*, Grand Rapids: W. B. Eerdmans Pub.

Gowens, K. (1998), "Perceiving the Past: Renaissance Humanism after the 'Cognitive Turn,'" *American Historical Review* 103: 55–82.

Gregory, B. (2001), *Salvation at Stake: Christian Martyrdom in Early Modern Europe*, Cambridge, MA, and London: Harvard University Press.

Hay, D., ed. (1965), *The Renaissance Debate*, New York: Holt Rinehart and Winston Inc.

Hillar, M. (2002), *Michael Servetus: Intellectual Giant, Humanist, and Martyr*, Lanham, New York, and Oxford: University Press of America.

Klassen, W. (1992), *Living at the End of the Ages: Apocalyptic Expectation in the Radical Reformation*, Lanham, New York, and London: University Press of America.

Levine, J. M. (1997), "Erasmus and the Problem of the *Johannine Comma*," *Journal of the History of Ideas* 58: 573–96.

Sartorelli, E. C. (2011), "Strategies of Construction and Legitimization of an Ethos of True Christian in the *Restitutio* of Michael Servetus," in J. Naya and M. Hillar (eds), *Michael Servetus: Heartfelt. Proceedings of the International Servetus Congress, Barcelona, October 20–1, 2006*, Lanham, Boulder, New York, Toronto, and Plymouth: University Press of America.

Servet, M. (1980), *Restitución del Cristianismo*, trans. A. Alcalá and L. Betes, Madrid: Fundación Universitária Española.

Servetus, M. ([1790] 1966), *Christianismi Restitutio*, facsimile edn, Frankfurt: Minerva.

Servetus, M. ([1531] 1965), *De Trinitatis erroribus libri septem*, facsimile edn, Frankfurt: Minerva.

Servetus, M. ([1532] 1965), *Dialogorum de Trinitate libri duo. De iustitia Regni Christi, Capitula Quatuor*, facsimile edn, Frankfurt: Minerva.

Teichman, J. (1986), *Pacifism and the Just War: A Study in Applied Philosophy*, Oxford: Blackwell.

Williams, G. H. (1962), *The Radical Reformation*, Philadelphia: Westminster Press.

Williams, G. H. and A. M. Mergal, eds (1957), *Spiritual and Anabaptist Writers*, Louisville: Westminster John Knox Press.

Wyneken, K. H. (1992), "Calvin and Anabaptism," in R. C. Gamble (ed.), *Calvin's Opponents*, 2–13, New York: Garland.

Chapter 5

Adler, E. (2016), *Classics, the Culture Wars, and Beyond*, Michigan: University of Michigan Press.

Appiah, K. A. (2018), *The Lies that Bind: Rethinking Identity,* London: Profile Books.
Bell, D. (2020), *Dreamworlds of Race: Empire and the Utopian Destiny of Anglo-Americans*, Princeton: Princeton University Press.
Blouin, K. (2018), "Civilization: What's up with that?," *Everyday Orientalism*, Feb. 23, 2018. Available online: https://everydayorientalism.wordpress.com/2018/02/23/civilization-whats-up-with-that/ (accessed March 28, 2022).
Bloxham, J. (2018), *Ancient Greece and American Conservatism: Classical Influence on the Modern Right*, London: Bloomsbury.
Bonnett, A. (2014), *The Idea of the West: Culture, Politics and History*, London: Bloomsbury.
Ferguson, N. (2012), *Civilization: The West and the Rest*, London: Penguin.
Greenberg, R., and Y. Hamilakis (2022), *Archaeology, Nation, and Race: Confronting the Past, Decolonizing the Future in Greece and Israel*, Cambridge: Cambridge University Press.
Hanson, V. D., and J. Heath (2001), *Who Killed Homer? The Demise of Classical Education and the Recovery of Greek Wisdom*, San Francisco, CA: Encounter Books.
Huntington, S. (1996), *The Clash of Civilizations*, London: Simon and Schuster.
Kennedy, R.F. (2019), "'On the History of 'Western Civilization,' Part 1," *Classics at the Intersections*, April 3, 2019. Available online: https://rfkclassics.blogspot.com/2019/04/on-history-of-western-civilization-part.html (accessed March 28, 2022).
Knox, B. (1993), *The Oldest Dead White European Males and Other Reflections on the Classics*, New York: W. W. Norton & Company.
Kuhl, S. (2002), *The Nazi Connection: Eugenics, American Racism, and German National Socialism*, Oxford: Oxford University Press.
Lavin, T. (2021), *Culture Warlords: My Journey into the Dark Web of White Supremacy.* London: Hachette UK.
Lefkowitz, M. (2008), *History Lesson*, New Haven and London: Yale University Press.
McInerney, J. (2014), *A Companion to Ethnicity in the Ancient Mediterranean*, Chichester, West Sussex: John Wiley & Sons.
Morris, I. (2010), *Why the West Rules—for Now: The Patterns of History and What they Reveal about the Future*, London: Profile Books.
Sen, A. (2007), *Identity and Violence: The Illusion of Destiny*, London: Penguin.
Sheth, F. (2009), *Towards a Political Philosophy of Race,* Albany, NY: SUNY Press.
Smith, R. O. (2019), "Disintegrating the Hyphen: The 'Judeo-Christian Tradition' and the Christian Colonization of Judaism," *ReOrient* 5: 73–91.
Stoddard, T. L. (1920), *The Rising Tide of Color: Against White World-Supremacy.* New York: C. Scribner's Sons.
Taylor, C. M. (1981), "WEB DuBois's Challenge to Scientific Racism," *Journal of Black Studies* 11: 449–60.
Thompson, W. S. (1917). "Race Suicide in the United States." *The Scientific Monthly* vol. 5 no. 1: 22–35.

Weller, R.C. (2017), "'Western' and 'White Civilization': White Nationalism and Eurocentrism at the Crossroads," in R. C. Weller (ed.), *21st-Century Narratives of World History*, 35–80, London: Palgrave Macmillan.

Zuckerberg, D. (2018), *Not All Dead White Men*, Cambridge, MA: Harvard University Press.

Chapter 6

Allison, G. (2017), *Destined for War: Can America and China Escape Thucydides's Trap?*, Boston: Mariner Books.

Appleby, L. (2021), "Academics and Social Media Hostility: Should We Give Up or Do More?," *British Medical Journal Opinion*, August 23, 2021. Available online: https://blogs.bmj.com/bmj/2021/08/23/academics-and-social-media-hostility-should-we-give-up-or-do-more/ (accessed March 14, 2022).

Bateman, O. (2017), "The Young Academic's Twitter Conundrum," *The Atlantic*, May 10, 2017. Available online: https://www.theatlantic.com/education/archive/2017/05/the-young-academics-twitter-conundrum/525924/ (accessed March 14, 2022).

Derakhshan, H. (2015), "The Web We Have To Save," *Medium*, July 14, 2015. Available online: https://medium.com/matter/the-web-we-have-to-save-2eb1fe15a426 (accessed March 14, 2022).

Ecker, U. K. H., et al. (2022), "The Psychological Drivers of Misinformation Belief and its Resistance to Correction," *Nature Reviews Psychology* 1: 13–29.

Farrell, H. J., and R. Perlstein (2018), "Our Hackable Political Future," *New York Times*, February 4, 2018. Available online: https://www.nytimes.com/2018/02/04/opinion/hacking-politics-future.html (accessed March 14, 2022).

Geva, H., G. Oestreicher-Singer, and M. Saar-Tsechansky (2019), "Using Retweets When Shaping Our Online Persona: Topic Modeling Approach," *MIS Quarterly* 43: 501–24.

Golder, S. *et al.* (2017), "Attitudes Toward the Ethics of Research Using Social Media: a Systematic Review," *Journal of Medical Internet Research* 19: e195.

Jaffe, S. N. (2017), "The Risks and Rewards of Thucydides' History of the Peloponnesian War," *War on the Rocks*, July 6, 2017. Available online: https://warontherocks.com/2017/07/the-risks-and-rewards-of-thucydides-history-of-the-peloponnesian-war/ (accessed March 14, 2022).

Kaurin, P. M. (2014), *The Warrior, Military Ethics and Contemporary Warfare: Achilles Goes Asymmetrical*, London and New York: Routledge.

Keene, E. (2015), "The Reception of Thucydides in the History of International Relations," in C. Lee and N. Morley (eds), *A Handbook to the Reception of Thucydides*, 355–72, Chichester, West Sussex: Malden-Oxford.

Lee, C. and N. Morley, eds (2015), *A Handbook to the Reception of Thucydides*, Chichester, West Sussex: Malden-Oxford.

Metzger, M. J., and A. Flanagin (2013), "Credibility and Trust of Information," *Journal of Pragmatics* 59: 210–20.

Mirowski, P. (2019), "Hell is Truth Seen Too Late," *Boundary 2* 46: 1–53.

Morley, N. (2013), "Thucydides Quote Unquote," *Arion* 20: 9–36.

Morley, N. (2014), *Thucydides and the Idea of History*, London: Tauris.

Morley, N. (2018), "Legitimising War and Defending Peace: Thucydides in WWI and After," *Classical Receptions Journal* 10: 415–34.

Morley, N. (2021), "Thucydides' Legacy in Grand Strategy," in T. Balzacq and R. R. Krebs (eds), *The Oxford Handbook of Grand Strategy*, 41–56, Oxford: Oxford University Press.

Noordally, B. (2020), "On the Toxicity of the 'Warrior' Ethos," *The Wavell Room*, April 28, 2020. Available online: https://wavellroom.com/2020/04/28/on-the-toxicity-of-the-warrior-ethos (accessed March 14, 2022).

Nyhan, B., and J. Reifler (2015), "When Corrections Fail: The Persistence of Political Misconceptions," *Political Behavior* 32: 303–30.

Peck, A. (2017), *The Memetic Vernacular: Everyday Argument in the Digital Age*, PhD Diss., University of Wisconsin at Madison.

Ruback, T. (2015), "Thucydides Our Father, Thucydides Our Shibboleth," in C. Lee and N. Morley (eds), *A Handbook to the Reception of Thucydides*, 406–24, Chichester, West Sussex: Malden-Oxford.

Sloan, L. et al. (2013), "Knowing the Tweeters: Deriving Sociologically Relevant Demographics from Twitter," *Sociological Research Online* 18: 74–84.

Sparks, J. R., and C. S. Areni (2008), "Style versus Substance: Multiple Roles of Language Power in Persuasion," *Journal of Applied Social Psychology* 38: 37–60.

Sperber, D. et al. (2010), "Epistemic Vigilance," *Mind Language* 25: 359–93.

Toma, C. L., and J. D. D'Angelo (2015), "Tell-Tale Words: Linguistic Cues Used to Infer the Expertise of Online Medical Advice," *Journal of Language and Social Psychology* 34: 25–45.

Townsend, L., and C. Wallace (2018), *Social Media Research: A Guide to Ethics*, Aberdeen. Available online: https://www.gla.ac.uk/media/Media_487729_smxx.pdf (accessed March 30, 2022).

Weismueller, J. et al. (2021), "What Makes People Share Political Content on Social Media? The Role of Emotion, Authority and Ideology," *Computers in Human Behavior* 129: 107150.

Williams, M. L. et al. (2017), "Users' Views of Ethics in Social Media Research: Informed Consent, Anonymity, and Harm," in K. Woodfield (ed.), *The Ethics of Online Research (Advances in Research Ethics and Integrity, Vol. 2)*, 27–52, Bingley, UK: Emerald.

Wu, L. et al. (2019), "Misinformation in Social Media: Definition, Manipulation, and Detection," *ACM SIGKDD Explorations Newsletter* 21: 80–90.

Chapter 7

Badian, E. (1993), "Livy and Augustus," in W. Schuller (ed.), *Livius: Aspekte seines Werkes*, 9–38, Konstanz: Universitätsverlag.

Borra, E. et al. (2015), "Societal Controversies in Wikipedia Articles," in *Proceedings of the 33rd Annual ACM Conference on Human Factors in Computing Systems (CHI '15)*, 193–6, New York: Association for Computing Machinery.

Briscoe, J. (2008), *A Commentary on Livy Books 38–40*, Oxford: Oxford University Press.

Cornell. T. J. (1995), *The Beginnings of Rome: Italy and Rome from the Bronze Age to the Punic Wars (c. 1000–264 BC)*, London and New York: Routledge.

Doody, A. (2009), "Pliny's Natural History: *Enkuklios Paideia* and the Ancient Encyclopedia," *Journal of the History of Ideas* 70 (1): 1–21.

Edwards, C. (1996), *Writing Rome: Textual Approaches to the City*, Cambridge: Cambridge University Press.

Feldherr, A. (1998), *Spectacle and Society in Livy's History*, Berkeley and Los Angeles: University of California Press.

Forsythe, G. (1999), *Livy and Early Rome: A Study in Historical Method and Judgment*, Stuttgart: Franz Steiner Verlag.

Forsythe, G. (2007), "The Army and Centuriate Organization in Early Rome," in P. Erdkamp (ed.), *A Companion to the Roman Army*, 24–42, Oxford: Blackwell.

Giles, J. (2005), "Internet Encyclopaedias Go Head to Head: Jimmy Wales' Wikipedia Comes Close to Britannica in Terms of the Accuracy of Its Science Entries," *Nature* 438/7070: 900–01.

Glassner, J. J. (2004), *Mesopotamian Chronicles* (n. 19), Atlanta: Society of Biblical Lit.

Gustafsson K. (2020), "International Reconciliation on the Internet? Ontological Security, Attribution and the Construction of War Memory Narratives in Wikipedia," *International Relations* 34 (1): 3–24.

Howard, A. A. (1906), "Valerius Antias and Livy," *Harvard Studies in Classical Philology* 17: 161–82.

Jahn, O. (1867), "Satura," *Hermes* 2: 225–51.

Keen, A. (2011), *The Cult of the Amateur: How Blogs, MySpace, YouTube and the Rest of Today's User Generated Media are Killing Our Culture*, London: Nicholas Brealey.

Laroche, R. A. (1977), "Valerius Antias and His Numerical Totals: A Reappraisal," *Historia* 26 (3): 358–68.

Last, H. (1945), "The Servian Reforms," *Journal of Roman Studies* 35: 30–48.

Leo, F. (1904), "Livius und Horaz über die Vorgeschichte des römischen Dramas," *Hermes* 39 (1): 63–77.

Levene, D. S. (2010), *Livy on the Hannibalic War*, Oxford: Oxford University Press.

Luce, T. J. (1977), *Livy: The Composition of His History*, Princeton: Princeton University Press.

Luce, T. J. (1989), "Ancient Views on the Causes of Bias in Historical Writing," *Classical Philology* 84 (1): 16–31.

Marincola, J. (1997), *Authority and Tradition in Ancient Historiography*, Cambridge: Cambridge University Press.

Marincola, J. (2009), "Ancient Audiences and Expectations," in A. Feldherr (ed.), *The Cambridge Companion to the Roman Historians*, 11–23, Cambridge: Cambridge University Press.

Marques, J. B. (2012), "Trabalhando com a história romana na Wikipédia: uma experiência em conhecimento colaborativo na universidade," *Revista História Hoje* 2 (3): 329–46.

Marques, J. B., and O. S. Louvem (2013), "A Wikipédia como diálogo entre universidade e sociedade: uma experiência em extensão universitári," *Anais do Workshop de Informática na Escola* 1 (1).

Marques, J. B. (2019), "Representação e visibilidade do mundo antigo na Wikipédia," *Revista do Museu de Arqueologia e Etnologia* 32: 2–17.

Miles, G. (1995), *Livy: Reconstructing Early Rome*, Ithaca: Cornell University Press.

Mommsen, T. (1887), *Römisches Staatsrecht*, III.1., 3rd edn, Leipzig: Hirzel.

Moreno, A. (2021), "¿*Patavinitas* más allá de Quintiliano? Sobre las interpretaciones morales del último siglo," *Politica Antica* 11: 191–220.

Muñiz Coello, J. (2009), "Livio, Polión y la *patavinitas*. El relato historiográfico," *Klio* 91 (1): 125–43.

Nielsen, F. Å. (2019), "Wikipedia Research and Tools: Review and Comments (January 24, 2019)," Danmarks Tekniske Universitet. Available online: http://www2.imm.dtu.dk/pubdb/edoc/imm6012.pdf (accessed January 14, 2022).

Nissenbaum, H. (1999), "The Meaning of Anonymity in an Information Age," *The Information Society*, 15 (2): 141–4.

Oakley, S. P. (1997), *A Commentary on Livy: Book IX*, vol. 3, Oxford: Oxford University Press.

Ogilvie, R. M. (1965), *A Commentary on Livy I–V*, Oxford: Clarendon Press.

Pailler, J.-M. (1988), *Bacchanalia. La répression de 186 av. J.-C. à Rome et en Italie: vestiges, images, tradition*, Rome: École Française de Rome.

Panciera, K. et al. (2009), "Wikipedians Are Born, Not Made: A Study of Power Editors on Wikipedia," *Proceedings of the ACM 2009 International Conference on Supporting Group Work*, Association for Computing Machinery.

Pelling, C. B. R. (2018), "Dionysius on Regime Change," in R. Hunter and C. de Jonge (eds), *Dionysius of Halicarnassus and Augustan Rome. Rhetoric, Criticism and Historiography*, 203–20, Cambridge and New York: Cambridge University Press.

Peterson, H. (1961), "Livy and Augustus," *Transactions of the American Philological Association* 91, 440–52.

Priedhorsky, R. et al. (2007), "Creating, Destroying, and Restoring Value in Wikipedia," in *Proceedings of the 2007 International ACM Conference on Supporting Group Work*, 259–68, Association for Computing Machinery.

Raaflaub, K. A., ed. (2013), *Thinking, Recording, and Writing History in the Ancient World*, Malden, MA, and Oxford: John Wiley & Sons.

Reagle, J. M. (2010), *Good Faith Collaboration: The Culture of Wikipedia*: Cambridge, MA, and London: MIT Press.

Rich, J. W. (2013), "Valerius Antias," in T. J. Cornell (ed.), *The Fragments of the Roman Historians: Introduction. Vol. 1*, 293–304, Oxford: Oxford University Press.

Richardson, J. H. (2018), "Valerius Antias and the Archives," *Materiali e discussioni per l'analisi dei testi classici* 80: 57–80.

Ridley, R. T. (2013), "The Historian's Silences: What Livy Did Not Know—Or Chose Not to Tell," *Journal of Ancient History* 1 (1): 27–52.

Roller, M. B. (2004), "Exemplarity in Roman Culture: The Cases of Horatius Cocles and Cloelia," *Classical Philology* 99 (1): 1–56.

Sailor, D. (2006), "Dirty Linen, Fabrication, and the Authorities of Livy and Augustus," *Transactions of the American Philological Association* 136 (2): 329–88.

Sanger, L. (2009), "The Fate of Expertise after Wikipedia," *Episteme* 6 (1): 52–73.

van Seters, J. (1997), *In Search of History: Historiography in the Ancient World and the Origins of Biblical History*, Winona Lake, IN: Eisenbrauns.

Smith, C. (1997), "Servius Tullius, Cleisthenes and the Emergence of the *polis*," in L. G. Mitchell and P. J. Rhodes (eds), *The Development of the Polis in Archaic Greece*, 208–16, London: Routledge.

Syme, R. (1959), "Livy and Augustus," *Harvard Studies in Classical Philology*, 64: 27–87 (repr. in (1979) *Roman Papers*, 1, 400–54, Oxford).

Tränkle, H. (1977), *Livius und Polybios*, Basel and Stuttgart: Schwabe.

Tsikerdekis, M. (2013), "The Effects of Perceived Anonymity and Anonymity States on Conformity and Groupthink in Online Communities: a Wikipedia Study," *Journal of the Association for Information Science and Technology* 64 (5): 1001–15.

Walsh, P. G. (1961), "Livy and Augustus," *Transactions of the American Philological Association* 4: 440–52.

Walsh, P. G. (1974), *Livy (New Surveys in the Classics)*, Oxford: Oxford University Press.

Walsh, P. G. (1996), "Making a Drama out of a Crisis: Livy on the Bacchanalia," *Greece & Rome*, 43: 188–203.

Waszink, J. H. (1948), "Varro, Livy and Tertullian on the History of Roman Dramatic Art," *Vigiliae Christianae*, 2: 224–42.

West, M. L. (1999), "The Invention of Homer," *Classical Quarterly* 49 (2): 364–82.

Woodman, A. J. (2011), "Cicero and the Writing of History," in J. Marincola (ed.) *Greek and Roman Historiography*, Oxford: Oxford University Press.

Yasseri, Taha et al. (2012), "Dynamics of Conflicts in Wikipedia," *PloS one*, 7 (6): e38869.

Chapter 8

Blue Star Storm (2015), "Effective Ways to Deal with CyberBullies," *SketNet*, 3 February. Available online: http://sketweb.com/effective-ways-to-deal-with-cyber-bullies (accessed November 24, 2021).

Cohen, E. (1995), *Law, Violence, and Community in Classical Athens*, Berkeley: University of California Press.
Cohen, E. (2000), *The Athenian Nation*, Princeton: Oxford Journals.
Daley, B. (2019), "Online Trolling Used to be Funny, but Now the Term Refers to Something Far More Sinister," *The Conversation*, February 3. Available online: https://theconversation.com/online-trolling-used-to-be-funny-but-now-the-term- refers-to-something-far-more-sinister-110272 (accessed December 17, 2021).
Dynel, M. (2016), "'Trolling is Not Stupid': Internet Trolling as the Art of Deception Serving Entertainment," *Intercultural Pragmatics* 13: 353–81.
Eemeran, F. E. van (2001), *Crucial Concepts in Argumentation Theory*, Amsterdam: Amsterdam University Press.
Gleason, M. (1995), *Making Men: Sophists and Self-Presentation in Ancient Rome*, Princeton: Princeton University Press.
Graham, P. (2008), "How I Disagree," *ConceptDraw Solution Park*. Available online: https://www.conceptdraw.com/examples/paul-graham-disagreement-pyramid (accessed November 24, 2021).
Gray, K. L. (2012), "Deviant Bodies, Stigmatized Identities, and Racist Acts: Examining the Experiences of African-American Gamers in Xbox Live," *New Review of Hypermedia and Multimedia* 18: 261–76.
Gray, K. L. (2014), *Race, Gender, and Deviance in Xbox Live: Theoretical Perspectives from the Virtual Margins*, London and New York: Routledge.
Huizinga, J. (1980), *Homo Ludens: A Study of the Play-Element in Culture*, London and Boston: Routledge and Kegan Paul.
Johnstone, H.W. (1978), *Validity and Rhetoric in Philosophical Argument*, University Park, PA: Dialogue.
Johnstone, S. (1999), *Disputes and Democracy: The Consequences of Litigation in Ancient Athens*, Austin: University of Texas Press.
Just, R. (1991), *Women in Athenian Law and Life*, London and New York: Routledge.
Koerner, B. (2018), "It Started as An Online Prank. Then It Turned Deadly," in *Wired*, October 28. Available online: https://www.wired.com/story/swatting-deadly-online-gaming-prank (accessed November 24, 2021).
Leigh, K. (2016), "Fantastic Internet Trolls and How to Fight Them. Trolling Trolls for Pleasure, Sport, and Peace of Mind," *Medium*, November 16. Available online: https://medium.com/snarketing/fantastic-internet-trolls-and-how-to-fight-them-bf0a221819ac (accessed November 24, 2021).
McGinn, A. J. (2014), "Prostitution: Controversies and New Approaches," in T. Hubbard (ed.), *A Companion to Greek and Roman Sexualities*, 83–101, Malden, MA and Oxford: Wiley-Blackwell.
Morrison, P. (2015), "Privilege Makes Them Do It—What a Study of Internet Trolls Reveals," in *LA Times*, July 1, 2015. Available online: https://www.latimes.com/opinion/op-ed/la-oe-morrison-phillips-20150701-column.html (accessed November 24, 2021).

Ortiz, S. M. (2020), "Trolling as a Collective Form of Harassment: An Inductive Study of How Online Users Understand Trolling," *Social Media + Society* 6 (2).

Phillips, W. (2015), *This Is Why We Can't Have Nice Things: Mapping the Relationship between Online Trolling and Mainstream Culture*, Cambridge MA: MIT Press.

Pothast, E. (2017), "Inverse Trolling Techniques for Net Activists," *Medium*, January 23, 2017. Available online: https://medium.com/form-and-resonance/advanced-trolling-techniques-for-net-activists-9dd43ed4d81d (accessed November 24, 2021).

Serafim, A. (2019), "Thespians in the Law-Court: Sincerity, Community and Persuasion in Attic Forensic Oratory," in A. Markantonatos, A. and E. Volonaki, E. (eds), *Poet and Orator: A Symbiotic Relationship in Democratic* Athens, 347–64, Berlin and Boston, MA: De Gruyter.

Sloane, T. O. (2001), *The Encyclopedia of Rhetoric*, Oxford: Oxford University Press.

Worthen, W.B. (2015), *Modern Drama and the Rhetoric of Theater*, Berkeley: University of California Press.

Walton, D. (1998), *Ad Hominem Arguments*: Tuscaloosa: University of Alabama Press.

Walton, D. (2001), "*Ad Hominem* Argument," in T. O. Sloane (ed.), *Encyclopedia of Rhetoric*, vol.1, 1–4, Oxford: Oxford University Press.

Woods, J., and D. Walton (1982), *Argument: The Logic of the Fallacies*, Toronto: McGraw-Hill Ryerson.

Chapter 9

Alfaro, L. (with R. Andújar) (2020), *The Greek Trilogy of Luis Alfaro: Electricidad; Oedipus El Rey; Mojada*, London: Bloomsbury Methuen Drama.

André, J.-M. (1966), *L'Otium dans la vie morale et intellectuelle à Rome des origines à l'époque augustéenne*, Paris: Presses Universitaires de France.

Balsdon, J. P. V. D. (1960), "*Auctoritas, Dignitas, Otium*," *Classical Quarterly* 10: 43–50.

Barker, P. (2018), *Silence of the Girls*, New York: Doubleday.

Beard, M. (2007), *The Roman Triumph*, Cambridge, MA; Harvard University Press.

Bradley, M. (2010), *Classics and Imperialism in the British Empire*, Oxford: Oxford University Press.

Brilliant, R., and D. Kinney (2011), *Reuse Value: Spolia and Appropriation in Art and Architecture from Constantine to Sherrie Levine*, Farnham and Burlington, VT: Ashgate.

Brooks, P., with H. Jewett (2014), *The Humanities and Public Life*, New York: Fordham University Press.

Brown, S., L. Stevens, and P. Maclaran, P. (2018), "Epic Aspects of Retail Encounters: The Iliad of Hollister," *Journal of Retailing* 94: 58–72.

Charles, M. B. (2015), "Remembering and Restoring the Republic: 'Star Wars' and Rome," *Classical World* 108: 281–98.
Connolly, J. (2005), "Border Wars: Politics, Literature, and the Public," *Transactions of the American Philological Association* 135: 103–34.
Connolly, J. (2014), *The Life of Roman Republicanism*, Princeton: Princeton University Press.
Dunkle, J. (1967), "The Greek Tyrant and Roman Political Invective of the Late Republic," *Transactions and Proceedings of the American Classical Association* 98: 151–71.
Dwyer, R. (2006), *Filming the Gods: Religion and Indian Cinema*, London: Routledge.
Esch, A. (2011), "On the Reuse of Antiquity: The Perspectives of the Archaeologist and of the Historian," in R. Brilliant and D. Kinney (eds), *Reuse Value: Spolia and Appropriation in Art and Architecture from Constantine to Sherrie Levine*, 13–32, Farnham and Burlington, VT: Ashgate.
Farrell, J. (2001), "The Vergilian Century," *Vergilius* 47: 11–28.
Felski, R. (2008), *The Uses of Literature*, Chichester: Wiley-Blackwell.
Fish, S. (1999), *Political Correctness: Literary Study and Political Change*, Cambridge, MA: Harvard University Press.
Forde, S. (2019), "Using Classical Reception to Develop Students' Engagement with Classical Literature in Translation," *Journal of Classics Teaching* 20: 14–23.
Giaccardi, S., et al. (2016), "Media and Modern Manhood: Testing Associations Between Media Consumption and Young Men's Acceptance of Traditional Gender Ideologies," *Sex Roles* 75: 151–63.
Gibson, C. (2014), "Better Living Through Prose Composition? Moral and Compositional Pedagogy in Ancient Greek and Roman progymnasmata," *Rhetorica* 32: 1–30.
Greenwood, E. (2010), *Afro-Greeks. Dialogues between Anglophone Caribbean Literature and Classics in the Twentieth Century*, Oxford: Oxford University Press.
Greenwood, E. (2013), "Afterword: Omni-Local Classical Receptions," *Classical Receptions Journal* 5: 354–61.
Gwyn, W. B. (1991), "Cruel Nero: The Concept of the Tyrant and the Image of Nero in Western Political Thought," *History of Political Thought* 12: 421–55.
Hanchey, D. (2013), "'*Otium*' as Civic and Personal Stability in Cicero's Dialogues," *Classical World* 106: 171–97.
Hammer, D. (2002), *The Iliad as Politics: The Performance of Political Thought*, Norman: University of Oklahoma Press.
Hammond, M., and S. Kim, eds (2014), *Rethinking Empathy through Literature*, New York: Routledge.
Haimson Lushkov, A. (2017a), *You Win or You Die: The Ancient World of Game of Thrones*, London: I. B. Tauris.
Haimson Lushkov, A. (2017b), "Genre, Mimesis, and Intertext in Vergil and G.R.R. Martin," in B. Rogers and B. Stevens (eds), *Classical Themes in Modern Fantasy*, 308–24, Oxford: Oxford University Press.

Haimson Lushkov, A. (2021), "Not Cricket, not Classics? A Case Study in the Limits of Reception," *Classical Receptions Journal* 13: 555–70.
Hardie, P. (1992), *The Epic Successors of Virgil*, Cambridge: Cambridge University Press.
Hinds, S. (1998), *Allusion and Intertext: Dynamics of Appropriation in Roman Poetry*, Cambridge: Cambridge University Press.
Jenkins, H. (2016), *Convergence Culture: Where Old and New Media Collide*, New York: New York University Press.
Jenkins, T. E. (2015), *Antiquity Now: The Classical World in the Contemporary American Imagination*, Cambridge: Cambridge University Press.
Johnson, M. (2019), *Antipodean Antiquities: Classical Reception Down Under*, London: Bloomsbury.
Keith, A. M. (2009), *Engendering Rome: Women in Latin Epic*, Cambridge: Cambridge University Press.
Kozak, L. (2017), *Experiencing Hektor: Character in the Iliad*, London: Bloomsbury.
Lange, C. H., and F. J. Vervaet, eds (2014), *The Roman Republican Triumph and Its Contexts*, Rome: Edizioni Quasar.
Lanham, R. (1993), *The Electronic Word: Democracy, Technology, and the Arts*, Chicago: Chicago University Press.
Louge, C. (1981), *War Music: An Account of Homer's Iliad*, New York: Farrar, Strauss and Giroux.
Macleod, C. (1983), *Homer: Iliad XXIV*, Cambridge: Cambridge University Press.
Marciniak, K., ed. (2016), *Our Mythical Childhood. . .: The Classics and Literature for Children and Young Adults*, Leiden-Boston: Brill.
Martindale, C. (2013), "Reception—A New Humanism? Receptivity, Pedagogy, the Transhistorical," *Classical Receptions Journal* 5: 169–83.
McCaffrey, G. (2020), *Nursing and the Humanities*, London: Routledge.
Muellner, L. (2016), *The Anger of Achilles: Mênis in Greek Epic*, Cambridge, MA: Harvard University Press.
Morgan, T. (1999), *Literate Education in the Hellenistic and Roman Worlds*, Cambridge: Cambridge University Press.
Olechowka, E. (2016), "J. K. Rowling Exposes the World to Classical Antiquity," in Marciniak, K. (ed.), *Our Mythical Childhood. . .: The Classics and Literature for Children and Young Adults*, Leiden: Brill.
Pittinger, M. R. P. (2009), *Contested Triumphs: Politics, Pageantry, and Performance in Livy's Republican Rome*, Berkeley: University of California Press.
Potter, D. (2018), *Ancient Rome: A New History*, New York: Thames and Hudson, 3rd ed. (1st ed. 2009).
Rabinowitz, N. and F. McHardy, eds (2014), *From Abortion to Pederasty: Addressing Difficult Topics in the Classics Classroom*, Columbus: Ohio State University Press.
Raji, W. (2005), "Africanizing 'Antigone': Postcolonial Discourse and Strategies of Indigenizing a Western Classic," *Research in African Literatures* 36: 135–54.

Richard, C. (2009), *The Golden Age of the Classics in America: Greece, Rome, and the Antebellum United States*, Cambridge, MA: Harvard University Press.

Rogers, B., and B. Stevens, eds (2017), *Classical Themes in Modern Fantasy*, Oxford: Oxford University Press.

Scodel, R. (1989), "The Word of Achilles," *Classical Philology* 84: 91–9.

Stegelin, D. A. (2005), "Making the Case for Play Policy: Research-Based Reasons to Support Play-Based Environments," *Young Children* 60: 76–85.

Torlone, Z., D. Munteanu, and D. Dutsch, eds (2017), *A Handbook to Classical Reception in Eastern and Central Europe*, Chichester: Wiley Blackwell.

Torrance, I., and D. O'Rourke, eds (2020), *Classics and Irish Politics, 1916–2016*. Oxford: Oxford University Press.

Vandiver, E. (2013), *Stand in the Trench, Achilles: Classical Receptions in British Poetry of the Great War*, Oxford: Oxford University Press.

Zuckerberg, D. (2018), *Not All Dead White Men*, Cambridge, MA: Harvard University Press.

Index

Achilles 17, 161–4, 169, 177
ad hominem argument 144–7, 149, 152, 154
Adeimantus 21–3, 25
Adler, E. 100
Aeneid 39, 160
Aeschines 149
Aeschylus 19, 169
Africa 11, 34, 89, 92, 94, 95, 98, 100, 102
Ahl, F. 32
Alberto, P. F. 49
Alcinous 24
Alcoff, L. 4
Alexander the Great 140, 168
Alexandre Júnior, M. 49
Alt-Right 106, 160, 161
alternative facts 9
Alvarado, S. de 62
Analogy 165, 167
Anchises 36
Andocides 151
Angola 135, 137
Annales 91
anonymity 2–3, 71, 75–8, 79, 82–3, 128, 137, 139, 144, 148, 153, 155
Antichrist 71, 75–8, 79, 82–3
Antiphon 147
anti-Semitism 107
ANZAC Day 112
Apollo 36
Appiah, A. 96, 103, 105, 106
Archangel Michael 77, 78, 80
Aristides 19
Aristotle 13, 35, 31, 39, 40, 47–50, 52, 62, 65, 66, 104, 112, 144, 146, 150, 155, 156, 168
Armistice Day 112
Artaud, A. 43
Assaracus 36, 41
Asso, P. 34
Athena 19–20, 35

Athens 20–1, 22, 123, 133, 146, 147, 148
Aub, M. 61–2
auctor 2
auctoritas 2, 138
Auden, W. H. 110
Aurelius, M., emperor 168
Aurelius Victor 32
Australia 90, 92, 95, 114, 167

Bacchanalia 131–2, 135, 137
Bachelard, G. 45
Balzac, H. de 55
Barker, P 169
Barthes, R. 3, 47, 59, 61
Bartsch, S. 36–7
Bataille, G. 43
belles-lettres 53–4
Ben Hur 165
Bénichou, P. 54
Bernal, M. 97
Bini, E. 49
biography 10, 54, 56, 61, 73, 110, 111, 116, 117, 118
Black Lives Matter 123
Bloch, M. 50
Blog 99, 107, 111, 143
Bloor, D. 45, 65
Bloxham, J. 95, 96, 103
Boeotia 16
Boethius 144
Bonaventure, St. 5
Bonnet, A. 87, 93, 104
Borges, J. L. 55, 62
Bourdieu, P. 4, 39
Brexit 114, 119
Briseis 169
Broyard, A. 2
Bucer, M. 69
Buffy 166
Burke, K. 3–4
Butler, W. F. 113, 122, 124

Cade, J. 52–3
Caligula, emperor 32
Calvin, J. 73–4, 79, 81
Camillus, M. Furius 34, 35, 41
Campalans, J. T. 61–2, 68
Canguilhem, G. 44–5
canon 9, 15, 33, 38, 46, 87, 96, 98, 159, 165
captatio benevolentiae 151
Caribbean 100, 167
Cassius Dio 32
Certeau, M. de 45, 60
Champel 74
Chapelain, J. 58
charis 151
Charon 20, 21
Charpentier, G. 55
Chicago Forum Council 106
China 89, 94, 102, 109, 112
Chios 19–20
Christianity 69, 70, 71, 73–6, 78, 79, 80, 81, 96, 98, 103–4, 108
Cicero 3, 15, 30, 32, 37–8, 41–2
Cleisthenes 133
Cohn, N. 72
Cold War 101, 106
Commodus 32, 168
communism 101, 108
Condell, H. 52
Condorcet, N. de 46, 47
Congregation of St. Maur 50
Connolly, J. 160
Constantine 50, 71, 76, 77, 83
Conte, G. B. 30
copyright 3, 5, 139
Corbyn, J. 117
Corinth 16, 21–3, 25, 42
Cornell, T. 133, 137
Covid-19 114, 117, 139
Crimea 114
Ctesias of Cnidus 15, 28
Culture Wars 96, 99, 104, 107, 108
cyber-bullying 145, 147, 153, 155
Cyme 19
Cypris 23
Cyprus 20
Cyrus 19–20

Dante 39, 167
decolonization 1, 3

Demosthenes 151
Derrida, J. 47
Detienne, M. 44
Diamond, J. 89, 94
Diodorus Siculus 15, 23, 42
Dionysius of Halicarnassus 10, 11–12, 18, 38, 124, 132
do Nascimento Pena, A. 49
Domitian 32
Donation of Constantine 50
Dothraki 162
Du Bois, W. E. B. 94
Dufour, M. 47, 48
Dunkle, J. R. 32
Duris of Samos 12
Dylan, B. 117

Eemeran, F. E. van 145
Egypt 15, 75, 82, 89, 94, 139
El Dorado 149
Elagabalus, emperor 32
elocutio 33
Ephorus 12
Erasmus of Rotterdam 69–71, 73–4, 76, 81
Euphrates 99
exaedificatio 140
exceptionalism 88, 90, 94, 95, 102, 103

Fabius Pictor, Q. 129
fake news 1, 119, 143, 152
falsehood 11, 16, 20, 22, 24, 35, 43, 57, 88, 103, 112, 118, 119, 124, 130, 148, 155
Farge, A. 59, 68
Faunus 33
Febvre, L. 91–2
Feldherr, A. 132, 134
Ferguson, N. 90, 91–2, 94, 95, 98, 106
Fertile Crescent 89
Fescennine verses 135
fides 49, 66, 80
Flavius Josephus 38
Forum, Roman 31
Foucault, M. 43–5, 56–7, 58–9, 64, 80
Freiburg 73
Freud, S. 167
Fronto, M. Cornelius 39
Funeral Oration of Pericles 12, 110, 112, 114
Furetière, A. 53, 59

Galba, emperor 32
Game of Thrones 161–2, 164, 165, 169
Gastaldi, S. 65
Gauls 34, 102
Geneva 73, 74, 79, 80
Giles 166
Ginzburg, C. 45–8, 50, 51, 54–5, 57–61, 65
Giza 102
Glaucon 19
Gleason, M. 153
globalization 92, 107, 159
Goodyear, F. 10–11
Grafton, R. 52
Graham, P. 145, 146
Greek Miracle 97, 102, 108
Gutenberg, J. 46

Habinek, T. 32
Hadrian's Wall 162, 168
Hall, E. 52
Hamblin, J. 144
Hamilakis, Y. 105
Hansen, J. 54
Hanson, V. D. 94, 99–103, 106, 107
Harry Potter 165, 169
Hartog, F. 31, 38, 49, 50
Harvey, W. 81
Heath, J. 99, 100, 102, 103
Hecataeus 12
Hedges, C. 122
Heidegger, M. 63
Heminges, J. 52
Henning, M. 147
Hercules 35
Herodotus 14–26, 27, 28, 31, 112, 129
Hesiod 27
Hesione 36, 41
Hesperides 35
Hilly Flanks 89–90, 92
Hitler, A. 94, 116
Holinshed, R. 52
Homer 13, 15, 24, 25–6, 99, 139, 165, 169
Hoover Institute 99
Hosukaï 56
House Stark 166
Huizinga, J. 148
Huntington, S. 87–8, 94

identification 3, 124, 126
Iliad 13, 17, 36, 70, 160, 162–3, 166, 168
imperialism 90, 92, 93, 97, 102, 104, 160
India 29–30, 94, 95, 161
Indus Valley 89
Inquisition 74, 80
International Relations 109, 117, 124
inventio 33

Jesus Christ 69, 71, 72, 75, 76, 77, 79, 83, 84
Jim Crow 101
Johansson, B. 32
Juba 34
Judaism 38, 82, 104
Julio-Claudians 166
Julius Caesar, C. 11, 30, 32, 36, 37
Jupiter 33

Kagan, D. 103–4, 108
Kandinsky, V. 61
Kant, I. 47
Kennedy, G. 48
Kierstead, J. 106
Klassen, W. 80
Knox, B. 96–9, 100
Koerner, B. 154

Laird, A. 30
Lanham, J. 160
Lefkowitz, M. 103–4, 107, 108
Leigh, K. 152
Leto 23
Lipsius, J. 53
Livy 10, 30, 31, 32, 33–4, 35, 38, 40, 31, 127–41
Locke, J. 144
logos 3, 44, 46, 144, 146, 147, 149, 150, 152, 155, 156, 157
Loras Tyrell 164
Lucan 29–42
Lydians 19
Lysias 147, 149, 150, 151

Mabillon, J. 50
Macedonia 112
McGinn, A. J. 149
Macrobius 11
Mahabharata 161
Man, P. de 47

Manetho 15
Manzoni, A. 54–5
Marincola, J. 31, 37
Mark Antony 37, 38
Matisse, H. 61
medical humanities 167
Mediterranean Sea 90, 97, 101, 102–3, 105
Melian Dialogue 110, 113, 114, 115, 117
Michon, P. 56
Miletus 20–1
Milton, J. 167, 170
Miraheze 130–1, 133, 134
Mommsen, T. 133
Mondrian, P. 61
Montfaucon, B. de 50
Morris, I. 89–95, 102–3, 106, 108
Muntzer, T. 77
Muse 27, 39, 66
muthologos 15
muthos 152, 155
myth 13, 29, 35–6, 64, 82, 88, 102, 104, 161, 164, 165, 167
Mytilene 19–20

Nazism 94, 107, 116
Neaira 149
Nero, emperor 32, 168
New Guinea 89
New Testament 70
New Zealand 167
Nicaea, Council of 71, 76
Nietzsche, F. 43, 46, 47, 50, 110
Nile 15, 90, 99
Numa Pompilius 33–5, 41

Oaxaca 89–90
Odysseus 24
Odyssey 13, 15, 17, 28, 169
Oecolampadius 73
Oenone 36, 41
Old Testament 70, 71, 72, 75
Orientalism 160
otium 159, 168
Ovid 33, 37, 39

Pactyes 19–20
Paillier, J.-M. 132, 136
Palmier, Cardinal P. 74
pathos 3, 146, 147, 149, 150–2, 153, 157

patriarchy 96–7
Paul of Burgos 82
Pericles 11–12, 110
Peloponnesian War 15
Pergamon 36
Perrin, A. 80
Persepolis 102
Persian Wars 14–16, 18, 19, 22, 24, 103
Persians 20, 22–3
Peru 89–90
Peter, St. 71
Petronius 148
Petrus Alphonsi 82
Pharsalus 38
Philip V of Macedon 16
Philippi 38, 42
Phillips, W. 153
Philosophes 46
Picasso, P. 61
Picus 33
pistis 48–9, 65, 66
Plato 9, 16, 18–19, 24–6, 28, 44, 47, 65, 104, 110, 112, 146
Plautus 3
Plebe, A. 65
Pliny the Elder 129, 140
Pliny the Younger 32
Plutarch 14–26, 28
Poe, E. A. 108
Polybius 10, 13, 27, 40, 129
Pompeius, Cn. 32, 34–5, 37, 38
positivism 51
Postumius Albinus, Sp. 132
Potter, D. 166
Powell, C. 122
Prince Joffrey 164
progress 89, 91, 93, 95, 104
proof 47–51, 63, 66, 122, 147, 149, 152, 156, 157
pseudonym 74, 128, 138
Pydna, battle of 37

Quignard, P. 56, 68
Quintilian 32–3, 37, 39, 50, 66, 160

racism 88–9, 93, 97, 102, 104–5, 108, 160
Ramayana 161
Ranke, L. von 63, 88

Rao, V. N. B. 29, 30
Reed, J. D. 36
Reeve, C. D. C. 48–9
Reformation 69–72, 76, 77, 80
Renly Baratheon 164
Richelet, C.-P. 53
Ricoeur, P. 62–3, 68
Roth, P. 1–2
Rowling, J. K. 169
Russia 87, 101, 105–6, 110, 114

Sahara 89, 90
Salii 33
Sallust 11, 27, 30, 32, 140
Samos 12
Sardis 20–1
Scaliger, J. J. 53, 67
Schake, K. 115
Schwob, M. 55–6, 57, 59
Sebastian, King of Portugal 82
Sen, A. 88
Senate, Roman 31, 132
Seneca 17, 39, 168
Serafim, A. 148, 149, 151
Servetus, M. 69–84
Servius 39
Servius Tullius 131, 132, 136, 137
Shakespeare, W. 52–3, 168
Shapin, S. 45, 65
Shelley, P. 97
Shulman, D. 29, 30
Sidon 102
Simonides 23
Sirtes 34–5
slavery 93, 96, 98, 104, 160, 163, 169
Socrates 19, 46, 143
Solon 25, 123
Sophists 17, 44, 46, 47, 50
Sophocles 16
Spence, J. 58
Star Wars 165, 169
Statius 162
Stoddard, L. 94–5, 101, 108
Stoicism 34, 160
Stow, J. 52
Subrahmanyam, S. 29, 30
Suetonius 32, 39
superstition 35
Sylvester I, Pope 51, 76, 77

Tabacco, R. 32
Tacitus 10–11, 32, 37, 38, 42, 140, 166, 168
Teichman, J. 69
Theocritus 167
Theopompus 12–13, 16–17, 26
Thespis 25
Thirty Tyrants 123
Thomas Aquinas 144
Thucydides 9–10, 11–12, 14–15, 22, 27, 109–26
Thucydides Bot 118–24
Thucydides Trap 109–10, 112, 114, 117, 126
Tiberius, emperor 32, 37
Tigris 99
Timaeus of Tauromenium 13–14, 26
Timarchos 149
Town, H. R. 61
Trilling, L. 10
Tritonis, Lake 34, 35
trolls 148–9, 150, 152–5, 157
Troy 36
Troy 165
Trump, D. 114–15, 116, 117
Tumin, M. 2
Turnbull, M. 114
Twitter 111–12, 114–26
Tyler and Straw, revolt of 53
Tyre 102

Ukraine 87, 106, 110, 114, 115
United Kingdom 100
United Nations 110
United States 101, 115, 117, 126, 163

Valla, L. 50, 70
Vandel, P. 80
Varro 129, 132, 140
Vasari, G. 69
Velleius Paterculus 32, 37–9, 42
Vergil 3, 36, 165, 170
Vernant, J.-P. 44
Vesta 34, 41
Veterans Day 112
Vieira, A. 72, 82
Vieira, B. V. G. 29
Vulgata 70

Walton, D. 144–5, 147
Western Civilization 87–108
Westeros 166
white supremacism 87, 88, 93, 94, 95, 96, 97, 100–5, 108
Wikipedia 1–2, 117, 128–41, 156
Williams, G. H. 71

Xanthus 36, 41
Xenophon 26, 28

Yellow-Yangzi Valleys 89
Yerushalmi, Y. 64

Zeus 36
Zuckerberg, D. 95, 160, 161

www.ingramcontent.com/pod-product-compliance
Lightning Source LLC
Chambersburg PA
CBHW061831300426
44115CB00013B/2328